W9-DEC-443

THE SOCIAL CONTEXTS OF METHOD

THE SOCIAL CONTEXTS OF METHOD

Edited by

MICHAEL BRENNER,
PETER MARSH and MARYLIN BRENNER

ST. MARTIN'S PRESS NEW YORK

Copyright ©1978 Michael Brenner, Peter Marsh and Marylin Brenner

All rights reserved.
For information write:
St. Martin's Press Inc., 175 Fifth Avenue, New York, N.Y. 10010
Printed in Great Britain
Library of Congress Catalog Card Number: 77-17903

ISBN 0-312-73165-5

First published in the United States of America in 1978

Library of Congress Cataloging in Publication Data

Main entry under title:

The Social contexts of method.

Includes bibliographical references and index.
1. Social sciences – Methodology. I. Brenner, Michael.
II. Marsh, Peter. III. Brenner, Marylin.

H61. S5897   300'.1'8   77-17903

ISBN 0-312-73165-5

Printed in Great Britain

CONTENTS

INTRODUCTION

Traditionally, as far as the empirical-positivist position is concerned, the methodology of the social sciences has emerged in the form of a conditional epistemological difference between theorising about social phenomena and empirically exploring, or more precisely, measuring them. Whereas theorising has mainly been seen as an activity geared towards an understanding of the social *qua* social, this has not been the case on the level of method. Research designs, data collection procedures, forms of error control in measurement and data analysis techniques have all been modelled after a paradigm which is essentially non-social and which is, in its epistemological assumptions, equivalent to the idea of method in the natural sciences.

Meanwhile, it has become apparent to many social scientists that the non-social paradigm of methodology in the social sciences is problematic. The fact, for example, that all data collected in the social sciences can only emerge from social interaction with the people under study, the subjects, respondents or informants, has led to great difficulty as far as the validity and applicability of natural science criteria of method in social enquiry is concerned. If the respondent's interpretation of the interview situation, for example, upsets the interviewer's plan for the interview, is this a contribution to data collection, or does it constitute error or bias? Is it possible to standardise interviewing procedures across all the interviewers involved in a survey, and across all the respondents? And if the answer is negative, is this an indispensable characteristic of the research interview, given its essentially social nature as social interaction between interviewer and respondent, with which we have to live? Similarly, does the deception experiment guarantee standardisation of measurement and, hence, precision of enquiry? And if there should be reason to assume this, does it not at the same time also guarantee the invalidity of the data obtained via such a method?

Many more such applied, and in a sense restricted, questions could be asked, and reflection along the lines of these questions will reveal that there is a fundamental paradox inherent in the application of a natural science paradigm of methodology to social enquiry, that is, to research which generates data by means of social interaction with the people under study. Let us, on a more abstract level, consider some of the lines of this paradox.

The science paradigm of methodology, for a start, does not involve, nor need, any *social* knowledge about the methodological processes, and here particularly data collection procedures, themselves. The logic of method is, and can be, conceptualised in a socially clean language. Forms of standardisation, for example, are recommended in order to achieve the independence of observations from experimenter influences and laboratory, and other, conditions, that is, to achieve unbiased measurement and the precise reproducability of results. But, as any practitioner of social research knows, in social enquiry, in the practice of conducting interviews, experiments and observations, we have to set up our measurement designs in *social* terms. We have to train interviewers in the skills of interviewing, these including the skills of social interaction with strangers in a well-defined situation of questioning. If experimenters deceive their subjects, they have to do so in social terms throughout the experiment. They must use credible techniques of interaction with subjects, that is, they must lie or pretend skilfully, in order to realise the intended purposes of the experiment. Indeed, the whole atmosphere of any experiment must be socially constructed in such a way that subjects find it meaningful to act. Similarly, in observational studies, access has to be negotiated in social terms, and modes of observation have to be implemented within environments in such a way that observation appears as a socially credible event to the people observed and to bystanders.

To conclude, methodology, if modelled after the traditional science paradigm, is underidentified in two ways. First, it does not elaborate, systematically and on the level of adequate social theorising, the social processes that constitute the practice of method. In other words, the present paradigm of empirical-positivist research does not understand methodology, axiomatically, in terms of a *social* structure. Rather, methodology is conceptualised as a measurement structure which is thought to be *independent* of the social platform on which any measurement act stands in social enquiry. Given this situation, it follows, secondly, that the relationship between postulates of measurement, as conceptualised, adequately, in the science paradigm of methodology, and the actual social practices necessary and sufficient to realise social measurement, is underidentified. For example, does the fact that a subject may define the experimental situation differently from the experimenter constitute error or bias, or is this a socially normal, perhaps even desirable, aspect of the social experiment, and in the case of the deception experiment, even an essential aspect?

The fact that methodology is understood in terms of axioms and postulates which are essentially non-social and, hence, conditionally different from axioms and postulates used in theorising *about* social phenomena, can produce paradoxical effects in actual social enquiry. Basil Bernstein (1971), for example, postulates two social languages for two social classes in modern Britain, these languages being functionally, perhaps causally, related to the social reproduction of the class system. One of the bases for postulating this relationship is the argument that the two social languages involve their speakers in different conceptions of social reality, and, hence, in different models of situations of action and the social rules relevant to them. This sociolinguistic contribution to a theory of social reproduction is intriguing because Bernstein, in the footsteps of Sapir and Whorf, elucidates the role which cognitive-sociolinguistic processes have in the social construction of reality, be it micro or macro.

On this particular level of theorising, one would then assume that Bernstein would use, or ensure that his collaborators would use, his *interpretative* insight about the functions of social language in social processes to conceptualise the forms of social interaction needed in measurement in order to validate, or empirically elucidate, his theory. But this has not been the case. In fact, on the level of method, that is, in Bernstein's case, on the level of research interviews and social experiments, the theory which is under empirical investigation is completely *abandoned*. For example, it is implicit in the theory that the two social languages influence the ways in which respective speakers define and recognise situations of action. However, in the conduct of experiments, Bernstein and his collaborators assume that children coming from two different social and sociolinguistic backgrounds can and do share the same definitions of experimental situation, experimenter and tasks involved, so that experimental responses are comparable. Let us consider the experiment in which children were given a series of four pictures representing a story and were then invited to tell that story (see Bernstein, 1971, p. 178), for our further arguments.

If taken at face value, the experiment revealed that middle-class children tell stories which listeners are able to follow without watching the pictures at the same time. The working-class children, however, do not. Here we need the pictures in order to be able to follow the stories, to comprehend their full meaning. The explicit meanings that make up the stories of the middle-class children are due, in grammatical terms, to a differentiated use of nouns, where working-class children tend to use pronouns instead. Hence, Bernstein concludes, middle-class children generate context-independent, universalistic meanings. In other words, the experimental results seem to validate, quite unambiguously, part of Bernstein's sociolinguistic theory. But, as Rosen (1974, pp. 12-13) has pointed out, this is only so because Bernstein is unable, as are his collaborators, to interpret the experiment as a *social* situation, involving the very determinants of action he is theorising about. Or in Rosen's words:

> If there is a route from these bare little stories, elicited on *demand* and not from a genuine wish to tell anyone a real story, to the Millers' universalistic flights [Rosen refers to an earlier criticism], then we are given no description of it. There is a vast lacuna to be filled in. And there is another interesting point here. The argument runs [in Bernstein's theory] that the working-class child takes up a communalized role as against an individualized one. Yet in this instance, bearing in mind that the researcher and the child are both looking at the same set of pictures, it is clear that it is the working-class child who is *responding to the person*. What needs to be explained is why the middle-class child *ignores* him (our italics).

In other words, Rosen points out that the social structure of the experiment does not resemble, necessarily, forms of social relationships in everyday life. Hence, the stories may perhaps only be indexical of the very situation in which they were produced. Now, if this is so, then the experiment constitutes at least one social situation in which Bernstein's assumptions concerning class-specific role identities do not hold. In fact, the actual role realisations of the children seem to falsify some of Bernstein's assumptions.

But back now to our more general arguments. It is interesting to conclude, for the case of Bernstein, that he seems to employ a two-level model of social relationships. There are social relationships which are strictly dealt with in his theory. But all social relationships which generate the data needed to empirically elucidate his theory are of a different kind. They are construed as non-social measurement acts, as if we could have a method which is based on interaction *without* the very fact of people, experimenter and children, interacting with each other.

Similarly, in the surveys carried out by Bernstein's team, his theory is not used to understand differences that may be expected to arise from socially different forms of symbolisation and expression of experience towards questions, and from socially different constructions of the interviewing encounter. Again, the interview situation is treated as socially unproblematic, questions are thought to be of equal communicative relevance to all the respondents involved, and so on. This paradox, that a form of interpretation of the social which is relevant on the level of theorising is abandoned on the level of method, enables the rhetoric of verification and falsification in the very way suggested by the philosophers of science. But the price for this procedure is high: what is thought to be true, adequate and relevant on the level of theory, is thought to be wrong, inadequate and irrelevant on the level of method. In other words, the price for consistency, as far as conformity to the empirical-positivist paradigm of enquiry is concerned, is, actually, gross theoretical and practical inconsistency.

There are various positive consequences which can be derived from the situation described above. Here, we are interested in only two. The first is that, even if the researcher wishes to avoid social theorising on the level of method, something social is always bound to happen in designs which have been intended as enabling disambiguated measurement. Hence, *any* measurement design, which is part of *social* enquiry, will take on, in its realisation, a definite social interactive format. If the researcher dismisses the sociology involved in methodology as uninteresting or superfluous, he is simply acting mindlessly, because there *is* a sociology in methodology. The second consequence, derived from the first, is that a sociology of methodology can only be developed, fruitfully, on the level of explicit social theorising. There is no difference between theorising about the social and theorising about social method. Both are attempts at the same subject-matter: understanding social life.

This implies that the rhetoric of verification and falsification has to be abandoned. It is not the data which decide the empirical propriety of theory *per se*. It is theory which is needed, *always already*, to justify the genesis, the validity and the communicative power of data, which can then, on these grounds, be used to *reflect* the legitimacy and empirical accuracy of theory. In this sense, theory and method form a dialectic, they are each other's condition, which is asymmetrical due to the primacy of theory. That is, empirical enquiry within the actual social formats which methods take is only an explicit process to the extent that we *understand* what goes on in method, in the social relationship the researcher wishes to build with people in a particular enquiry. On the other hand, it is empirical evidence, *Einsicht*, which is needed to propel forward theorising. The more systematic, in terms of socially structured enquiry, empirical insight becomes, the greater the possibility for theory to reflect its boundaries. In this sense, it is theory which ultimately draws the boundary between what has been understood, what is clearly known, and what is out of reach. What is not known in theory is *unknown*, but at the same time, this is *known* and provides, hence, the incentive for more adequate and imaginative theorising.

So far, some basic problems in the sociology of methodology have emerged. There are many others which find expression and treatment in this book. Our contributors have in many ways their own paths towards a new understanding of the role of method in social enquiry. These paths are certainly diverse and, perhaps, there are only a few points where arguments in the sociology of methodology converge at the present time. This is a healthy state of affairs. Hence, no attempt at elaborate paradigm-building is made in this introduction. Determination of overall consistencies and inconsistencies in our move towards a new concept of social enquiry may be left to our critics. Yet, given the dialectic of theory and method, there is a common ground on which this book is based. It is a major task to develop adequate social theory for methodology. This is an endeavour strictly on the level of theorising itself, and many contributors, in different contexts of argument, develop interpretative insights into the social on which method, as theory and practice, must ultimately be based. Another major task is to reconstruct the social forms which enquiry takes. This leads straight towards an empirical investigation of methods. What happens in the experiment, in the interview, in observation? What *can* be known by virtue of these instruments? Perhaps this book will provide only a few answers, but we hope that at least the problems of method in social enquiry will come out clearly.

Michael Brenner
Brenner Collet Marsh Research Ltd, Oxford

Peter Marsh
Department of Experimental Psychology, Oxford University

Marylin Brenner
Department of Psychology, Reading University

References

Bernstein, B. (1971). *Class, Codes and Control. Vol. 1, Theoretical Studies towards a Sociology of Language*. London: Routledge and Kegan Paul.

Rosen, H. (1974). *Language and Class, A Critical Look at the Theories of Basil Bernstein*. Bristol: Falling Wall Press.

1 ON NEGATIVE RATIONALISM IN SCHOLARLY STUDIES OF VERBAL COMMUNICATION AND DYNAMIC RESIDUALS IN THE CONSTRUCTION OF HUMAN INTERSUBJECTIVITY

Ragnar Rommetveit

An enlightened layman who tries to assess what linguists, psycholinguists and socio-linguists have achieved since he left school twenty years ago will very likely – as was the case with Molière's Jourdain – take a novel pride in his own mastery of prose. A joint scholarly explication of his communicative competence in terms of some appropriate collection of general syntactic, semantic and pragmatic rules may indeed be read as a scientifically established passport for entry into a strictly and rationally ordered semiotic universe in which whatever can be *meant* can also be *said* and *understood*. Thus, Searle (1974, p. 20) takes it to be an analytic truth about language that '. . . for any speaker S whenever S means (intends to convey, wishes to communicate in an utterance, etc.) X then it is possible that there is some E such that E is an exact expression of, or formulation of, X.' 'What is meant', moreover, may be further explicated in terms of rules that connect what is said to 'actions being performed with words'. These are rules of interpretation (and their inverse: rules of production). In addition, there are rules of sequencing which connect 'actions being performed with words' in everyday discourse. The major task of socio-linguistic discourse analysis is to analyse all such rules and '. . . thus to show that one sentence follows another in a coherent way' (see Labov, 1972, pp. 121-3). In order to hit upon the exact expression of what he intends to convey in any particular context of social interaction, the speaker must hence also have the ability '. . . to select from the totality of grammatically correct expressions . . . forms which appropriately reflect the social norms governing behaviour in specific encounters' (Gumperz, 1972, p. 205). His communicative competence must therefore include '. . . knowledge of the different aspects of dialectal and stylistic variation . . . within the more inclusive speech community of which he is a member (Pride and Holmes, 1972, p. 10). The communicated meanings, however, are, according to Habermas, identical for all members of such a speech community. And 'pure intersubjectivity' may hence be attained under conditions of unlimited interchangeability of dialogue roles, i.e. '. . . when there is complete symmetry in the distribution of assertion and disputation, revelation and hiding, prescription and following, among the partners of communication' (Habermas, 1970, p. 143).

However, as our friend the enlightened layman continues his study with the aim of improving his own capacity to understand and make himself understood, his initial pride is bound to turn into despair and feelings of alienation. His everyday communication takes place in a pluralistic, multi-faceted, only fragmentarily known and only partially shared social world, a world fraught with ideological conflicts, generation gaps, and uneven distribution of power, knowledge and expertise. He may hence often have the feeling that he has hit upon the exact and socially appropriate expression of what he intends to make known, yet fail to make himself understood. And who is to decide, on such occasions, which expression is 'the exact expression' of what is being meant?

I shall in what follows try to argue that the despair of our friend, the enlightened layman, is well founded and that Habermas' promised land of 'pure intersubjectivity' is a convenient fiction which allows scholars of human communication to pursue their trade with scientific rigour, formal elegance and academic success while evading practically urgent and basic existential issues of human intersubjectivity. It is certainly true that not only socio-linguists but also 'pure' linguists today are far more concerned with what people actually say than was the case twenty years ago. Their theoretical account of what they observe, however, testifies to a confounding of normative linguistics and descriptive social science. The 'rules' they reveal are accordingly not easily understood by the enlightened layman: they are in part by definition intuitively mastered and hence of no practical value whatsoever in his attempts to improve himself, and in part rules by which what is actually said and understood may be gauged against what *should* be said and understood under Utopian conditions of perfect commonality with respect to interpretation and fully shared knowledge of the world. Searle's 'principle of expressibility', Labov's notion of production rules as the inverse of rules of interpretation, and Habermas' formulation of prerequisites for 'pure intersubjectivity', I shall argue, are thus manifestations of a 'negative rationalism'. They are *not* axiomatic assumptions capturing basic prerequisites for human intersubjectivity, but normative conditions imposed upon human discourse which are at variance with the actual conditions under which such discourse takes place.

Acquisition of knowledge entails systematic comparison, and we may often gain knowledge of something initially unknown by examining how it resembles and in which respects it differs from something we assume to be known already. Thus, human thought may be studied and in part made known to us in terms of resemblance to and deviance from the operations of some particular logical calculus. Acquisition of semantic competence within some field, moreover, may be assessed as an approximation to be given, systematically elaborated, scientific framework. These are perfectly legitimate and useful strategies, of immediate diagnostic and evaluative relevance in educational settings aiming precisely and explicitly at mastery of such calculi and scientific frameworks. The resultant knowledge is bound to be of a negative nature, though in the sense that our initial ignorance is being replaced by knowledge of shortcomings. And our interpretation of results is to a large extent contingent upon how we conceive of those formal models against which human performance is being gauged.

I have elsewhere (Rommetveit, 1974, pp. 6-7) questioned the rationale for applying criteria from formal logic in semantic analysis of ordinary language. The calculus of propositions, for instance, was developed for particular purposes and with carefully considered gains and losses: an algorithm for assessing truth values of composite expressions was gained at the cost of the semantic flexibility inherent in everyday discourse. A recourse to criteria from formal propositional logic in the analysis of segments of such discourse may hence, of course, serve to reveal those very shortcomings of natural language which motivated the creators of the propositional calculus. We may for instance, as Katz and Fodor (1963, p. 200) have done, claim that a sentence, such as 'My spinster aunt is an infant,' is contradictory or even 'ungrammatical'. What we do then, however, is simply to impose upon an isolated segment of discourse a strait-jacket of 'propositional content' contrary to the intersubjectively established premises and presuppositions of the dialogue in which it is embedded.

More subtle forms of negative rationalism are revealed in characteristic sins of omission: What is 'meant' by single words is thus often explicated with reference to scholarly taxonomies without any account of the relationship between such taxonomies and lay notions. It is certainly true, for instance, that *butterflies are insects*. Since dictionaries are supposed to contribute to the dissipation of such taxonomic knowledge, it may even be proclaimed part of the 'public' meaning of the word *butterfly*. This, however, does by no means imply that such knowledge of class membership is entailed in intuitive mastery of the word in everyday discourse. The question of 'scientific' versus 'lay' anchorage of 'public' word meaning has thus been raised by Deese (1962, p. 174) who maintains that '. . . contrary to zoology, associative *butterflies* are as closely related to the birds as to the moths.' This bird-like quality of *butterfly* within the 'Lebenswelt' of ordinary people, however, is hardly ever considered worthy of serious linguistic enquiries and hence never taken into account in explications of the 'public meaning' of the word.

Lay notions at variance with established scientific taxonomies are thus – in dictionaries as well as in theoretical semantic analysis – as a rule relegated from the sphere of 'public' and 'literal' meaning. They may reappear, though, in attempts to account for 'connotative meaning' and 'metaphorical use'. This is particularly transparent in semantic analysis of kinship when the meaning of words such as *uncle, brother* etc. are defined in terms of class membership and degree of consanguinity without any reference whatsoever to kinship roles. Thus, Chomsky compares the following three expressions:

> John's uncle.
> The person who is the brother of John's mother or father or the husband of the sister of John's mother or father.
> The person who is the son of one of John's grandparents or the husband of a daughter of one of John's grandparents but is not his father.

And he maintains (Chomsky, 1972, p. 85): 'If the concept of 'semantic representation' ('reading') is to play any role at all in semantic theory, then these three expressions must have the same semantic representation.'

I have elsewhere (Rommetveit, 1974, pp. 18-19) explored some rather puzzling implications of such a claim. Of particular interest in the present context, however, is Chomsky's sin of omission: 'Synonymy salva veritate' (and hence: the possibility of 'pure' intersubjectivity) is achieved by relegating from the 'public' meaning of *uncle* those aspects that in ordinary discourse about kinship are subject to modification by evaluative adjectives. '*John's good uncle*', for instance, is thus clearly *not* synonymous with '*the good person who is the brother of John's mother or father or the husband of the sister of John's mother or father*'. The particular person referred to by the expression may in fact be a *bad* person whose kinship role relationship to John stands out in marked contrast to his morals in all other interpersonal relations.

Incapacity to cope with relational aspects of kinship is, according to Piaget, characteristic of egocentric thought. The point of departure for some of his enquiries is the 'three brothers' problem' from the Binet-Simon test. The child is told about a family consisting of three brothers, and he is requested to place himself at the point of view of one of them so as to count the latter's brothers. Lack of mastery of *brother* as a relation is then revealed in conclusions such as: '*I have three brothers, Paul, Ernest and myself*.' What happens, according to Piaget (1951, p. 88), is thus that '. . . judgments of relations are constantly transformed into judgments of inherence (inclusion or membership).'

This, however, is also precisely what – for entirely different reasons – happens to *uncle as a relation* in Chomsky's explication of the meaning of that word and to *brother* (*uncle, father*, etc.) *as a relation* in conventional dictionary accounts. Let us therefore examine somewhat more closely the relationship between the dictionary meaning we take for granted when we count heads of relatives *and* kinship as a role relation. Consider, for instance, a family consisting of the four brothers Paul, Ernest, Jean and Noam. The *brother* relations involved are in that case the set of all twelve possible ordered pairs (1) Paul, Ernest; (2) Ernest, Paul; (3) Paul, Jean; (4) Jean, Paul, etc. Each such ordered pair represents one discrete and autonomous *brother relation* in the sense that, e.g. Paul may be a good brother to Ernest even though Ernest is bad brother to Paul. And such a complete enumeration of relations is of course as 'objective' and 'referential' – and no more 'connotative' – that the counting of heads. The number of *brother* relations in the family described above is thus increased by four the moment a sister is born.

Such specific relations, moreover, constitute the very matrix of social interaction out of which the child's initial mastery of kinship words develop. As his semantic competence expands so as to encompass knowledge of descent and marital institutions, it may even come to entail semantic potentialities such as Chomsky's 'readings' of the word *uncle*. Such 'readings' may in fact prove essential in order to establish intersubjectivity when he, being asked *who* are his uncles, engages in a counting of heads. Potentialities mirroring purely relational aspects of kinship, however, may be essential in other contexts. Suppose, for instance, that Jean's relationship to his brother Noam is devoid of that shared dependency upon adult providers, that attitude of solidarity etc. that may be said to constitute distinctive features of *brother* as a relation. Noam, moreover, being greatly distressed by such a deplorable state of affairs, may want to make that known to his best friend. And he may in fact succeed in doing so by saying: 'Jean and I have the same parents, but he has never been a brother to me.'

The use of *brother* in such a context is, according to Chomsky and Searle, an illustration of 'metaphorical', 'parasitic' use. The claim that such use is 'parasitic', however, seems in part to be founded on the assumption that a logic of relations is contingent upon class logic. This implies, in the present case, that you have to be able to count the heads of your brothers in order to assess some characteristic quality of their relations to you. The lexicographer may hence feel justified in his general practice of treating such brotherly qualities as mediated by a connotative fringe contingent upon a 'literal' core. He may, in addition, refer to his own role as an educator of the general public: his commitment to a technologically oriented society is such that he should not confuse people who consult him by exposing them to fragments of 'soft' social sciences in cases when relevant wisdom from more established academic fields is at his disposal. Role relationships are thus – unlike the biological mechanisms of procreation – subject to cultural variation and social change. Whatever is implied by, e.g. *uncle* and *brother* as *relations* is hence necessarily *negotiable*. And any armchair inference from *what is said* to *what is meant* and vice versa (and hence also: Searle's 'principle of expressibility') is of course jeopardised if a word such as *uncle* (*brother, mother*, etc.) is allowed to convey class membership and/or some only partially defined and negotiable role relation. The aims of the lexicographer as an educator and the scholar engaged in the construction of formally elegant semantic theory are thus different, but convergent. The 'public' meanings proposed by the lexicographer are accordingly stripped of residual fringes of lay notions and, with minor modifications, endorsed by the theoretical semanticist – while lip-service is being paid to the native speaker-hearer. Possible complaints, moreover, are easily overruled by powerful and compelling scholarly arguments. It is an essential part of the duties of theoretical semanticists and lexicographers to establish order, and order is impossible without internal consistency. Composite word meanings must hence be explicated in the form of conjunctions of semantic markers, not as veljunctions of only partially determined semantic potentialities.

The stories about Chomsky's *uncle* and the lexicographer's *brother* may accordingly be supplemented with similar case studies of *infant, man, democracy, sell, buy, kill, die, poor, short, heavy*, etc. (see Rommetveit, 1974 and 1977). What invariably happens to such words when trapped in scholarly nets of negative rationalism is that very significant – though often negotiable – semantic potentialities get lost.

These are potentialities mirroring options with respect to categorisation and attribution and hence polysemics and genuine ambiguities of discourse in and about a multi-faceted, pluralistic, only fragmentarily known and only partially shared 'Lebenswelt'. And this has to be so because utterances have meanings only in the stream of life and because our mastery of words borders on our imperfect knowledge of the world and only partially explicable ontological assumptions (Wittgenstein, 1962, p. 739). Polysemy due to the manifold of possible social realities and human perspectives can thus never be eliminated by recourse to prestigious, but monistic, 'conceptual realities', nor by lexicographical legislation. We may of course attempt to disambiguate a word such as *human* by anchoring its interpretation in zoological taxonomy, and we may even decide to make that interpretation 'a semantic marker', i.e. an Archimedian point, in our assessment of the 'public' meanings of a set of other words. This may indeed seem plausible '. . . after three hundred years of science and criticism of religion . . .' (Habermas, 1970, p. 137). But it will not prevent religious people engaged in conversations or preaching from exploiting other 'lay' (or 'theological') potentialities of the word such as those revealed in contrasts like *human/divine, human/saintly*, etc. Archimedian points in assessment of human meaning are hence necessarily provisional and contingent upon some 'world view', never entirely neutral with respect to competing ontologies. And even a zoologically founded interpretation of 'human' is bound to contain some residual ambiguity. Indeed, this may be revealed, in principle, by lack of referential consensus if we should happen to encounter on some other planet entirely novel forms of living beings. Suppose, for instance, that some of them grow like plants. They are in possession of a sign system similar to our languages, however, are clearly extremely intelligent according to earthly criteria, and are also engaged in a variety of creative and communicative activities. Some astronauts may hence maintain that they are human, others may argue that they are not. And how could we, on the basis of a taxonomy constrained by our earthly experiences of variants of life, resolve that dispute?

The moral of this excursion into metaphysics and science fiction is very simple: the semantic system inherent in our everyday language is orderly and borders on our knowledge of the world, yet is ambiguous and open. The order exists in the form of constraints upon semantic potentialities, however, and not in unequivocal 'literal' meanings. Such meanings exist only in dictionaries but are nevertheless, as Wright (1977, p. 56) has observed, a convenient fiction in the British philosophy of ordinary language in the fifties. This is also Goffman's conclusion. He maintains (Goffman, 1976, p. 303):

> 'Literal' . . . is a wonderfully confusing notion, something that should constitute a topic in linguistic study, not a conceptual tool to use in making studies. Sometimes the dictionary meaning of one or more words of the utterance is meant, although how *that* meaning is arrived at is left an open question. And the underlying, common-sense notion is preserved that the word *in isolation* will have a general, basic, or most down-to-earth meaning, that this meaning is sustained in how the word is commonly used in phrases and clauses, but that in many cases words are used 'metaphorically' to convey something they don't really mean.

The practice of reading unequivocal 'literal' meanings into semantic potentialities, however, paves the way for the assignment of 'propositional content' to sentences whose message potentials are legion, though constrained by the combinatorial possibilities of semantic potentialities inherent in the words of which they are composed. 'John's uncle' is thus doomed the moment Chomsky starts assigning a 'reading' to the expression: his kinship *role* is sacrificed with lip-service to *John*'s intuition, but for *Chomsky*'s purpose of securing unequivocal readings of sentences in subsequent analysis of texts containing such kinship words. Issues such as genuine vagueness and ambiguity, negotiability of meaning, and social control of criteria for proper interpretation are hence evaded. What is meant by what is said is assumed not to be subject to negotiation, but fully determined by linguistic rules. And this practice of reading unequivocal 'literal' meaning into mere semantic potentialities and assigning propositional content to only partially determined message potentials seems to pervade semantic analysis by transformational linguists like a hereditary sin, in spite of recent concern with presuppositions and other signs of a pragmatic counter-revolution against Chomsky's Cartesian rationalism (see Rommetveit, 1974, pp. 79-101).

The notion of linguistic competence we encounter in generative-transformational theories of language may be conceived of as a heavenly version of our mastery of a common code, a version devoid of dialectal variations, stripped of ambiguities, and dyed in pure reason. Chomsky's postulation of unequivocal literal meanings and evasion of the issue of negotiable residuals may hence be defended by reference to some of his own Cartesian, explicitly stated, metatheoretical assumptions: his ideal speaker-hearer's communication is a monologue in disguise because it is assumed to take place in a society characterised by perfect commonality with respect to interpretation. Socio-linguistics, on the other hand, is by definition a study of human discourse under conditions of linguistic and cultural variation, and for that reason, one should expect, precisely of negotiable residuals in human communication. It is very strange, therefore, to witness how its theoretical foundation nevertheless is being infiltrated by assumptions about unequivocal meanings very similar to those of the transformational-generative semanticists. A Trojan horse in this enterprise seems to be Searle's theory of speech acts. Let us therefore return to his basic 'principle of expressibility' (see p. 16).

Some of the consequences of this principle are explicated as follows (Searle, 1974, pp. 20-1):

> . . . the principle that *whatever can be meant can be said* does not imply that whatever can be said can be understood by others; for that would exclude the possibility of a private language, a language that it was impossible for anyone but the speaker to understand . . . It has the consequence that cases where the speaker does not say exactly what he means – the principal cases of which are *non-literalness, vagueness, ambiguity,* and *incompleteness* – are not theoretically essential to linguistic communication. But most important . . . it enables us to equate rules for performing speech acts with rules for uttering linguistic elements, since for any possible speech act there is a possible linguistic element the meaning of which (given the context of the utterance) is sufficient to determine that *its literal utterance* is a performance of precisely that speech act (my italics).

Notice, first of all, that the principle as such says nothing about the hearer. His interpretation of what is said is assumed to be identical to that of the speaker, however, provided that the latter '. . . is *speaking literally* and that the context is appropriate' (Searle, 1974, p. 18; my italics). Socio-linguistic rules of discourse are accordingly based upon the assumption that rules of interpretation are the inverse rules of production and '. . . connect what is said to the actions performed with words . . .' (Labov, 1972, pp. 121 and 123). They are not only supposed to reveal how what is meant is converted into exact expressions and vice versa, but also to account for what happens when tacit though contextually appropriate and shared propositional knowledge merges with literal speech. Thus, Labov maintains (1972, p. 122):

> *If A makes a request for information Q-S_1, and B makes a statement S_2 in response, that cannot be expanded by rules of ellipsis to the form XS_1Y, then S_2 is heard as an assertion that there exists a proposition P known to both A and B:*
>
> If S_2, then (E) S_i, *where (E) is an existential operator, and from this proposition there is inferred an answer to A's request: (E)S.*
>
> This is a rule of interpretation that relates what is said (S_2) to what is done (the assertion of P and the answer to Q-S_1). Note that there is no direct connection between the two utterances Q-S, and S_2, and it would be fruitless to search for one.

The rule is then applied in an analysis of the following fragment of a dialogue:

A: Are you going to work tomorrow? (Q-S_1)
B: I am on jury duty. (S_2)

The tacit proposition P assumed to be known to both A and B is in this case that *B cannot go to work the next day if he is going to be on jury duty then*. This appears to be a valid inference since we may safely assume that knowledge about work and jury duties constitutes part of A's and B's shared social reality. B's response entails therefore a 'no' to A's question even though no direct semantic connection can be established between Q-S_1 and S_2. Labov can thus by his rule apparently reveal what is meant by what is said solely on the basis of literal meaning and shared propositional knowledge of the world.

Suppose, however, that A's question is being addressed to B as they are bumping into each other outside the courthouse, and that B responds while hurrying away from B and toward the entrance. Or let us imagine that A and B are friends engaged in an informal conversation. The latter may then take a variety of different courses, for instance:

1. A: *Are you going to work tomorrow?*
   B: *I'm on jury duty.*
   A: Couldn't you get out of it?
   B: We tried everything.
   A: Well, it's a pity you are not free. I hoped we could go fishing together.
2. A: *Are you going to work tomorrow?*

B: *I'm on jury duty.*
A: Lucky you! I wish I too had some legitimate excuse to evade the issue of tomorrow's strike.

3. A: *Are you going to work tomorrow?*
B: *I'm on jury duty.*
A: But the doctor has allowed you to start working again, then?

4. A: *Are you going to work tomorrow?*
B: *I'm on jury duty.*
A: But you'll be driving to the city then, won't you?
B: Yes.
A: Fine. I have some errands there, and I had sort of relied on you for transportation.

5. B: You look terrible. For how long do you think you can continue like this without consulting a psychiatrist?
A: *Are you going to work tomorrow?*
B: *I'm on jury duty.* Why do you ask, by the way? Why do you always switch to some other silly topic whenever I try to talk some reason into you?

These are all possible – and even plausible – expansions of that very fragment of a dialogue Labov himself has chosen in order to show what can be achieved when his formally very impressive rule is applied in analysis of real-life discourse. I have refrained from potential esoteric and 'metaphorical' interpretations of expressions such as, for instance, that of 'jury duty' when it is used by teachers as a label for that part of their work that consists in oral examinations. What I have done is simply to insert Labov's pair of consecutive utterances into different social encounters and then, within the general friendly-conversation-frame, to imagine alternative intersubjectively established *here*-and-*nows*. We may thus explore whether his inference from what is said to 'the actions performed with words' is valid across our range of contexts. Labov claims, we remember, that B's response '*I'm on jury duty*' entails a '*no*' to A's question '*Are you going to work tomorrow?*' because both of them know that a person on jury duty is relieved of his daily occupational obligations.

The outcome of our enquiries, however, is very depressing as far as the validity of such a claim is concerned. The only case in which it seems entirely plausible is in fact case 5, i.e. when A's question appears to be an evasive manoeuvre of 'empty talk'. And this, I shall argue, is a sad but by no means incidental outcome of our validation study. Case 5 is also the only case in which A's question can be treated as an 'exact expression' of a proposition in the interrogative mode, i.e. as fully determined and (according to Searle's criteria) '*complete*' in the sense that it can be unequivocally answered in terms of '*yes*' or '*no*'. Propositions are namely by definition immune to semantic infiltration by 'streams of life', and utterances approach the status of propositions (and grow asymptotically empty) the more they are detached from patterns of meaningful human action and interaction. The '*no*' which Labov claims is entailed in B's response is thus a perfectly satisfactory answer in case 5 because whether B is going to work the next day is a topic of no relevance whatsoever to, for example, A's recreation plans, his concern with B's health, or any other issue of significance to him.

But let us now return to the cases in which Labov's claim appears to be false or misplaced and keep in mind that neither of Labov's explicitly stated premises is altered when we do so: the proposition P (that jury duty implies absence from work) is part of the sustained shared social reality of A and B, and the very same pair of consecutive utterances reappears in every case. Why, then, is Labov's conclusion plausible in case 5, while absurd in the outside-the-courthouse case and – at best – very questionable in the remaining four cases? Is his rule simply false, or is it correct in principle but incomplete with respect to specification of significant dynamic aspects of the dialogue that cannot be captured either by what 'literally' is said or by what is said in conjunction with shared propositional knowledge? And, if so, what are these residual dynamic aspects?

What happens outside the courthouse seems fairly simple. The very location of the encounter and B's hurried locomotion become significant features of an immediately shared *here*-and-*now* in which B's response to A is embedded as soon as it is uttered and understood. What is made known is thus the simple truth that B is on jury duty today, and this also explains why he has no time to engage in a conversation with A. This, I shall argue, is very likely how B's reply is meant and 'heard'. We have therefore no reason to believe that what both of them know about jury duty and legitimate absence from work (Labov's proposition P) enters their temporarily shared social reality at all.

Common to cases 1, 2, 3 and 4 is that A on every occasion has some particular *reason* for engaging in the dialogue. His introductory question, moreover, is the first move in a game, the rules of which are at that stage not yet fully revealed to B. What he says is accordingly an incomplete expression of what he means. This, however, will in principle always be the case unless what actually is said is fully transparent with respect to the underlying *why* of communication (see Ducrot,

1972).

The reason why A asks B whether he is going to work tomorrow is in case 1 that he wants B's company when going fishing. The alternative prospects entailed in his question are thus whether B will be tied up (with work) or free to engage in recreational activities. An appropriate 'proposition P' can thus in view of these prospects hardly be Labov's P. The incompatibility between jury duty and recreational activity, however, may also be said to constitute part of A's and B's sustained shared world knowledge. And this fragment seems also to be made part of the immediately shared *here*-and-*now* of their dialogue as A reveals more of what he meant with his introductory question. Case 2, on the other hand, seems at first glance to corroborate Labov's conclusion. What A initially sets out to find out, however, is whether B will go to work or join those who plan to go on strike. B's response brings into the temporarily shared social reality of possible prospects a third alternative, one that has not been foreseen by A. It entails therefore no unequivocal answer at all to A's question as it was meant the moment A uttered it. The same may be said about B's response in case 3. The issue presupposed in A's initial question in case 4, finally, is whether B will go to work tomorrow and hence be able to provide transportation to the city or stay at home. What 'actions' A and B perform with words in that situation, moreover, are clearly contingent upon which issues and prospects are proposed and/or presupposed by them in an only partially shared *here*-and-*now*. Labov's conclusion is thus also in this case highly questionable. There is no compelling reason at all why shared propositional knowledge about jury duty and absence from work should enter A's and B's temporarily shared, dialogically relevant, social reality, and B's response can hence hardly be said to entail a 'no' to A's intended, though incompletely expressed, question.

Labov maintains (1972, p. 121) that '. . . formalization is a fruitful procedure even when it is wrong . . .' This is true and his own formalization of rules of discourse may indeed serve to illuminate what is basically wrong with the foundation of current socio-linguistic theory. The assumption that one can infer what actions are being performed with words on the basis of what is said is thus, in view of the general outcome of our 'validation' study, obviously false. Such an assumption may prove valid in accounts of meta-communicative frames, for instance in Labov's account of how members of a youth subculture in Harlem distinguish between personal and ritual insult (Labov, 1972, p. 157). What happens when it is converted into an axiom in general discourse analysis, however, is that socio-linguists need not any longer concern themselves with the very complex issue of what is made known when something is said and understood. Which particular fragments of shared world knowledge enter a dialogue may then be inferred from what is said without enquiring into which issues and prospects are taken for granted by the speaker only, the listener only, and both of them at the moment it is said. Lack of consensus with respect to such prospects as well as with respect to only partially determined semantic potentialities of words is simply prohibited because production is assumed to be the mirror image of interpretation. What is meant in a verbal exchange such as '*Are you going to work tomorrow? – I'm on jury duty*' is accordingly supposed to remain the same across variant dialogically established *here*-and-*nows*. Searle's notion of '*what is meant*' in speech acts is thus in current socio-linguistic theory elaborated into a hybrid of Utopian literal meanings and vaguely described '*actions being performed with words*'. The resultant picture is bound to be a masterpiece of negative rationalism, replete with shared world knowledge and literal meanings, but devoid of the essential dynamic aspects of human communication. And the dynamics involved in the construction of human intersubjectivity can hardly be captured by adding a few auxiliary rules to a conceptual framework based on erroneous assumptions. Let me therefore, very briefly, suggest some features of an alternative approach.

The futility of postulating 'literal meanings' and fully determined propositional content follows from the fact that ordinary language is semantically open and embedded in 'the stream of life'. We cannot, therefore, attain closure in our theoretical account of verbal communication without prejudging a multi-faceted, only partially known and opaque reality. What in normative linguistics has been labelled a semantic rule may hence from a socio-linguistic point of view more appropriately be conceived of as a linguistically mediated draft of a contract concerning categorisation or attribution. The entire set of basic semantic potentialities inherent in ordinary language may be thought of as constituting a common code of such drafts, i.e. of potentially shared strategies of categorisation and cognitive-emotive perspectives on what is being talked about. Institutionally, ritually and situationally provided frames for social interaction, moreover, may determine which more restricted subsets of semantic potentialities are intended within different kinds of contexts. A word such as *democracy* may thus be 'heard' in very different ways, depending upon whether it is encountered in a demagogical political speech or in an academic lecture by a political scientist. And what is made known by what is said is always in part contingent upon what at that moment is tacitly taken for granted.

Transcendence of the 'private' worlds of the participants in acts of communication, i.e. states of partial intersubjectivity, presupposes the capacity for decentred categorisation and attribution, reciprocal role-taking, and complementarity of intentions. Reciprocity and complementarity may indeed be conceived of as generative 'pragmatic postulates' in the construction of intersubjectivity. I have, for instance, to assume that my partner in the dialogue is trying to answer my question in order to make sense of his response to it. This is also the case when his response sounds odd. My faith in him, however, will make me search for some potentially taken-for-granted (by him) aspect of our only partially shared *here*-and-*now* which may confirm my faith. If I succeed, our shared *here*-and-*now* IS immediately expanded, and we have an instance of 'prolepsis' (Rommetveit, 1974, p. 87). Additional shared presuppositions may then also immediately provide an answer to my question. But this is not necessarily so; and probably very seldom in authoritarian school situations. The participant making the request for information, moreover, is, as a rule, by firmly established tacit and mutual understanding in control of the criteria by which the odd response is judged to entail an answer or not. What was meant by his question cannot be decided by the respondent if the two of them happen to disagree. Asymmetry with respect to power and expertise, however, may also override such a rule, and so may a symbiotic relationship between a small child and an adult (Bateson, 1973, p. 185). What is meant by a question from an ignorant pupil may be decided by his teacher, and what kind of information is sought by a small child may under the conditions of pathological mother-child relationships rather arbitrarily be decided by the mother. The first case is an instance of a quasi-dialogue, the latter very likely part of a pattern leading to autism.

The plausible essence of Labov's rule relating some odd response S_2 to a preceding question Q-S_1 (see p. 25) may hence be converted into a generative 'pragmatic' postulate and embedded in our alternative, more dynamic approach. And so may even Searle's entire 'principle of expressibility' (see p. 16). The anticipation that persons *will* understand is according to Garfinkel (1972, p. 6) a sanctional property of common discourse, and Schutz (1945, p. 534) maintains that '. . . the world is from the outset . . . an intersubjective world, common to all of us . . .' Mutual understanding is based upon mutual faith in a shared social world, and the anticipation that others will understand us may be enhanced and in some sense corroborated because we, *qua* speakers, are in control of the intersubjectively shared *here*-and-*now*. Rules of control constitute part of the basic complementarity of intentions and control is unequivocally linked to direction of communication: it is the speaker who (unless he is responding to a question) has the privilege of deciding which entities within a sustained shared social reality are going to enter the temporarily shared *here*-and-*now* of the dialogue. Searle's assumption that everything that can be meant can also be said may thus be an analytic fallacy about ordinary language. That fallacy, however, can be converted into a true, even though semi-paradoxical generative 'pragmatic' postulate: we must, naively and unreflectively, take the possibility of perfect intersubjectivity for granted in order to achieve partial intersubjectivity in real-life discourse with our fellow men.

References

Bateson, G. (1973). *Steps to an Ecology of Mind*. Suffolk: Paladin

Chomsky, N. (1972). *Studies on Semantics in Generative Grammar*. The Hague: Mouton.

Deese, J. (1962). The structure of associative meaning. *Psychological Review, 69*, 161-75.

Ducrot, O. (1972). *Dire et ne pas dire. Principes de Semantique Linguistique*. Paris: Hermann.

Garfinkel, H. (1972). Studies of the routine grounds of everyday activities. In D. Sudnow (ed.), *Studies in Social Interaction*. New York: Free Press.

Goffman, E. (1976). Replies and responses. *Language in Society, 5,* 257-313.

Gumperz, J.J. (1972). Sociolinguistics and communication in small groups. In Pride and Homes (eds.), *Sociolinguistics*.

Habermas, J. (1970). Toward a theory of communicative competence. In P.E. Dreitzel (ed.), *Recent Sociology*, No. 2. London: Macmillan.

Katz, J.J. and Fodor, J.A. (1963). The structure of a semantic theory. *Language, 39,* 170-210.

Labov, W. (1972). Rules for ritual insults. In D. Sudnow (ed.), *Studies in Social Interaction*. New York: Free Press.

Piaget, J. (1951). *Judgement and Reasoning in the Child*. London: Routledge and Kegan Paul.

Pride, J.B. and Holmes, J. (1972). Introduction. In Pride and Holmes (eds.), *Sociolinguistics*. Harmondsworth: Penguin Books.

Rommetveit, R. (1974). *On Message Structure*. London: Wiley.

Rommetveit, R. (1977). On Piagetian operations, semantic competence, and message structure in adult-child communication. In I. Markova, *The Social Context of Language*. London: Wiley.

Schutz, A. (1945). On multiple realities. *Philosophical and Phenomenological Research, 5,* 533-76.

Searle, J. (1974). *On Speech Acts*. Cambridge: Cambridge University Press.

Wittgenstein, L. (1962). The Blue Book. In Barrett and Aiken (eds.), *Philosophy*

in the Twentieth Century, vol. 2. New York: Random House.
Wright, E.L. (1977). Words and intentions. *Philosophy*, *52*, 45-62.

2 TOWARDS A SOCIAL PSYCHOLOGY OF EVERY-DAY LIFE: A STANDPOINT 'IN ACTION'

John Shotter

In this chapter I have space to treat of one question only but it is, I feel, a crucial one: 'Is it possible to devise as part of a new approach to the study of actual everyday life activities, a special way of 'seeing' them which will not, on the one hand, distort their nature, but which will, on the other, allow us as professional social scientists to deepen and enlarge our understanding of them?'

It is necessary, I think, to pose such metamethodological questions as this, for, if the professional's way of seeing the world is no different from the layman's, then it is difficult to see in what consists the professional's claim to have access to any special knowledge, unavailable to laymen.

But if the professional's way of seeing the world distorts or is from a different standpoint to the layman's view, then we have a situation in which the very nature of the scientific knowledge meant to help us solve our own everyday life problems brings into question, and apparently denies (Joynson, 1974), the common-sense assumptions about ourselves that we would use in applying that knowledge to the solution of such problems. The professional's account lacks, in the current jargon, 'ecological validity'; but much worse: if believed, rather than resolving our moral confusion and bewilderment, the studies of social scientists may play no small part in compounding and augmenting it.

My claim in this chapter is that it *is* possible to have such a special viewpoint; although, only as a theoretical construction (for if we try to catch ourselves in the act to see *how* we do what we are doing, we stop the temporal flow of our action): we can learn, but only with great difficulty, to see everyday activity *as if* from a standpoint *in action*, 'seeing' it not as an external observer but as an actor, not as an objective pattern of events but as meaningful activity which, in its temporal flow from less to more realised states, may be perceptually (but not physically) divided into coherent acts which can be taken as expression of an intention. And such a new viewpoint 'in' action is, perhaps, all that one needs to embark upon a new approach; *a* methodology as such being not only unnecessary but at the moment at least, difficult to decide upon. For what one seeks from such a new standpoint is to 'see' *the ways* that men do things: the methodologies (Garfinkel, 1967) they use become the subject matter of our new approach.

Undermining Our Confidence in Our Own Common Sense

Let me begin my argument for a new standpoint by first discussing how at least some of us, as tyros, come to a study of the social sciences: quite without knowing how it is that we can make sense of it, we wake up in the world one day, finding ourselves able to make at least some sense of it – and in it. And of course, if we were not able to do so, then we would be unable to conduct our daily lives as we do. So it is not *in* our daily life's activities that our problems with the nature of our own abilities usually occur; it is when we disengage ourselves from such activities and pause to reflect upon what it is that enables us to act as we do that we run into difficulties. It is thus from our knowledge of what we can do – or strictly, from our accounts of it – that problems arise.

Facing such problems, some of us turn to academic psychology, and try to become professionals in studying them; for surely, we feel, a disciplined and scientific investigation of them must yield some solutions. But – after much struggle and hard work to become trained in the discipline – we find it, strangely, of little help.

It begins in a plausible enough manner, by suggesting to us that a special way of seeing ourselves and of formulating our problems must be fashioned to replace the inadequate stories that we have told ourselves in the past. For we must admit that our common-sense 'folk psychology' *is* full of fallacies, fantasies and falsehoods; and is most certainly lacking in precision . . . it was a sense of common sense's inadequacies that drove us to academic psychology in the first place. Accepting, then, the truth of such remarks, we are not at all surprised to hear it suggested next, that all our 'social problems' – our criminal tendencies and mental illnesses, etc., etc. – continue *because of* its inadequacies, because of our ignorance, the unreasoned attitudes enshrined in our common-sense ways of going on. And that if we were to redesign our culture (or at least aspects of it) upon a scientific basis, much conflict and hardship, fear and confusion, in short, much that is bad in social life could be eliminated, and, of course, we would all vote for that. Thus it is that the first step in the education of a psychology student is the undermining of his confidence in the importance *and* the reliability of the knowledge of everyday affairs *that he already possesses*, and the institution in him of the unrealistic ideal of a conflict-free, logically structured social life. Surely, real life is intrinsically conflictful and vague . . . isn't it?

Learning to 'See' Objectively

Instead of introductory textbooks beginning, then, with both practical and imaginary exercises designed to awaken in the student a special awareness of that knowledge – an awareness of how he actually does use it in regulating his own affairs, and how he acquires and transforms it – texts begin by showing what psychology as a science of behaviour is, and how it goes about its business. They have to do this because, as they all without exception point out (because it's true), there is a great difference between popular conceptions of things psychological and their proper scientific formulation; the novice has to learn – to quote from a popular early text – 'to think in a new way about the living organism and the activity we [psychologists] call behaviour' (Hebb, 1958, p. 1).

And we (psychologists) all know what that new way is – we have all been trained in it – it is the method of studying human activity objectively from the standpoint of external observers. Rather than seeking from a standpoint in action to understand the sense of their actions, we have to view people's activity as an orderly sequence of movements, seeking, by use of an experimental methodology, the cause-and-effect laws supposed to govern *all* such movements. And, as it is maintained that all the concepts and distinctions important in daily life should be abandoned, what one sees should be described within a supposedly 'neutral' language designed to replace everyday terms.[1] We have had to try to learn, for instance, to see a smile not as a smile but as a certain pattern of facial movements; we have had to try to work with – as Hull (1943, p. 25) put it – 'colourless movements', and attempt to build up complex human behaviour from its atomic parts.

Now I say 'try' here because it is not at all clear that it is actually possible to 'see' human activities in this way, as those who know for example of Birdwhistell's (1970) work on smiling will realise. After a great deal of work attempting to correlate 'smiling' with a particular, well-defined pattern of movements, Birdwhistell (p. 33) could only say to sum it all up: 'Only [as a result of my analyses] have I been able to free myself from an ethnocentric preconception that I know what a smile is.' In other words, there seems to be no such well-defined pattern of movements to be discovered at all. To adapt St Augustine's statement of his problem with time, we could say 'What is a smile? If nobody asks me, I know, but if I want to explain to some one, then I know not.' And in general the same result turns up time and again; we find in different social contexts the same pattern of movements being different things, and different patterns of movement being the same thing. Evidently, our ways of identifying things in real life, the methodologies that we use there, are quite different from the methodology we are meant to apply in the pursuit of our science – that methodology, including as it does 'seeing things objectively', will become an item in the subject-matter of our new approach; for, how we agree amongst ourselves as to what are the objective aspects of a particular situation is problematic.

Mowing Down Straw Men?

The difficulty with our standard 'objective' methodology is, I think, a real one, and in a moment I shall suggest that to meet it we must abandon – not our common-sense ways of going on – but that standard methodology which currently we feel makes our profession a scientific one. But before I do, I want to point out something to those who say that to attack psychologists who use behaviourist and other such-like methodologies is to attack 'straw men'. I want to point out to them that it is only our methodology at the moment which unifies all the various specialisms within psychology, and it is only in virtue of it that we can claim access to a form of knowledge which competes in truth and accuracy with common-sense knowledge. It is only by use of our methodology that we can transform the observations we make into data. Thus it is no use saying that all psychologists now recognise and take account of the fact that people think, and feel, and so on, and that few apply *the* methodology strictly. For without our methodology, our special way of 'seeing' the world and seeking truth within it, we have nothing to distinguish us from laymen – and there are many laymen with experience at least equal to if not greater than our own in the special fields we have chosen for study. Thus we cannot in one breath legitimate our special status as professionals by reference to our methodology, while in the next, having gained access to the corridors of power in the meantime, revert merely to common-sense modes of analysis and explanation; at least, that is, not if we want to remain honest (and rational).

So, whether it is a real possibility for us or not – and the prospect is of course still debatable – if we want to claim the status of a science, then we must possess as part of a methodology, a special way of 'seeing' the world, a special technique for making a proper contact with the subject-matter of our science – whatever that subject-matter may be.

We are Responsible for at Least Some of Our Own Actions: Our 'Methodologies' are the Subject-Matter of Our New Approach

Now I do not want to argue any further here about the inadequacies of the behaviourist methodology we borrowed from the natural sciences long ago. Many, including my colleague R.B. Joynson (1974), seem to me to have produced quite devastating accounts of its shortcomings. And were it not for the fact that in this modern world there is nowhere else to turn for help in life's problems, except to the social sciences in general and to psychology in particular, many psychologists might well have felt tempted in the force of such depressing prognostications, to shut up shop and go home. But we cannot, not now, for many reasons other than merely personal ones (like not having any other job to go to): it would be to give up our dream in the power of rational thought as an instrument of progress; it would be to give up the task of constructing a methodological framework within which successive generations of men could contribute to the same tasks and move towards the same goals.

Thus, the task of reconstructing psychological enquiry is an important one. For no deliberate and continuous progress is possible without a method for comparing what we are doing now with what we used to do in order to assess whether there is any improvement or not.

Now one way of putting what seems to me to be wrong with our classical methodology while offering at the same time an alternative to it – if I may be permitted here merely to sketch what I think is the difficulty rather than arguing it properly – is that *while claiming to replace our everyday ways of doing things with a 'scientific' method, it still relies heavily upon them*. In other words, it does not offer, as it claims, knowledge that can compete with common sense, as common-sense procedures still lie at the heart of the method it uses.

When illustrating this point in the past (Shotter, 1974a, 1975), I have introduced it, under the influence of work in the philosophy of human action (Winch, 1958; Peters, 1958; Taylor, 1966), by way of discussing the distinction between *actions* and *events*, between what we do and what merely happens, to, within, or around us. I have pointed out that not only *can* we all make the distinction, but that we *must* make it if we are ever to conduct scientific investigations: for the only way of ever testing scientific theories necessitates that we recognise, when acting in accord with the theories, whether the consequences of our actions accord with or depart from the expectations engendered by those theories. Thus I took it that, being able to assess our responsibility for things – which is of course at the heart of everyday life – was also at the heart of doing science and was quite irreplaceable, for scientists without any sense of responsibility for their own actions would be unable to do experiments. Thus I took it that, no matter what metaphysical notions one may believe about universal determinism, etc., in everyday life, it seems, people can themselves cause at least some of their own motions; not all, but at least some of them.

But even more than this: I also took it that men face the task of acting, even when all alone, in ways which make sense to others. And the main force of Winch's (1958) argument – which still seems to me valid in spite of devastating attacks upon his cultural relativism – is that one cannot find the sense or meaning in a person's action just by looking at the logical structure of the movements in which it consists; one must study how these movements are put to use in a social context. Thus it is that, learning-to-make-sense-to-others is not just a matter of learning to make a well-defined pattern of responses – that is, learning something objective – it is a matter of learning how to adapt and modify one's actions continually in the face of changing circumstances in relation to an ideal or standard – that is, it is a matter of learning a practical skill. Given this approach, one's focus of concern becomes not behaviour, not the pattern of people's movements as viewed from the outside by someone merely as an observer, but people's *actions*, the ways that people do things as understood (not merely viewed) from the inside by someone involved in some manner in the action being studied – people's everyday-life methodologies become one's topic of research.

Self-Mystification in the Formulation of Problems

In this chapter I would like to present that same issue – that 'scientific' accounts rely heavily upon common-sense knowledge – in another way to do with how we formulate our problems for ourselves. As an example of how, upon reflection, 'a problem' about our own abilities might occur to us, consider the following: we know, for instance, that in the context of their daily use we understand the meaning of words without being continually baffled and bewildered by them; it presents us with no problems until one day, someone suggests to us that we only ever have waves of activity in the basilar membranes of our ears, and, to make matters worse, all other types of sounds, as well as speech sounds, make waves similarly. Thus – they go on to suggest – hearing speech sounds 'as having a meaning' is 'a problem' to us. And we, seeing the force of their argument (why?), agree, and begin as scientists to study it 'as a central problem of auditory perception'.

But, perhaps, we mystify ourselves in allowing ourselves to be faced with such a problem, in such a way: that is, by letting it be taken for granted that we already know what it is we actually do when we hear sounds – we understand meanings – and that thus 'the problem' is simply that of explaining how we do it. For such an approach:

> (1) biases us towards a search for that within us (a 'mechanism') which *causes* us to hear the sounds of speech 'as having a meaning'; (2) leads us to treat 'a meaning' as a product rather than a process, a noun rather than a verb; and (3) directs our attention towards just the behaviour of (and within) individuals, and away from the social arena of exchanges between people.

The activity of meaning, the process by which people make sense to and of one another, and themselves, in the course of their daily lives, is thus left unstudied.

This is, of course, exactly the point Garfinkel (1967, p. 31) makes in discussing the sociologist's professional concern when he says:

> In short, a common understanding, entailing as it does an 'inner' temporal course of interpretative work, necessarily has an operational structure. For the analyst to disregard its operational structure, is to use common sense knowledge of that society in exactly the ways that members use it when they must decide what persons are really doing or really 'talking about', i.e., to use common sense knowledge of social structures as *both* a topic and a resource of inquiry. An alternative would be to assign exclusive priority to the study of the methods of concerted actions and methods of common understanding. Not *a* method of understanding, but immensely various methods of understanding are the professional sociologists' proper and hitherto unstudied and critical phenomena.

A Phenomenological Approach from a Standpoint 'In' Action

Rather than taking it for granted, then, that on hearing words we do in fact simply perceive their 'meanings', and seeking the 'mechanisms' within us supposedly responsible for such an achievement, is there another way in which we could begin?

Well, perhaps we should, even before we begin, notice that the statement of our initial problem – 'what is it that enables us to act as we do?' – is ambiguous, in that we might be asking either:

(1) 'what *in us* enables us to do it?' (the classical question); or
(2) 'what enables us *ourselves* to do it?'

(1) requires as an answer a description of some 'mechanism' within us, whereas (2) requires a description of some process of social exchange productive of increased self-directed, self-regulated, or self-determined behaviour; an account of what goes on *between* people rather than *within* them. In (1) and (2) then, one has two quite clearly different foci of interest, with two quite different aims; needing in their pursuit – presumably – two quite different guiding frameworks of thought. One should notice too that in (1) and (2) two quite different images of man (Shotter, 1975) are involved: while in (1), man is a special nexus of causal mechanisms, in (2) he is a peculiar bifurcated thing, manifesting partly natural processes or *powers* (Harré, 1970) outside his agency to control, and partly personal processes or powers which *are* within his own self-control – and allowing, also, of the former to be transformed into the latter in a process of social exchange (Shotter, 1973). It is thus perfectly legitimate to ask of such bipartite beings as these, 'what is it that will enable them to act as they *themselves*, rather than their circumstances require?', in a way not possible when addressing causal mechanisms.

If that is the first point to note, the next in constructing our new point of departure is that we must avoid taking as given the world simply as it appears to be – as being full of acts and objects, words and things, all being just as we believe and describe them to be – and then attempting simply to explain how it is that we can do and see all these things; for that is a statement of 'the problem' that leads us, as we saw above, to study products rather than process, our achievements rather than how we achieve them; in short, it leads us into self-mystification. Instead, we must start *phenomenologically*, with – what is extremely difficult to describe, as we shall see – an analysis of psychological and social psychological processes *as we experience them*; that is, we must deal with that which in each and everyone's *experience* makes it possible for us to live our daily lives in processes of exchange with both one another and our physical surroundings. For instance, here I mean the distinction in our experience, mentioned above, between that which we, as individual personalities, experience ourselves as doing, knowing that we intended to do it, and that which we merely find ourselves doing (and often only recognise as an act for which we could possibly be responsible when our attention is drawn to it by others). Such a distinction can only be made by those who reject the behaviourists' view of people's activities as consisting in a sequence of objective events; but in rejecting such a view, what view of or in *action* could we have?

A 'Copernican Revolution'

If we are to take the standpoint *in* action that I am proposing (rather than that of the external observer), then the methods that people actually do use in their concrete, everyday-life situations to bring off certain socially intelligible achievements would become the topic of our enquiries. But, rejecting the behaviourists' 'view' of people's activities as consisting in a sequence of objective events, what 'view' of *action* could there be?

The problem is a difficult one for it entails, as John Macmurray (1957, p. 85) who has discussed this issue puts it, a 'Copernican Revolution': if we do try to view ourselves in the middle of our acting and to think about how we are doing it, while we are doing it, we usually trip ourselves up or something in the process. Such a standpoint in action is not one that we actually can have in practice – *but we can have it in theory*, Macmurray points out. Just as the astronomer can conceive of the planetary system from a standpoint on the sun (even though he cannot actually have such a standpoint), so we too must conceive of action as if from a standpoint in action (even though we cannot actually have one there). In other words, just as in many other areas of science, we must *construct* a *theoretical view* of our everyday-life world; the world from such a standpoint 'looking' quite different, surprisingly perhaps, from how it looks to us when we ordinarily just look at it, uninvolved in any action in it. Thus in the approach I am proposing, the professional's view of the world *is*, as with the behaviourist's, a view quite different from the layman's, it is, however, a 'view' from a position of involvement in the real affairs of the everyday-life world, in which the professional hopes to see *more* than the layman, rather than from a position that disregards or distorts the reality of those affairs, in which the professional hopes to see, not more, but something quite *different* from the layman.

'Seeing' the 'Meanings' and 'Uses' in the Everyday-Life World

To construct such a theoretical view is not, of course, an easy task. It involves, I think, at least to begin with, asking oneself over and over again the question: 'What must my world and the other people in it be like in order for this particular way, that particular way, for all the particular everyday ways of going on that I can make myself aware of, to be possible at all?' Now luckily for us, a great deal of this kind of question asking has already been done. And while no doubt the answers given are controversial, they at least provide us with a starting point. To me, this much about the everyday-life world seems clear: as Schutz and Luckman (1974) or Berger and Luckman (1967) point out, we begin by finding ourselves in a world that presents itself to us as in large part self-evidently 'real'. It was there before we were born and it will be there after our death. It has a history which antedates our birth and which is not available to our introspective recollection. This history, as the tradition of the existing institutions, has the character of objectivity. That is, it is something which we as individuals cannot 'wish away', neither can we change it merely by wishing that it were other than it is; even though as such it is a history made by men. A world with such a history to it has an 'objective structure' with which people must learn to cope if they are to execute their practical projects within it successfully; this objective structure being present, not in their heads as an idea available to introspective examination, but in the shape of their social practices – practices which they learn in the course of their everyday practical exchanges with those who already execute such practices successfully (Shotter, 1974b; 1976). Thus, to begin with, Schutz suggests, such a world is experienced pre-theoretically, simply as the prevailing and persistent condition of everyone's projects. It is experienced too as an intersubjective world, known or knowable in common with other people.

These and other properties of the everyday-life world are, for any child born into it (to borrow Merleau-Ponty's phrase) 'always already there'. Our world, however, the world of the professional psychologist – not the world of the behaviourist seeing only objective events, nor the world of the layman seeing more than the behaviourist, but still only seeing the products of his own processes rather than the processes themselves – but the world of methodical human action in which the professional studies the ways in which people make themselves, and their world, understood, to one another, and to themselves, is indeed a strange place. None of us can ever see it directly, but it is one which, with effort, we can none the less understand. With such a 'view', we could hope to see more than, but not differently from, the layman; and presumably we would be able to see both *better and worse* ways in which we all might act. And, unlike the behaviourist's view in which man's behaviour is seen merely as the effect of a cause, in this view man himself would still have to choose, and his choice would bear upon the degree of responsibility he could have for his own actions.

Note

1. One may find this view very clearly stated, for example, in Broadbent (1969), where he says: 'In summary then the traditional terms which are sometimes regarded as referring to mental activities or states give us grave difficulty when we try to apply them to detailed experimental analyses of the way people work. . . . There is no obvious and clearly correct way of identifying the traditional with the experimental concepts. One needs therefore to abandon the older mental terms, and rather to generate new technical languages for considering particular psychological problems. One such language is that of information processing . . .'

References

Berger, P.L. and Luckman, T. (1967), *The Social Construction of Reality*. Harmondsworth: Penguin Books.

Birdwhistell, R.L. (1970). *Kinesics and Context*. Philadelphia: University of Philadelphia Press.

Broadbent, D.E. (1969). On distinguishing perception from memory. *Theoria to Theory*, *3*, 30-41.

Garfinkel, H. (1967). *Studies in Ethnomethodology*. Englewood Cliffs, New Jersey: Prentice-Hall.

Harré, R. (1970). Powers. *British Journal of the Philosophy of Science.*, *21*, 81-101.

Hebb, D.O. (1958). *Textbook of Psychology*. London: Saunders.

Hull, C.L. (1943). *Principles of Behaviour*. New York: Appleton-Century-Crofts.

Joynson, R.L. (1974). *Psychology and Common Sense*. London: Routledge and Kegan Paul.

Macmurray, J. (1957). *Self as Agent*. London: Faber and Faber.

Peters, R.S. (1958). *The Concept of Motivation*. London: Routledge and Kegan Paul.

Schutz, A. and Luckman, T. (1974). *The Structures of the Life-World*. London: Heinemann.

Shotter, J. (1973). Acquired Powers: The Transformation of Natural into Personal Powers. *Journal for the Theory of Social Behaviour*, *3*, 141-56.

Shotter, J. (1974a). What is it to be human? In N. Armistead (ed.), *Reconstructing Social Psychology*. Harmondsworth: Penguin Books.

Shotter, J. (1974b). The development of personal powers. In M.P.M. Richards (ed.), *The Integration of a Child into a Social World*. London: Cambridge University Press.

Shotter, J. (1975). *Images of Man in Psychological Research*. London: Methuen.

Shotter, J. (1976). The growth of self-determination in social exchanges. *Education for Teaching*, *100*, 10-18.

Taylor, R. (1966). *Action and Purpose*. Englewood Cliffs, New Jersey: Prentice-Hall.

Winch, P. (1958). *The Idea of a Social Science and its Relations to Philosophy*. London: Routledge and Kegan Paul.

3 ACCOUNTS, ACTIONS AND MEANINGS – THE PRACTICE OF PARTICIPATORY PSYCHOLOGY

Rom Harré

Introduction

Mistakes in methodology may sometimes seem to be only superficial flaws in a science, but on reflection they can usually be seen to be consequences of quite deep confusions about its subject-matter. This is no more so than in social psychology. Early attempts at social psychology were marred by an almost exclusive reliance on mass methods and statistical analysis. It was assumed that this was the only proper way to deal with empirical data in such a way as to render the psychology legitimate as a science. The social character of social psychology was assumed to be guaranteed by confining the study to people engaged in mutual interaction. The distinctive characteristics of interaction episodes and the criteria for reclassification into kinds were, and still are, taken as unproblematic and *given* to common sense. Paradoxically it has become clear that the use of mass methods and the reliance on unexamined common sense (often disguised as adherence to blind empiricism) has made social psychology less rather than more 'scientific', since it has taken its practice further away from classical exemplars of 'science', like chemistry.

The source of these mistakes, I suggest, is a confusion about the relation of individuals to the social collectives to which they belong. It was supposed that merely by averaging or performing some more elaborate statistical operation upon the properties of individuals, a psychology would automatically become scientific and general, that is, its results nomothetic. But a social collective is not a statistical aggregate of individuals. It is a supra-individual, having a distinctive range of properties. A psychology becomes scientific when it includes an investigation of the way individuals record and represent to themselves certain properties of some of the collectives to which they belong, and how they use this knowledge in generating the co-ordinated actions which continue to reproduce their collectives more or less accurately. General principles may emerge, but only on a foundation of detailed particularistic studies. The example of chemistry should be kept in mind. Chemical laws have emerged only after intensive study of hundreds of thousands of individual compounds to determine their composition, structure and mode of preparation. It is of the utmost importance for the theory of social change that we take account of the imperfections in individual representations of the properties of collectives and consequently of imperfect reproductions of social collectives through time.

If these points are understood, one must as a consequence devise a new and characteristic methodology. In this methodology the intensive design is favoured over the extensive, that is, detailed studies of individual people selected as typical members of social collectives, and of particular occasions identified as typical examples of kinds of social events, are to be preferred to studies of large numbers of individuals and of social occasions based upon external manipulations of only one or two variables. Emphasis on the intensive design leads on to a revival of interest in how people understand the social worlds they are creating. This leads to a change in the role given to individuals under study and a quite new attitude to their contribution to the study. Their views must be taken seriously as contributions to the investigation and their accounts given the status of theories since their actions are co-ordinated with those of other people by reference to their version of the shared interpretations of action and rules for conformative behaviour which define and so create distinct social occasions.

The complementary problem, attention to which completes the social aspect of psychology, concerns the way an individual co-ordinates his intentions with those of other people in the mutual construction of fragments of a social order in the course of lived episodes, that is, how he recognises what their interpretations and social theories are and how a working consensus is brought about. Emphasis shifts from trying to foresee responses to externally imposed treatments, to a study of the semantic structure of episodes, the co-ordinated actions of people in situations or scenes, and to an investigation of the way their intentions are formed, co-ordinated and realised in action, and most particularly to the talk with which episodes are anticipated, corrected and renegotiated in the course of daily life. In sum, a psychology becomes social by:

(1) Cultivating an interest in the way and the degree to which members 'contain' a representation of the properties of the collective to which they belong, that is in members' social knowledge.
(2) Cultivating an interest in the conditions under which members are able to act in co-ordination to reproduce fragments of these collectives with approximately the properties they intend.

(3) Cultivating an interest in the methods by which members routinely deal with threats to and infractions of social order and show themselves to be socially worthy as persons, that is represent themselves as autonomous rational beings who have right motives and act intentionally. Human beings generally use talk to accomplish these ends.

A human society is a dynamic structure because both the individual representation of collectives and their social reproduction are imperfect. As a consequence actions which are aimed at offering the properties of collectives directly usually fail in varying degrees. This relative failure introduces a further element of imperfection into the system — the imperfection in the degree to which a plan can be realised co-ordinatively in the social world.

The ethogenic approach derives from the attempt to realise these interests in serious theoretical and empirical work, coupled with a systematic attempt to fashion psychological studies in the image of the way natural science really proceeds, eschewing philosophical caricatures such as the deductive-nomological theory of explanation, the operationalist theory of empirical concepts, indeed repudiating the whole positivistic approach.

In this paper I hope to indicate the style of ethogenic investigations by picking on certain characteristic ideas of that approach, choosing from among both theoretical doctrines and empirical practices. My exposition will be incomplete in many ways, but I hope illustrative of the style of the method, its theoretical stance, and some of its philosophical presuppositions.

1 General Principles

An understanding of the approach can be achieved by illustrating the operation of five main principles:

(1) The social dimensions of the study are to be based upon an explicit distinction between synchronic analysis, the analysis of social practices and institutions as they exist at any one time, and diachronic analysis, the investigation of the stages and the process by which these practices and institutions are created and abandoned, change and are changed. The ethogenic approach makes no assumptions about universality. In particular, synchronic analysis of the practices of culturally limited populations must not be assumed to lead directly to the discovery of any universal social psychological principles or laws. The practices and institutions of human society

may be so various, and the psychological processes by which they are created may be so differentiated that there may be no common principles. In a word, the universality of any 'result', even if achieved in an ethogenic study of some institution or practice, is taken to be problematic. A claim to universality would have to be made out empirically by very widespread comparative studies based upon the interpretations and social theories of each local culture. Nor can it be assumed that the diachronic processes by which practices and institutions are constituted and changed are the same at all times. That is, the processes of creation and change may involve different social psychological mechanisms in different societies at different times (Gergen, 1973). More generally, though, it seems reasonable to adopt a generally evolutionary approach to understanding social change. There is a continuum of specific theories between strict Darwinism and a pure Lamarckian form, depending on the degree to which selection and mutation conditions interact, a different specific form of evolutionary theory being appropriate under different historical conditions.

The distinction between synchronic and diachronic analysis ought to be maintained for individual members and participants too. While we would expect to find that at any given moment individual social aptitudes are a unique combination of habit and knowledge, it should also be remembered that the processes by which they are acquired and changed may be culturally specific and even peculiar to that individual (De Waele, 1971).

(2) Social interaction is to be analysed under the assumption that action takes place through the endowment of intersubjective entities with meaning, and the understanding or reading of those meanings by the interactors. The physical properties of the media of interaction, gestures, speeches, symbols, etc., are taken to have only a minimal constraining effect upon what they can mean, and to be of only marginal interest to microsociologists and social psychologists whose attention is to be concentrated on the meaning system.[1]

This programmatic principle has two important methodological consequences:

(a) The ethogenic analysis of action-sequences makes use of an analogue of the semantics/syntax distinction, and proposes to draw upon the technique of language study as a resource for both methods and concepts. For example, the structure of an action-sequence is to be given in terms of the *kinds* of semantically distinct meaning units it contains, as, for example, a greeting may involve symbolic physical contact, exchange of intimacy formula, and a formula reincorporating each in the social regard of the other. The specific elements of the sequence, say a handclasp, are treated as identified and individuated by their meanings. Only as the bearers of those meanings do they have a place in the sequence. Their physical properties are almost irrelevant to their social effectiveness (Harré and De Waele, 1976), though of course, physical distinctiveness is an important condition for their usefulness as media for meanings.

(b) Ethogenic analysis involves attribution of meaning to the elements of action-sequences, but the meaning of elementary actions depends upon the social meaning of the whole sequence by which a social act is achieved in an episode. The understanding of episodes as act-performances necessarily draws upon common sense or folk understandings of the social significance of the performance of an action-sequence. To take a very simple case to illustrate this point, the utterance 'You're an idiot' has one kind of social meaning when embedded in an action-sequence taken as a reprimand, and quite another when it is the last element of an action-sequence taken to be a psychological testing procedure. Reprimands and diagnoses are social acts and exist only as nodes in a network of relations with the acts of other members of a social collective, whose membership depends on the sharing of interpretations and some coherence of social theories.[2]

In what sense of meaning can we speak of the social meaning of gestures, utterances, and so on? De Saussure (1974) distinguishes between two aspects of a sign, *signifié* and *valeur*. In general, a socially meaningful performance at the action level has an act as its *signifié*, that is the meaning of a wave (or its verbal equivalent, 'Hi') is greeting. Unlike linguistic meaning, social meaning is devoid of referential aspects. An action does not refer to or indicate the act it means in the way a name refers to or signifies the thing it means. Gesture, action and act are different aspects of the same thing. This marks a difference between social meaning and linguistic meaning, in that linguistic meaning includes reference *beyond* the sign to another entity which is the signified.

But for a sign-system to be possible, actions must be experienced as semantically distinct. This can be understood in terms of De Saussure's concept of *valeur*. The value of a sign is defined in terms of the internal relational properties of the *system* of actions, by which one action-sign is differentiated from another. *Valeur* is defined by the intersection of the action-sequences into which a sign can fit, with the set of alternative signs it excludes. For example, understanding the social meaning of a smile involves not only differentiating one smile from another phenomenologically, but knowing the various action-sequences into which a smile of a given type can fit with propriety, and recognising those in which it would be socially bizarre. It also involves knowing the range of actions which as alternatives are excluded by the presence of a smile at that place in the sequence. In some sequences an eyebrow flash can serve the place of a smile, a contrast which preserves the meaning of the act, while in another context the change from smile to forced grimace can alter the meaning of the whole sequence. Putting these dimensions together creates a network of relations with other actions. The totality of these relations is the *valeur* of a semantically distinct item.

Common-sense or folk understanding of social life is ineliminable from the social psychological analysis, not only for empirical reasons (e.g. its essential role in picking out act-action sequences), but for deeper, philosophical reasons. Since a social act is *constituted* by its place in a humanly constructed social reality, it is what the folk take it to be. Individuals, of course, may be deviant in both the production and the understanding of the acts their actions accomplish, but the folk cannot be. If the perceptions of culture are changed, say by politicising, the meaning of actions (say accumulating personal wealth) may change from being read as a mark of moral virtue to being interpreted as theft from the toiling masses. There may be diachronic change in meaning. But synchronically the meanings are what they are, from the point of view of social psychology, since it is as those meanings that they are operative in the day-to-day management of social life and the constitution of the self as virtuous and worthy of respect. Clearly differentiating the synchronic and diachronic features of meaning allows for the politically important point that folk interpretations may lead people to generate actions and acts to their disadvantage. Change of social consciousness leads to change of social interpretations, which leads to change of social reality. New interpretations generate new acts – they do not reveal the 'real' meaning of the old acts. On this view, 'false consciousness' has to be more carefully construed than it often has been. The phenomenon of acting in accordance with the meaning system that leads to one acting to one's own disadvantage is real enough.

(3) Social life is lived by a medium that is an intimate blend of speech and action, so intimate that there are many social acts where it is a matter of indifference whether the medium of meaning is the one or the other. A wave, or 'Bye, bye' are equally successful devices for ending a personal encounter with that degree of civility that ensures a civil re-opening of the next. Examination of the speech component of action reveals a working distinction between speech which accomplishes action (identified first by Austin (1965) in his rather loose category of performative utterances) and speech which accompanies action, serving to smooth over the rough patches of interaction by making meanings and intentions (understood as aims and plans) clear. Such speech allows for looseness of articulation in the system providing opportunities for the revision of meanings and plans as action runs into incomprehension and opposition.

The speech which accompanies action has the general role of making actions and the speech which accomplishes action, intelligible and warrantable; that is, transparent as to meaning, and justified as occurring at the place it did in the sequence of unfolding and co-ordinated action. Such speech is *accounting*. For example, the behaviour of a stranger kissing the hand of a lady on first acquaintance can be made warrantable by an account which mentions that the stranger is a Pole. This implies, via common knowledge, that the action-sequence which accomplishes the act of greeting is culturally idiosyncratic and amongst Poles involves the hand-kiss. The action is made intelligible as a version of the body-contact phase of greeting and warranting the placement of that particular form of body contact *there*.

The blend, between accomplishing action and accounting for it, extends to the next level, so to speak, since it seems that accounting may, on occasion, be a way of accomplishing some social act. For example, an account may lead to the discrediting of the action it purports to justify and that discredit may spread to the actor. An action which would otherwise be taken as creditable to the actor may discredit him because his account reveals a 'hidden motive'.

I shall return to outline the techniques of account analysis after I have laid out the technical underpinnings in more detail and made the principles of the general ethogenic theory clear. Suffice it to say that it must be, in part, a reflexive analysis in so far as accounts are socially meaningful, and hence it must be possible to ask for accounts about accounts. The discovery of the social force of an account, as distinct from its explanatory efficacy with respect to its apparent subject-matter, requires a linguistic analysis of the grammar of the accounting language, an analysis of the content of the account and, on the basis of what these reveal, a sociological analysis of the theories of the social world revealed in the account.

(4) Ethogenics proposes a coherent cluster of sociological and psychological theories whose moral and political content is explicit and fundamental. It is our view that part of the psychological and social reality of our epoch is founded upon the sociological and psychological theories of the preceding epoch. A human being tends to be the kind of person his language, traditions and tacit and explicit knowledge tells him he is. I do not propose to offer evidence or argument for that here. I take it it is now widely regarded as uncontroversial. If psychological and social theories influence subsequent psychological and social realities it is open to a social critic to ask about the moral quality of the realities which those influences create. The problem of the relation between the empirical truth of social and psychological theories and their moral quality has not yet been satisfactorily resolved.

The moral basis of ethogenics is the emphasis on the enhancement of autonomy, self-control and self-determination, within an overlapping system of human collectives, only with respect to which can these apparently individualistic ideals be defined. People are human constructs within the *Umwelt*, the environment as endowed with social meaning (Harré, 1977b). Along with and partly as a consequence of the emphasis on an ultimate autonomy, and its associated moral quality, dignity, and partly as a consequence of independent argument as to the constructed character of the social collectives in which human beings define themselves as persons, ethogenics takes a radical political stance. But it is not the radicalism of the confrontation radical, in which the existing 'system' is confronted and attacked as such. Rather, it proposes a defence on social and psychological grounds of alternation radicalism, the politics of alternative societies conceived as social mutations. Ethogenics provides the means for the construction of social forms as alternatives to the dominant society by making existing social practices and theories explicit by drawing on anthropological and historical data, providing for alternative social practices and theories explicit by drawing on anthropological and historical data, providing for alternative social practices. These alternatives then become available for selection as alternatives to the present, existing society (Harré, 1978).

(5) Finally, as I hope to show in more detail, the skills which are drawn upon in empirical studies of social life are more like the skills of literary and dramatic criticism and of poetics than the skills of physical scientists. I have already hinted that the method makes essential use of common-sense understandings of the social world. However, these common-sense understandings, though a natural attitude, must be set aside and subjected to examination. As yet there are unsolved problems as to the mode of understanding that this *epoché* involves. If it takes the natural attitude to be a topic for analysis it cannot be based upon the natural understanding and the natural ways of endowing social practices with meaning, of which that understanding in large part consists.

2 The Old Methodology

Another range of insights into the ethogenic method derives from the way that method resolves the problems raised by the current critique of 'traditional' experimental methods in social science and particularly social psychology.

In an attempt to utilise the skills of the physical scientist in studying human society and social practices traditional social psychologists tried to partition the social actions and their effects and products into dependent and independent variables, and to manipulate them according to what they took to be the standard methods of the physical sciences, isolating the effect of variation in each 'variable'. But a causal condition (or an effect) is social only in so far as it has social meaning. If we understand this as parallel to linguistic *valeur*, the condition etc. only is what it is, in its place in a system of relationship with other meaningful elements. If the attempt to use the skills of the physical scientist in this area of investigation leads to the abstraction of that condition from its place in the structure, it loses its social character. This is a direct violation of Vigotsky's Maxim, the principle that a method of analysis must not so partition the elements of a structure that the relevant property of the structure is destroyed. In this case, the elementary variables, abstracted and isolated as units, fail to have the meaning that they had in the original structured set of conditions, the very property upon which their social effectiveness depended. A classical example is the study of the role of 'frequency' in the genesis of liking. As mere frequency, it has, of course, no social meaning and no effective role in generating a feeling one way or another towards another person. Frequency is a meaningful factor only in case it is located in that complex of other social actions, etc., we could call a 'slice of life'. Compare the likely effect of frequency as a result of accidental propinquity, marriage, of common job location, of deliberate contrivance by an interfering relative, etc. In each case it seems clear that it has a specific interpretation and is likely to have a different effect. Only as *having a meaning* is frequency a relevant item in the study of the conditions under which people come to say they like each other.

What is the source of our understanding of the meanings of isolable features of the social conditions for the genesis of actions and acts? There are two possible answers. The source of our understanding may be a sociological theory as to what is going on, or our understanding may come from drawing upon common sense and folk knowledge in our interpretations. The first way leads to functionalism, the second to ethnomethodology. We reject the functionalist way out of hand, since it could not be an adequate base for addressing the problem of how an individual, created as a person by the collectives of which he is a member, is related to his social actions. Functionalism seems to require psychologically implausible theses of a culturally imperialist kind, implying that the members, taken individually, do not know what they are doing. Of course, members may know what they are doing in this sense, and yet be brought to realise that what they are doing is to their own disadvantage (or advantage, for that matter).

Our rejection of functionalism is restricted to microsociology and social psychology. Functionalist theories may have a place in macrosociology, where indeed, since the ramification of consequences may pass beyond the purview of any individual and many of those consequences may be unintended and even unknown, knowledge of overall structure may be available only to a sociologist who has assembled the jig-saw of individual views and actions. With respect to that structure and its properties he may attribute functions to individual or collective actions.

The idea that statistical methods are adequate to cope with human variety and variability is another consequence of the assumption that the skills of the natural scientist are appropriate to solve the problems of the social sciences. It has long been pointed out (though the phenomenon has only recently been named) that statistical generalisations can lead to two distinct conclusions. For instance, if it is known that 80 per cent of a population have developed a property A in certain circumstances and that 20 per cent have not, this can imply:

(1) the probability law that every individual is 0.8 likely to develop the property A in the circumstances; or

(2) the two non-probabalistic laws that every individual of the domain A determinatively develops A, while every individual of the domain B determinatively develops some property which excludes A, or perhaps no determinate at all of the determinable over A.

Case 1 involves properties which are said to be distributively reliable, that is the propensity to develop the property A can be attributed as an objective property to every member of the original domain. The probabilistic distribution is explained as an effect of individual fluctuations. On this view individual manifestations of the property under study are not determinate. The adoption of this approach requires the acceptance of the prior condition that every member of the domain has A amongst its repertoire of possible properties.

Case 2 involves properties which are distributively unreliable. Frequency cannot be automatically transformed into an individual propensity. The statistical frequency must be interpreted as a measure of the relative size of two or more domains in each of which the mode of manifestation of the property(ies) under study is determinate. For instance if, in a converse domain, the property under study is not manifested, then if that property is distributively unreliable, individuals in that domain might not have the property amongst their repertoire of *possible* properties.

The use of Fisher-type confidence levels obscures this vital distinction since whatever may have been Fisher's intention, confidence levels are used almost without exception as if the properties, or in this case the behaviour in question, were distributively reliable. This is not a criticism of statistics, but of the interpretative naivety of some of those who use it.

A similar interpretative problem infects that other great statistical science, 'quantum mechanics'. Is PSI the measure of the propensity of an individual microparticle to behave in a certain specific manner, or is it a measure of the distribution of individuals each behaving in a specific way in a population? Since the internal structure of electrons etc. cannot be explored at present, there is no empirical way of resolving the problem.

These points are nicely illustrated in Mixon's reworking of Milgram's (1974) 'obedience' experiments. Mixon (1972) was able to show that 'obedience to recognized authority' is distributively unreliable, that is, of the population of 'subjects' in the Milgram experiments, there were those who, given the circumstances, their personal history and their individual construals of the situation, had to obey, while there were others for whom obedience in the conditions of the 'experiment' was impossible. The outcome for each 'subject' could be made determinate if the analysis of the conditions for action was elaborated to the point where individual interpretations and theories were included. But this move was not open to Milgram himself, working with an externalist, manipulative paradigm in the original study. Mixon was able to show that in the circumstances arranged by Milgram, some 'subjects' were capable of obeying an experimenter in circumstances which, had they been real, would have led to someone's death, while others were incapable of such action. Whether a 'subject' pressed a switch or not depended on his individual knowledge of science and his individual trust in experimenters. Thus, it would be improper to draw the conclusion that everyone is (reasonably) likely to kill another person in obedience to authority.

The use of statistical methods to identify distinct individual patterns which then become the focus of detailed study I shall call the idiographic transition.

In cases where empirical study involves distributively unreliable properties, the existence of a nomothetic level, even within an apparently homogeneous local culture, becomes problematic. The best hope for revealing any universal features of human social life would perhaps be by a search for *underlying* structural homologies rather than for universal laws at the level of action. This follows the way linguists tend to treat the problem of universality, whether or not they subscribe to particular views as to what universals there are and how they are grounded.

In sum, then, the role of statistics in psychology should be comparable to the role of purification techniques in chemistry, that is statistics should be a device for selecting the typical member for intensive study. In real sciences the work begins by idiographic investigation of the selected typical member.

If we follow Mixon in supposing that, in general, social practices and institutions are based upon processes involving distributively unreliable human social attributes, such as the meanings attributed to cultural artefacts (say the presentation of a person as 'scientist'), then the idiographic transition leads to more and more culturally specific meaning relations being revealed. The step back to principles applicable to understanding the social behaviour of every human being within the same explanatory and interpretative framework must then involve the attempt to identify universals which cross cultural boundaries. The observation and analyses of social anthropology and social history must, then, be incorporated as essential elements in a social psychology which pretends to any degree of universality beyond the modest but decent aim of revealing the form and content of the local ethnography or social practice. Further, the history of literature and drama as representations of social practices, institutions, meanings and interpretations presents us with an important source upon which we might begin the long road to universality. The incorporation of these matters as essential elements in social psychology carries us further and further from the naive experimental approach still distressingly prevalent in psychology departments.

Psychologists sometimes fail to recognise that they commit the fallacy of false distribution. Their failure to see this is closely related to the issue of causality. Is causality a mass phenomenon or an individual one? Since Durkheim, many social scientists have supposed that there was mass causation and that Fisherian statistics was its inductive logic. But the nexus of causation is always individual since it is individuals who act and are acted upon. Of course, each may be influenced in his actions by properties of his collectives, and his actions may have collective consequences, but the basic mechanisms of causation are always located in individuals. So if a social scientist claims that Fisherian statistics lead him to formulate causal principles he is making one of two possible errors – false distribution or the fallacy of collective causation.

Paradoxically, the idiographic transition need not involve loss of generality. Scientific practice recognises two routes to the general. In the extensive design the properties of the type of the set of individuals are revealed by some form of averaging on the properties of the members. In this design all members are examined and the type is generated by an intellectual act of abstraction. In the intensive design an individual is chosen as typical and its properties ascertained in detail. In this design the class of which it is a typical member is generated by an intellectual act of enlargement.

Each design incorporates an element of risk. The use of the extensive design risks the elimination of nearly all individual properties in the genesis of the type, that is for a given extension the intension may be minimal. The intensive design risks the shrinkage of the supposed class to a few or even only one member, that is for a given intension the extension may be minimal. Physics, aiming at universality, uses the extensive design; chemistry and anatomy, aiming at detail, use the intensive design.

3 The Structural Explanation Schema

The problems that arise from trying to develop a methodology based upon the independent/dependent variable technique and the use of statistics to ground laws at the level of overt behaviour need not lead to a total collapse into a multitude of idiosyncratic individual psychologies. Even at the level of the deliberate actions of individuals a collective grounding is presupposed since there must be some degree of shared interpretation for an action to be understood in fairly close correspondence to the way it was meant. To get a grip on communality of meaning we need to break with the philosophical tradition that sees all causal production in terms of efficient causes, that which stimulates or prompts to action. There is more to a scientific explanation than efficient causes. One perspicuous way of bringing to light the components of a scientific explanation is to turn our attention to the objects of an explanation, that is to look at what we are required to explain. In the most general case we seem called upon to explain items 1 to 3.

(1) The coming-to-be of some product of human or natural activity. For this the normal explainer would be an agent, an individual capable of exercising a power appropriate to generating such a product; for example, an electric charge is capable of producing a flash of lightning.

(2) The coming-to-be of the product at a particular place and time and in a specific situation. For this the normal explainer would be some combination of circumstances such as a change in the spatial relationships of agent and patient, the charged cloud comes close to a tree; or the occurrence of a stimulus to a generative mechanism, a tiny crystal falls into a super-saturated solution; or the removal of an impediment that was preventing a potent agent manifesting its activity in action, pulling away the support of a heavy body in a gravitational field.

(3) The properties of the product: for this the normal explainer would be some property or properties of the agent, or the properties of the material on which the agent works to generate the material, or sometimes the properties of a template followed by the agent in the genesis of the product.

This analysis can be summarised as follows: a causal explanation requires an agent, a stimulus or releasing condition, and a template. The notorious Humean or regularity theory of causality, and its psychological version SR behaviourism, restricted scientific investigation of causal production to (2). The continuance of manipulative 'experiments' as a prime empirical method tacitly preserves the old theory because the only aspects of causal production that can be readily studied in this way are the conditions sketched in (2) since they are the only 'external' features of the action which generates the social behaviour as product.

It could be argued with some plausibility that the study of specific conditions for action at a particular place and time has almost no place in psychological studies. For example, there are many cases where the genesis of the flow of activity is physiological, but that activity is shaped in a particular way to have a specific structure that conveys a certain social meaning. Schachter's (1974) discovery that there is a physiological cause prompting someone to light a cigarette at a particular moment, a cause which is not registered in the consciousness of that person or anyone in social contact with him, is a typical case. The social meaning of the lighting-up is derived within a fragment of autobiography that assigns to it a definite social meaning in accordance with the style in which a person presents himself. The psychological aspect of the study of this phenomenon would involve an attempt to identify the 'template' which shaped the activities of the person in such a way that 'lighting-up' had a meaning within them as part of the presentation of a certain personal image, for example.

The external, manipulative experiment as a model of action-determination involves the idea of the production of action as a cause/effect sequence on the model of the processes described in the event-laws of the physical sciences. In these cases we simply correlate one kind of change with another kind of change. So far as we can tell, this kind of causal determination in human social affairs is highly idiosyncratic if it is part of the subject-matter of psychology at all.

Borrowing a phrase from traditional philosophical analysis, we could call the way the properties of a product are produced by an agent on the basis of a template *formal cause determination*. This suggests that there may be communality of structure between them, or the even stronger communality which occurs when the product is an actual transformation of a template into a product. In the case of formal causality it is a necessary condition of the template being the formal cause of the product that they come, in the measure of their isomorphism, under the same description.

Examples of the way the distinction works in social science are very common. For instance, it may be that what brought a particular individual to suicide was a unique combination of factors, both biographical and environmental, physiological and social. But the form that that suicide takes is not idiosyncratic. It depends upon the templates available in the society and known to the person involved, that is individually represented in his cognitive resources for this *type* of action-sequence. It is quite essential for the person performing the act to conform to the local template of action, for otherwise he may fail altogether to have his death read as having just that social meaning, and his actions fail to be a successful performance of that act of suicide. To put the same point in terms of prediction, while we may not be able to complete an idiographic study sufficiently detailed to say whether *he* will commit suicide, let alone when and where, if we know enough about the available conceptions of proper suicides in his community we will be able to predict the form of the action-sequence that any suicide of his would take. At a more explicitly formal level, what brought someone before the altar with a particular other may be highly idiosyncratic, and hence that they should so appear be extraordinarily difficult to predict, but the form their actions will take in the course of the wedding proceedings is highly determined, since the structured product, the ceremony, is produced by the following of another structured object, the order of service, which serves as template, according to which the various agents involved model their actions.

In general, the production of structured objects from structured objects can occur in three ways.

(1) By the putting together, under certain constraints, of structured components. For instance, a crystal is a structured object and is a product of the structural properties of the component ions constraining the way a multitude of ions can be assembled. Sometimes the overall structure is an isomorph of the structure of the components, as in the case of diamonds and the tetrahedral valencies of carbon, but sometimes it is not.

(2) By the projection of the structure of the template onto the product, each being a distinct existent. This again may take two forms, in that sometimes the material in which the structure is represented may be different in template and product as in the musical score and the tune, and sometimes it may be the same as in a desert terrain and a sand map of it.

(3) By the evolution of the template into the product under the constraint of some invariant. This may involve a change of material or medium; sometimes it does not.

In general it is the second and third ways of production of structured objects that we find in social science. The second way is exemplified in acting according to plan, where the action-sequence is the production of the plan into the medium of overt action, and both template and action-sequence are distinct existences. The third way is exemplified in some kinds of intentional action where the intention evolves into the action, and in the coming-to-be of the action-sequence the intention ceases to be a distinct existent.

Conceived according to this prescription, a science that seeks to understand the relation of individuals to their social actions must seek to reveal the structure of the products, action-sequences and the structures which, as templates, serve to determine the form of these sequences. The ethogenic method depends upon the assumption that the structured action-sequence endowed with meaning as both actions and act is not the only product of that template and not the only manifestation of this form in a publicly available object. It is also revealed in the content and socio-grammar of accounts, the speech which accompanies action, and which serves to underline the meaning of the action and by reinterpreting or remedying failures and mistakes, smoothing the flow of microsocial interactions.

If both action-sequences and accounts are manifestations of the templates of formal causes of a matching, structured element in each, how is the template represented in individual people? Clearly, it can neither be in the mode of speech, nor can it be in the mode of action. From the point of view of social science we must develop an abstract mode of representation that is neither action nor speech. But we must beware the formalist temptation of seeking the means of this mode of representation in formal logic, since that study highlights only content-free or content-neutral structural properties of speech, whereas we are very much concerned with content itself, with specific understandings and theories of the social world, and our places in it.

4 Empirical Methods

Phase I – Action Analysis

The complexity of ethogenic analysis of what people are doing is to be understood against the background of the realisation by philosophers of science that the inductivist picture of scientific method is almost wholly mistaken. According to that picture, data are collected and general laws and theorems derived from them later. The failure of this picture to depict scientific method comes from the fact that there is no such thing as 'data' *from* which theory can be derived. 'Data' are a product of the interaction of theory with experience in the course of which the matter under study is selectively perceived and interpreted. To discover what the action is becomes a complex and intellectually demanding task. However, a method for the analysis of human action can be devised, in accordance with the theoretical position outlined in the earlier sections of this chapter. It is built up from the results of an analysis of the various influences that go into the genesis of action.

The first point to notice is the relativity of actions to episodes, the larger slices of social life within which actions occur. A kiss exchanged on leaving a friend's house is not the same action as a kiss exchanged on the parade ground of St Cyr, or in the garden of Gethsemane. Notice too that in identifying episodes I am not simply defining an abstract social interaction, but locating the occurrence in a setting in both space and time. Notice further that in certain settings in certain spaces and times the characteristics of the people engaged in the activity bear upon the interpretation of the activities. For instance, if the kiss is exchanged between two men, it is taken for granted and in need of no special accounting in St Cyr and Gethsemane, but on the doorstep of a private house in an Oxford suburb would, even these days, be an occasion for comment (though not if the very same two men were exhibiting ritual joy at a goal scored by a football team for which they both play).

Actions are defined and identified at the intersection of several lines of investigation – the setting, the people as they are engaged in the action, the episode they are realising, and the historical lines of convergence not only of the specific society in which all this is occurring and sustaining that society in being, but of the biographies of the actors. When we come to consider the people as they are present in the episode, we are forced to a further duality in the relation between their public representation of themselves as persons of a certain kind (their presented personas), the intentions and plans they each know themselves to have and believe of the others; intentions and plans which are an unstable and continually reconstructed background to the unfolding of the action.

The action, then, to use a mathematical metaphor, is a time-dependent function of setting, personas and social intentions, each of which is itself a time-dependent function of the local beliefs about the circumambient society and of the lives of the participants, as they conceive them to have been.

Action-analysis can be undertaken according to the following schema.

Stage 1: Act-action Structures

(i) Common sense or intuitive knowledge can be used by the investigator to identify the social acts achieved in the interaction he is studying.
(ii) His identification of the acts is then checked against the act-identifications made by the participants in their commentary upon the episode.
(iii) The investigator is now in a position to identify the actions by which those acts are routinely accomplished by those participants.
(iv) His identification of the actions is then checked by constructing scenarios of the action-structure of possible episodes and staging the action-sequences, calling for intuitive judgements of social propriety from competent participants.

At this stage the investigator has a representation of an act-action structure (or perhaps several act-action structures) for the episode. On the basis of this he can now define the episode as being of a particular social type or types. There is no suggestion in ethogenic studies that each episode is a single reality. It is more likely to be a multiple reality.

Stage 2: Expressive Presentations

In performing the tasks required of us as contributors to act-action structures in different styles we can display our social selves. The expressive aspect of a person's social performances is particularly effective in defining his public reputation. Change and development in public reputation constitute our 'moral careers'. Social reputations are recognised and ritually marked by a separate class of interactions. Here we see, with the help of Goffman's brilliant perceptions, the exchange of conventionalised expressions of social recognition, the giving of deference and respect; and their reciprocation in condescension; social censure by ceremonial acts of denigration and debasement; rituals for the amelioration and remedy of offence, actual and possible. Each society has its own conventions determining by what means (action) these person-defining acts of social life are carried out. It is an open question whether the acts Goffman (1972) has brought to light as the core of Anglo-American social life have any universality. I think we can be sure that the actions by which they are accomplished have only a local validity in time and place.

On the basis of these analytical studies we can *attribute* items from three categories of social knowledge to competent actors.

(1) Knowledge of the acts demanded of a human being as a particular kind of person in a particular social setting. This knowledge is usually explicit.

(2) Knowledge of the actions locally required for the accomplishment of such acts. This knowledge is usually implicit.

(3) Knowledge of the conventions by which the kind of person one is for that occasion is expressed. The degree of expressiveness of this knowledge differs greatly (Rosser and Harré, 1977).

Phase II – Account Analysis

At various moments in the use of the empirical procedure outlined in the last section, the interpretations offered by participating actors were called for in an essential definitional role. The next phase of an ethogenic study calls for the systematic study of participants' accounts to form the basis of a second way of founding an attribution of social knowledge to competent actors. The analysis of accounts is aimed at revealing the basis of the intellectual skills exercised in the methodic control of action. Such control usually falls short of the self-consciousness of the Machiavellian, whose lightest act is calculated and probably rehearsed. Account analysis reveals the knowledge of social meanings, situations, standards of propriety and so on required by a competent social actor in the continuous meta-activity of interpreting and justifying what has been done in this or that episode. For example, schoolchildren's accounts of violent goings-on in the classroom revealed, when analysed, a well-articulated and systematically applied theory of situations and their meanings, and rules for the conduct which would be 'proper' in those situations, that is conduct socially approved by their peers (Marsh, Rosser and Harré, 1977). This is the knowledge needed by anyone who is to be competent at a particular mode of social action. Competence has nothing to do with whether the action would be approved or not. Disruptive kids are, from one point of view, bad at school, but from another they are good at disruption.

The product of ethogenic analysis of accounts (Harré, 1977a) includes much material that would naturally be called 'rules', that is statements representing a structured content, say if A occurs, then do B, qualified by some action-modality. For example, the consequent action could be obligatory, permitted or forbidden. The content of the rule has a structure isomorphic with the action-sequence 'A happens, followed by the doing of B'. Rules, then, would be one form of verbal representation of the templates of the forms of action and so available for justifying action and hence for accounting. Whether or not that rule was actually used for the production of that action is irrelevant to its role in accounting since the role of the account is to re-interpret 'what happened' to complete a proper social event. Accounts, of course, can be offered prior to an event to ensure against misunderstandings though they can never guarantee the univocality of interpretation once the episode has begun.

I have already referred to the dominance of the episode in determining what the action is by heavily restricting act-interpretations. This is reflected in the use of situation as the taxonomically prior category in classifying the material revealed in accounts.

But since accounting is itself a kind of social action it lends itself to the presentation of selves under particular personas and the censure of improper presentation. So the first step in account analysis is to try to identify, with respect to the episode of which the giving of an account is part, what sort of expressive task is being carried on. In this way the illocutionary force of the statements making up the account can be 'creamed off' and their locutionary force as interpretations and explanations revealed.

The final stage is to order the statements as to content and modality with respect to the kind of episode they are relevant to, and then classify them as they serve for the definition of the episode, the formulation of the principles of the proper expression of suitable personas, the guidance of action of the people involved within the limits of their self-presentations, and finally the identification of those for whom the action is performed.

Renegotiation of these materials with typical participants allows us to amplify and correct our attributions of social knowledge. Amplification can be taken a stage further by the kind of explorations of creative cognitive activity proposed by Kelly. It now becomes clear why we recruit participants as actors, defined as social scientists. In proposing this role to them, and in their adopting it, they take on the expressive task of being that category of persons, with truth-telling and sincerity as ways of illustrating that one is a kind of scientist.

The cognitive processes by which this complex structured mass of social knowledge issues in individual co-ordinated actions are, I believe, currently unknown. Some version of an intention theory based upon a generalisation of the practical syllogism is probably the way forward, but at present this can be no more than speculation.

Notes

1. This is not to be confused with the important physically mediated processes of 'non-verbal communication', by which a background of interaction is sustained.
2. Such differences of meaning may be marked by paralinguistic differences (say intonation) but they may not.

References

Austin, J.L. (1965). *How to do Things with Words*. New York: Oxford University Press.

De Saussure, F. (1974). *A Course in General Linguistics*, translated by Wade Baskin. London: Fontana, Collins.

De Waele, F.P. (1971). *La Méthode de ces Programmés*. Bruxelles: Dessart.

Gergen, K. (1973). Social Psychology as History. *Journal of Personality and Social Psychology, 26*, 309-20.

Goffman, E. (1972). *Interaction Ritual*. London: Allen Lane, The Penguin Press.

Harré, R. (1977 a). The Ethogenic Approach: Theory and Practice. In L. Berkowitz (ed.), *Advances in Experimental Social Psychology*. New York: Academic Press.

Harré, R. (1977 b). Architectonic Man: the structuring of lived experience. In S.M. Lyman and R. Brown (eds.), *History, Structure and Society*. New York: Cambridge University Press.

Harré, R. (1978). Apropos des changements sociaux. *Sociĕtĕ et Sociologie.* Montreal

Harré, R. and De Waele, J.P. (1976). The Ritual for Incorporation of a Stranger. In R. Harré (ed.), *Life Sentences*, Ch. 10. London and New York: Wiley.

Marsh, P, Rosser, E., and Harré, R. (1977). *The Rules of Disorder*. London: Routledge and Kegan Paul.

Milgram, S. (1974). *Obedience to Authority*. London: Tavistock.

Mixon, D. (1972). Instead of Deception. *Journal of the Theory of Social Behaviour, 2*, 145-77.

Rosser, E. and Harré, R. (1977). Explicit knowledge of personal style. *Journal of the Theory of Social Behaviour, 7.*

Schachter, S. (1974). The physiological basis of smoking, lecture delivered to the Psychology Department, Oxford University (unpublished).

Shotter, J. (1975). *Images of Man in Psychological Research*. London: Methuen.

Wittgenstein, L. (1956). *Remarks on the Foundations of Mathematics*, v. 48. Oxford: Blackwell.

4 METHOD AND SOCIOLOGICAL DISCOURSE

Stewart Clegg

Introduction

The chapter begins by considering the appropriateness of Kuhn's 'paradigm' argument for the analysis of social scientific discourse, particularly the task of explaining changes in this. The applicability of Kuhn's framework, even in the form of a *modified naturalism*, is rejected in favour of metaphors derived from *archaeology* and *geology*, as employed in the analysis of discourse by Levi-Strauss and Foucault. Criteria of the rationality of such analyses are argued to be decisively different from those that might be appropriate in a *logocentrically* constructed discourse. Sociology's logocentrism is discussed in terms of its own metaphoricality: that of a *socius-logos*. It is argued that the metaphoric primacy of either of these constitutive elements within sociological discourse indicates the unreflexive presence of logocentrism, and as such, presents the formal possibilities within which sociology can inscribe itself substantively. This is explored through the historical tendency of sociology to have evolved around the model of positive science first rigorously formulated by Durkheim, analysed here in terms of a theological solution to the problem of order posed by *theodicy* for Christian religion. However, where metaphorical primacy is given to the 'socius' this does not resolve the contradictions engendered by the theodical problem. It merely restates them in a more sophisticated, because more critical, form. Theodicy, it is suggested, has generated its own demonology: one which is essentially *nihilistic*. This nihilism derives from the failure of discourse to transcend what Habermas terms the *transcendental framework*. It is argued that sociology, as a *socius-logos*, could not transcend itself in its debates, such as those of the sociology of power, without transcending the form of the framework. Through such a transcendence, it is argued, an alternative to the 'rationality' of logocentrism may be found in a treatment of discourse which can explain changes in that discourse through the formal contradictions of the possibilities of the discourse, rather than through the environmental determinism of an external social factual nature or society. At the same time, this analysis is premised on a dialogic practice which presents the possibilities of social change beyond that of formal contradiction.

Method and Sociological Discourse

As a consequence of the publication of Kuhn's (1962) work *The Structure of Scientific Revolutions* it has become conventional to regard the history of substantive scientific discourse as one of changing 'paradigms'. It is argued that these paradigms function as conventional ways of seeing and communicating within scientific communities. They serve to distribute scientific legitimacy and authority. Changes in legitimacy and authority, which is to say changes in paradigm, are explained by a model of epistemologically 'normal' discourse incorporating or annihilating 'abnormal' or 'extra-territorial' discourse. The latter, when it is not successfully ignored, annihilated or incorporated, will actively promote the 'revolutionary' doctrine implicit in any systematic discourse excluded from, or opposed to, the current consensus.

In 'normal science' it might seem to be an easy task to map a highly bounded, classified and framed discourse which is relatively insulated from interaction with ordinary concerns and language. Modern physics would in this sense be an ideal paradigm. In such an instance, abstracted and formal definition can maintain the paradigmatic zone of discourse as pure as if it were within a *cordon sanitaire*. As Ryan (1972, p. 90) suggests, Kuhn's paradigm functions in an analogous manner to the Kantian Idea of Reason: 'it provides a framework of assumptions about the nature of the phenomena and about the sort of lower level theories we can put forward to explain the phenomena, but it itself is not empirically testable.' In addition, it has a profound symbolic value: it constitutes the parameters of the scientist's scientific and social world. To be a legitimate member of the scientific community one has to be seen to use the paradigm: to use the paradigm is to see the world as a legitimate scientist would.

Ryan, amongst others, has pointed out some of the incoherencies of this position. It admits of no factual status for the material world other than that mediated through the auspices of the paradigm. If this were empirically so, and if the paradigm were so absolute as Kuhn has had occasion to suggest, at least in his earlier work (Kuhn, 1962), then Kuhn's conception of puzzles and anomalies given by nature to the paradigm, would be, at the least, inconsistent.

Perhaps the most easily conceded aspect of the Kuhnian argument is that, historically, discourse can be constituted as if it were paradigmatic, and this can be achieved by noting, empirically, the strategic importance of certain key texts as exemplary grammars of a specific discourse. In the natural sciences, these texts are important because of their elegant solutions of key problems within the prescribed limits of the paradigm. It is on these criteria that one would agree with Kuhn that the social sciences are not paradigmatic: whether one would argue that they are pre-paradigmatic is another issue, and one which provides the point of departure for this paper.

The history of social and political thought is overwhelmingly un-self-consciously unparadigmatic in the above sense. Key texts in these areas of discourse have been more frequently read for the possibilities they frame rather than the limits they prescribe and for the contradictions they engender rather than the light of absolute clarity with which they shine. Such texts are embedded in a discourse which is operative at many simultaneous levels and in many simultaneous contexts to a degree far greater than any paradigmatic idealisation could ascribe. Certain key texts will crystallise this significance in their 'indexicality',[1] and the compelling fascination which they present for renewed reflection and meta-reflection as objects in their own right. What this 'right' may be is liable to transformation in the light of subsequent reflection, as historians have long been aware.[2] The meaning of a text is less than self-evident. It would seem that the limits of sense and intelligibility appear to reside not so much in what any text says – because it can be interpreted as saying many different things – but may be instead located, in a 'modern' formulation, in the underlying 'grammar' of the text, its 'deep structure',[3] the hidden and buried grounds of the textual superstructure – what is, and is not, said.[4] The metaphors which would seem to be appropriate to tracing such subterranean features are those of an 'archaeology' (Foucault, 1970) or a 'geology' (Levi-Strauss, 1969), rather than a 'paradigm'.

Geology attempts to slice through time, to disrupt our passive trust in the surface, the appearance of things, by providing us 'with a concrete manifestation of a perfectly accomplished transformation of time into space' as Donato (1973, p. 14) says of Levi-Strauss's use of the geological metaphor. Such an enquiry reveals a constantly changing surface, subject to erosion, attrition, sedimentation and addition, rather than any constant geological feature. For long periods it may seem that the surface remains relatively stable, relatively 'the same'. This deceptively constant surface may all the time be subject to climatic erosion or accretion, or may contain beneath its visible face a hidden energy potentially capable of a transformation almost beyond recognition. Beneath the surface, if only we can contrive to see them, will be clues and traces which function as signs of previous times discontinuously present in each other.

The text, or succession or discourse of texts, presents parallels with this sedimentation in time. Texts can also have hidden depths capable of transforming the seeming security of their surface.[5] Time present, time past and time future are, as Eliot (1952, pp. 117, 119) says, 'unredeemable': 'do not call it fixity, where past and future are gathered.'

Our explorations will be temporal rather than static. They will be of a constantly changing subject as object through the reflexive medium of the discourse. Our own explorative activities will act as agencies of change which find expression through the metaphors of 'archaeology' in the retrieval and re-ordering of the discourse into linked spatial and lineal configurations in the form of a narrative. The difference that is our text is the inscription of a journey of discovery which it is our privilege to narrate, or better – translate – because every writing, just as much as every reading, is always an act of translation. The archaeologist's translation may involve an imaginative reconstruction of the possibilities of time past, on its way to the present, as these are gleaned from the minutiae, the debris and rubbish of yesterday. Sociologists have the same care for the rubbish of tomorrow, be it today's words, relationships, facts or things. As narrators and translators we inscribe the texts of our life and times with a meaning barely glimpsed on the surface.

One's contribution must be capable of explicable translation if it is not to be arbitrary, isolated and vain.[6] It is our obligation to assist others to engage us. This engagement does not speak of our mastering the voices of others as servants, or followers. Such would be to deny the extent to which we are mastered by the voice – the 'theorising power' – of that through which we speak. It would also be to deny one's own voice as one striving to be distinguishable, as one which makes a difference. In this respect, a social discourse is quite unlike one which speaks of phenomena which may be legitimately treated as something not rooted in language. In instances such as these our terms may legitimately be stipulative, operational and extra-ordinary in the way that a British Imperial measure is. However, this provision requires qualification. The legitimacy of a system such as that of British Imperial measurement was dependent upon the agreement of the Empire's subjects to be ruled by such measures. Frequently they had no choice. The growth of a system of measurement is not infrequently closely related to the ability to terrorise or cajole subjects into its use.[7] The repressive potential of such systems of measurement, particularly where they might deal with socially evaluative words and concepts, should not be too lightly dismissed.

Where the object of the measuring system is composed of evaluative concepts which have differential relations of material interest to competitive and unequal power groups in the social world, then it is unlikely that the legitimacy of free and open discourse can prevail. Where discourse attempts to map and measure discourse, this will almost certainly be the case. We cannot measure the words of men and women through the absolute word of man, as if the latter were the embodiment of *logos*, without domination.[8] In the past, this domination has been accepted as part of the 'natural attitude' of men towards nature. Sociology has only too often expressed the same attitude to its sphere of enquiry. Recently, the realisation that this 'natural attitude' may be the fallacious ideology of an epoch, rather than the wisdom of the ages, has become more widespread.

The proper relationship between the geosphere of geology, or the biosphere of ecology, and their respective *logos*, have been the subject of considerable discussion in recent years – particularly with the emergence of ecology as a subject of popular speculation in the 1960s. The relationship between 'sphere' and 'logos' has taken on a new criticality which centres on the indissolubility and irreversibility of the relationship of 'logos' to 'sphere', which Commoner (1972, p. 33) has crystallised as the 'first law of ecology': everything is connected to everything else. In terms more familiar to sociology, one might say that all the sciences would seem to be increasingly characterised by a growing awareness of the reflexivity of their enquiries. The passivity of subjected spheres such as nature, or mankind, or, in particular, womankind, can no longer be assumed. To use Derrida's (1967) phrase, it is the fallaciousness of *logocentrism* which enables us to think in terms of oppositions such as object/subject, viewer/viewed or *logos*/sphere. *Logos* cannot be regarded as something originally or separately present from the sphere it thinks. Their inter-existence is already there at the moment, in the moment, of the thinking and the thought because *logos* and what-ever-is-subjected are always interpolated – the text will always be corrupted. This corruption, as will shortly be suggested and argued for the case of sociology, already carries within itself, as a prefiguration, the subsequent history of the concept which bears its sign.

Following Derrida (1970), one can say that *logos* is not a signifying system transcending individual *socius* as signifiers and signified. It cannot be outside the charmed circle of language. The presence of signifier/signified will always be as one in language. Neither can stand apart from the other, despite that the metaphors of 'logos' attempt to trace their difference. In ecology this difference is in terms of our relationship to the material world, rather than our dwelling-within-it, while in sociology it is in terms of our relationship to, and our dwelling-within, the material word. Signifier (logos) and signified (socius) are one within language, but are posed as oppositions within sociology. As this paper will go on to argue, the resolution of this opposition has tended to be in terms of either the assimilation or the annihilation of either one of the constituent parts of sociology by the other.

Sociology, as a metaphor, stands as a figure of speech which implies but does not explicitly state a comparison between two objects or actions, between the signifier *logos* and the signified *socius*. To investigate the metaphor of sociology is to question what it implicitly is. It is to seek its essence between that which it is of, but which it is not. 'Essence is expressed by grammar' says Wittgenstein (1968, par. 371). Essence is not a thing but the underlying relation between any one thing and another which makes a specific something or other. So sociology is the relation between society and *logos*.

Originally *logos* meant that order which pervaded and grounded all things with intelligibility. This order represented, as *The Penguin English Dictionary* so concisely puts it, 'The Word of God incarnate'. A *socius-logos* would thus be the Word of God embodied in the words of men about the words and doings of men.

Comte's title for the new positive science of society preserved God at its very centre, albeit in charade. Comte's priesthood were to be the embodiment not of God's word, but the word of Reason as it charted the positive laws of society from its ascendancy in post-Newtonian consciousness. Comte's proposed sociology was a programme for the moral regeneration and guidance of a society which, in the conservative view, required protection from critical Reason. If the French Revolution was the result of Reason, then it would reasonably seem to be that this faculty required restraint. Moral, conceived as traditional, authority had to be fostered in order to ensure that the restored social order be preserved from chaos. Comte's *savants* should not be taken as a grotesque misconception of the infant sociology at its christening. As a concrete version of *logos* they are implicit in the sociological metaphor.

One possible version of the subsequent history of sociology might depict it as the rationalisation of the ideal of moral authority, initially formulated by Comte in the archaic idea of the *savants*, through the rationalisation of method. This rationalisation merely serves to reconstitute the metaphor monadically: sociology becomes a discipline whose recurrent motif would seem to be a desire for the annihilation of one or other of its constituent parts by the other. Stated prototypically, this nihilism has been most frequently expressed in the desire to submit the *socius* to the *logos*, with the reverse movement sometimes being posited as a radical departure (viz. enthnomethodology) rather than as a mirror image, a mere reflection. Another way of expressing this would be to say that one way of showing sociology – one way of formulating it – might be to inscribe it as an oscillation between epistemological authoritarianism and liberalism.

This tension results from the following. Sociology presumes to produce morally authoritative words about the conversation and happening of mankind, words the authority of which, if not indubitable, will at least be taken seriously. In this respect it is, as Comte and Saint-Simon correctly formulated it, the heir to religion. Conventionally, the Christian religion had solved its problem of authority by counterposing the priesthood between men and God.[9] Only they could interpret the sacred texts correctly, and mediate between God and the mundane world. They were in this respect the rationalised bearers of the originally prophetic and charismatic message.

Sociology, as *the* social *logos* (that which aspires to One speech about the many), if it were not to perish with the sects of time, had to have its Durkheim. As a specific someone or other, Durkheim was historically necessary in order to routinise the charismatic conception of the secular *socius-logos*, through *The Rule of Sociological Method*. For, if there were no rule to sociological method, then how could its pronouncements be valued? And if its pronouncements were not valued, how could it ever produce social order?

Durkheim attempted to found sociology on reasonable ground by an act of faith and wilful stipulation. This involved re-defining and re-placing God in *logos*. Henceforth, *logos* was to be conceived as the rule of method. Durkheim's programme consisted precisely in its intent to subject human intelligence to 'the facts' as Bauman (1976) has argued. But 'the facts', like God, are not immediately accessible to the layman, who may be so easily bewitched by 'crudely formed concepts':

> Man cannot live in an environment without forming some ideas about it according to which he regulates his behaviour. But, because these ideas are nearer to us and more within our reach than the mental realities to which they correspond, we tend naturally to substitute them for the latter and to make them the very subject of our speculations. Instead of observing, describing and comparing things, we are content to focus our consciousness upon, to analyze, and to combine our ideas. Instead of a science concerned with realities, we produce no more than an ideological analysis (Durkheim, 1938,

p. 14).

Ordinary conceptions of ordinary men about their ordinary environment are to be distrusted as 'dangerously incorrect', so much so that they might lead to 'art' rather than to 'science' (an argument which Schutz (1967) and ethnomethodology were to reverse at a much later date). Such dangerous notions had to be re-formed. *Socius* must submit to the *logos* if the 'idols' of 'everyday experience' are not 'to exercise undue ascendancy over the mind and to be substituted for the study of facts' (Durkheim, 1938, p. 17). Facts require method to be visible.

Durkheim's strictures on method may be regarded as a way of producing the social order that will be sociology. Sociology's version of the problem of order is precisely this: if men are left to their naive judgements they will fail to focus on ideas as if they were factitious, as if they were things. Instead, ideas 'as products of everyday experience' will have as 'their primary function' the task of putting 'our actions in harmony with our environment' according only to their 'useful or disadvantageous qualities'. Empirically, for Durkheim, such a self-interested relationship would be represented by the metaphor of 'egoistic suicide'.

Sociology's methodological solution to its problem of order is to consist in treating of itself through its own idea of treating all phenomena as if they were things. Treat the sociological method as a thing and 'facts most arbitrary in appearance will come to present, after more attentive observation, qualities of consistency and regularity that are symptomatic of their objectivity' (Durkheim, 1938, p. 28). *Logos* is rationalised into method as an idea and then treated as if it were a thing. As Durkheim (1938, p. 28) advises, '*The voluntary character of a practice or an institution should never be assumed beforehand*.'

> Classically, where faith has been invested in the conception of a transcendent unitary god who is universal, the more there arises the problem of how the extraordinary power of such a god may be reconciled with the imperfection of the world that he has created and rules over (Weber, 1964, p. 138).

The distinctive problem of theodicy resides in the fundamental presupposition that 'even a meaningful world order that is impersonal and supertheistic must face the problem of the world's imperfections' as Weber (1965, p. 139) raised the issue.

In terms of sociology, and its own theoretical social order, the problem of theodicy has generated an entire epistemological debate stalked by the demons of nihilism.[10] Nihilism pertains where evaluation proceeds either by wilful stipulation, which may as easily be negated as affirmed, or through liberal-plural epistemologies. In these, a number of equally wilful stipulations coexist in a state of more or less peaceful coexistence or competitive incommensurability. Where this is the case, any one paradigm may be as valid as any other, within its own commitment.

The nihilism of wilful stipulation seeks ascetic salvation through the rationalisation and purging of doctrine. The nihilism of liberal-pluralist doctrine seeks salvation through the aesthetically joyful expression of polytheism. It proposes a relativistic world of distinctively ordained deities and practices. Monadism, or relativism, come to be the twin poles of our contemporary epistemology. They are the demons of our sociological existence.

How does one drive the demons out? Certainly not within the terms of the demonology itself. One might instead want to insist that the problem resides within a framework in which such demons are possible, on the assumption that demons, however apparent they appear to be, will always be the result of alienated human practice. Such practice can provide no solution for the salvation of social theory from the fall from grace that it exhibits in the polymorphous complexity of its own genesis. The problem is the problem. It results from a situation where the ideal discourse is posited on an essentially nihilistic standard, so that whatever might be said or written is irredeemably valueless. This is because both monadism and relativism are locatable within the

> problem posed by the system of primitive terms (or the 'transcendental framework') within which we organize our experience *a priori* and prior to all science, and do so in such a manner that, of course, the formation of the scientific object domains is also prejudiced by this (Habermas, 1974, pp. 7-8).

This 'transcendental framework' is ontologically rooted within two distinct realms of ordinary life. These are the realms of *instrumental* and *communicative* action (Habermas, 1974, p. 8). The practical interest of the person engaged in instrumental action is in the control and manipulation of objects. In it is grounded the empirical-analytical project which slowly developed into the positive sciences. In the realm of communicative action is rooted the hermeneutic project which has culminated in the interpretive sciences of which ethnomethodology is the most recent and positive flowering. These sciences result from the systematic objectification of these two concerns of daily life: control of objects and communication between subjects. The minutes of this process of 'systematic objectification' are to be found in any account of methodological procedures and puzzles.

The objectifications of positive science have clustered around the icon of the methodological purity of the one science. This has been premised on the ideal of the exact natural sciences as the perfect practice. This perfection would be most fully realised in causal explanation which was capable of being replicated across comparable data.[11] The objectifications of hermeneutic science have clustered around the interpretation of meaning, in particular the problem of privileged access to the 'intentions' or 'motives' of the 'other' as causal springs of social action.

These two modes of the 'transcendental framework' each present particular types of problems in any substantive research pursued under their auspices. What might at first acquaintance appear to be problems of the field in which one operates, or of the concepts with which one is working, can on further reflection frequently be seen to be posed by the constraints of the transcendental framework. Within the general area of the concept of 'power', for example, one can immediately think of the debate between Dahl (1957) and Bachrach and Baratz (1971) as falling within this scope.

Dahl (1957) has consciously tried to develop a behavioural political science. He is located squarely within the transcendental framework of the positive sciences.[12] Epistemologically, Dahl's (1957) gambit has been to secure knowledge on the agreement of measurements which are operationally defined in overtly observable and causal terms. Such an enterprise predicates a number of problematics, some of which concern the 'internal' coherence ('reliability') of the measuring instruments, while some others concern their coherence with a world of 'external' data ('validity'). While questions of internal coherence are of interest in posing the limits of ingenuity within the framework, criticism becomes socially potent when it is focused upon the terms of the 'possible society' in which the theorist predicates his formulations.[13] Criticism concerns the validity, rather than the reliability, of a body of knowledge or discourse under consideration. The reliability of a knowledge-domain is not its primary critical interest. The first stage of criticism is to move from a purely technical interest in reliability, to also incorporate a concern with the validity of the 'possible society' which is formulated. This entails asking to what extent does the 'possible society' enable us to assemble a theoretical object and practice which captures the diversity of that everyday life it purports to depict? This first stage of criticism involves the comparison of the theoretical object – the 'possible society' – not only with those formulated by other theories, but also with the living, and lived, history of daily life. These are the substance of Bachrach and Baratz's (1971) critique of Dahl's work.

Bachrach and Baratz (1971) elect not to live within the 'possible society' that Dahl's theory formulates because, as they argue, it only enables us to see overtly measurable power. They argue that although this may seem a hard-headed and scientific premise from which to produce scientific work, it may none the less fail to account for decisively important 'unmeasurable elements' which are not part of the world of observable behaviour. Such 'unmeasurable elements' do not derive their social significance from what is, but from *what is not*. Their significance as meaningful action is precisely that they do not issue in observable and measurable behaviour. In this way they introduce the concept of 'non-decisions' into discussion of power. This concept is meant to index the type of situation where power is displayed not in the frequency with which some person's proposals are followed, and the significance of these according to some theoretically internal criteria, but one in which power can be seen in the way in which these proposals do not significantly affect the interests (again decided on some internal theoretical criteria) of some agent or agency, almost as a matter of course. Proposals and action which would significantly affect these interests remain unarticulated: they are 'non-decisions'.

The crucial distinction between Bachrach and Baratz and Dahl, is that Bachrach and Baratz do not simply rely on the outcome of decision-making as their guide to power. For them, it is members' questioning of prevailing definitions which show us what the key issues are. Lukes quotes them to this effect, that a key issue is 'one that involves a genuine challenge to the resources of power or authority of those who currently dominate the process by which policy outputs in the system are determined' (Bachrach and Baratz, 1970, p. 47; quoted in Lukes, 1974, p. 18). With Bachrach and Baratz the concept of interests enters the debate. It does so in the shape of articulated grievances – that is, through an awareness of subjective interests. But, as Lukes points out, Bachrach and Baratz still insist on observable conflict as a criterion for a non-decision, and hence remain within the terms of a *behavioural* science – one that depends on manifestations as its only source of reliable data (Lukes, 1974, pp. 18-20). Their model is 'two-dimensional' because it enables us to see that the maintenance of surface order against the expressed interests of lower participants also qualifies as a 'face' of power. This formulates the 'two dimensions' of power on observable 'decision-making' and 'non-decision-making', on observable 'action' and 'inaction'. This kind of dualistic problematic is given to the discourse by the way in which it bears the traces of classical mechanics. Bearing these traces, power will invariably be discussed in such a way that the positive interest, even where articulated against, as in Bachrach and Baratz, will shape the subsequent range of discussion. Hence, the Bachrach and Baratz debate with Dahl is an argument concerning what are the (behaviourally) admissible grounds and parameters of tangibly visible 'power-effects', where 'effect' will be indexed by some change of state in the subject.[14] Notwithstanding any such reservations, that Bachrach and Baratz are able to raise such criticisms of the terms of a discourse shows its re-centring away from a location within a positive to a hermeneutic interest. It raises issues of understanding and interpreting behaviours, not as actions assembled by the conventions of the scientific enterprise, but in terms of an understanding of the actions through their intrinsic meaning.

This re-centring introduces a new interest and a concomitant problematic as the focus of enquiry. The interest is in the communicative acts and meaning of the other. The new problematic will revolve around 'action' concepts such as the 'intentions', 'reasons' or 'motives' of the other. Thus, in studies of power, once one has decided on some criteria to distinguish what class of action one will include in the exercise of power, one is obliged, within the hermeneutic interest, to decide whether or not to limit power solely to instances of 'intended action' (White, 1971, for instance). Invariably, such discussions founder on the impossibility of direct access to what the other *really* meant, said or intended. Cognitions are private. One way around this unfortunate aspect of social life has been that proposed by Winch (1958).

Winch (1958) can be interpreted as saying that we can take our interpretation of the other's acts from what one can conventionally assume the act to mean or be, within (in Schutz's (1967) phrase) the socially available common stock of knowledge. But this is not really very satisfactory as a way of answering the critical question raised under the hermeneutic interest. To do this would be to accede to the tyranny of public opinion polls or common usage as determinant of what things are. Just because one, or many, think a thing to be so does not make it so. Common meaning may not be the key to interpretation so much as that which locks us within itself, and outside of interpretation. Again, an example from the area of enquiry into 'power' is particularly apt. It is another way of formulating Bachrach and Baratz's point about 'non-decisions' and of pointing toward the difficulty one has in resolving it within the hermeneutic interest.

Perhaps the most potent type of power is that which is rarely if ever exercised. There is little need for it to be so. Normal states of affairs, meanings and conventions routinely appear to be natural, as if they were without interest. What might once have been called 'legitimate authority' prevails.[15] In such instances all that the conventional attribution of meaning will do is to exhibit the dominant 'theorising power' which conceals the relation of meaning and social interest. To believe what people tell us, or to accept it as the standard of what we judge people to mean is to make of the *socius* a quite arbitrary *logos*. It is a suspension of judgement and the negation of wisdom.[16]

It might appear that the options that this theorising poses as possibilities for sociology are bleak. Either it is obliged to embody the rule of an arbitrary *logos* (positive science) or an indiscriminate and unenlightened *socius* (hermeneutic science) as its standard of discourse, or cease production. The three options are equally unattractive. Rationality cannot be said to be present where one submits to arbitrary scientistic criteria as one's monitor of reality any more than where one allows reality to be in terms of some *verstehende* grasp of what others say. And silence in the face of life is a sacrilege committed against both the living and the dead.

Perhaps we should consider socio-logy sociologically in terms of the order (or contradictions) which it engenders. This order is that of the dyad. Its members are the *socius* and the *logos*. I have suggested that in sociology there has been a recurrent tendency for either one to assimilate or annihilate the other. Simmel (1969) suggests that this may well be a formal property of all dyadic relationships. In a dyad the social structure

> rests immediately on the one and on the other of the two, and the secession of either would destroy the whole . . . This dependence of the dyad upon its two individual members causes the thought of its existence to be accompanied by the thought of its termination much more closely and impressively than in any other group, where every member knows that even after his retirement or death, the group can continue to exist. Both the lives of the individual and that of the sociation are somehow coloured by the imagination of

> their respective deaths. And 'imagination' does not refer here only to theoretical, conscious thought, but to a part or a modification of existence itself. Death stands before us, not like a fate that will strike at a certain moment but, prior to that moment, exists only as an idea or prophecy, as fear or hope, and without interfering with the reality of this life. Rather, the fact that we shall die is a quality inherent in life from the beginning . . . Ideally, any large group can be immortal. This fact gives each of its members, no matter what may be his personal reaction to death, a very specific sociological feeling. A dyad, however, depends on each of its two elements alone – in its death, though not in its life: for its life, it needs both, but for its death, only one. This fact is bound to influence the inner attitude of the individual toward the dyad, even though not always consciously nor in the same way. It makes the dyad into a group that feels itself both endangered and irreplaceable, and thus into the real locus not only of authentic sociological tragedy, but also of sentimentalism and elegiac problems (Simmel, 1969, pp. 57-8).

Simmel's solution to the instability and immanent death of dyadic sociation – of which, in my analysis, sociology would be a prime exemplum – is to introduce the third party: 'The appearance of the third party indicates transition, conciliation, and abandonment of absolute contrast' (Simmel, 1969, p. 59). The locus of the triad is the reappearance of sociology in the sight of the person as sociologist. Instead of the unreflexivity which issues in death – the annihilation of either of the constitutive parts by the other – this premises the reflexivity which is possible when a subject is able to act back upon itself. This subject is, quite simply and concretely, the speaking/spoken subject. In *socius* this may be the people and practices which one researches. In *logos* this will be the practice through which one speaks – the theorising power which, to put it somewhat oddly, but dramatically, speaks one.[17] And the one that writes this and the one that reads this is the mediating agency which completes the triad through formulating the possibility of the dyad. But this triadic reformulation is always in the process of becoming – it never is, for once it comes to be in any objectified or objective sense, then it simply re-collects itself dyadically under the auspices of the *socius* and the *logos*. It becomes. It is.

In the sociology that I am formulating it simply never is, unreflexively. If it were it would immediately become another part of the 'transcendent framework'. The triad would have been dissolved back into the dyad with its attendant instability and immanent death. Criticality and reflexivity cannot be within the 'transcendent framework'. Conventionally, substantive sociological discourse has been. Thus, in distinction to this discourse, critical sociology seeks its standard of truth neither in correspondence with what is (as positive science does) nor in terms of its internal coherence with what it allows to be (as hermeneutic science and relativist epistemologies must do). It deals with neither an immutable object domain nor aspires to an immutable knowledge domain. Both are capable of transformation through the dialogue which is its theoretical practice.

Such a critical sociology takes as its empirical domain all discourse, all theory, all texts, to treat each as seriously or as ridiculously as the other. It will not accept that the text, the discourse, or the theory resides in a possibility constitutable only by the reality which it reports and purports to correspond to. Nor will it accept that the text's possibility is purely a matter of convention. Instead it will commence analysis with the proposition that any text is inscribed in the relation between convention and correspondence, between the discourse and the interest expressed in the possible society constituted by the theorist.

Its critical interest is thus always primarily in rupture, interruption, discontinuity and damage to the sober conventions of discourse, both 'lay' and 'academic' wherever these can be shown to be premised on the reification of such conventions into a form of life. A 'form of life' concerns that which 'has to be accepted, the given' (Wittgenstein, 1968, p. 226). In general terms the 'form of life' need not be reified – indeed, it may be no more than a fundamental physio-biological framework which is determinate of human agency and activity, as some interpreters of Wittgenstein have suggested (e.g. Hunter, 1971). However, the determination of activity does not proceed only through nature's invariances, but can also exist as a 'given' where the determinant in question is reified as a form of life in conventional practice, as if were natural, but where in fact it can be shown to serve a definite social interest. Thus, I have rendered the notion of a form of life in a somewhat unorthodox version as:

> 'iconic': a material thing (*or practice*) whose being is inexplicable apart from the idea(l) projected on to it. The behaviour glossed by the phrase 'form of life' indicates that it is behaviour which may be shown as the embodiment of actions oriented towards a standard or measure of activity, where activity may be taken to stand for any manifestation of beings in the world who can be constituted as theoretic actors. To be a theoretic actor is to be one who could have

> been held to have done otherwise (Clegg, 1975, p. 35, my italics).

What this suggests is that not only the conventions which we study but also those through which we study them may be regarded as a 'form of life' in the above sense. Each practice may exist in the grasp of a theorising power which unreflexively formulates routine convention iconically: it may be invested with an almost mystical power such that it becomes that which we could not doubt, the ground of our being and time. As Horkheimer and Adorno (1944, p. 274, quoted in Jay, 1973) wrote: 'All reification is a forgetting.' The critical and reflexive mode of the triad as a way of attending to discourse enables us to show distorted communication in the reification of forgetfulness where

> To be disabled thus is use one's theorizing as one *used* by the rule of whatsoever theorizing power one theorizes the world with. This is to be as unremarkably mundane as everyday theorizers in that one allows forgetfulness to rule one's speech. One rules through, and is ruled by, concepts whose origins one neglects, or of which one is too much membered, to be able to speak. The result of this is that one proposes theories which can only be read as conventions (Clegg, 1975, p. 75).

To attempt to go beneath the surface of things in this manner is not to engage in some vain quest for influences or origins, which one plots like tributaries and streams of the great river of language and its ripples in discourse:

> We must renounce all those themes whose function is to ensure the infinite continuity of discourse and its secret presence to itself in the interplay of a constantly recurring absence. We must be ready to receive every moment of discourse in its sudden eruption; in that punctuality in which it appears, and in that temporal dispersion that enables it to be repeated, known, forgotten, transformed, utterly erased, and hidden, far from all view, in the dust of books. Discourse must not be referred to the distant presence of the origin, but treated as and when it occurs (Foucault, 1972, p. 25).

In this treatment one can interrogate the discourse for its rule of functioning, its mode of rationality inscribed in whatever form of life reflexively theorised as its origin, rather than locate this origin in the traces of some once determinate presence in either 'reality' or 'discourse'.

The purpose of the triadic resolution is this – it enables us to constitute criticality as a formal practice because it presents us with a method for attending to all discourse (lay or 'professional') as *discourse*, as a speaking spoken to *and* with. It does not simply resign us to a position in which we are unable to make any judgements about the discourse other than those imposed on it, spoken at it, through standards external to it, such as correspondence with *logos* or coherence with *socius*. It avoids the dismissal of a discourse as 'pre-paradigmatic' and hence prior to critical judgement.

It suggests a rational way of re-viewing debate in specific substantive discourses which does not subsume these debates to the working-out of competing 'paradigms', our starting-point, which have sprung up and appeared because of some unexplicated concept of 'anomaly' or 'puzzle' which is imported into the dominant paradigm by the realisation of 'pure fact'. Instead, it suggests that the types of anomalies and puzzles which occur, and the debates that these engender, are the result of the limits governing the universe of our discourse on any specific substance, in part, as they are given in the formal terms of our discourse. Our debates are thus neither purely empirical-factual, nor theoretical-paradigmatic. They are *the form* of our intellectual life, and its substantive history, as it engages its world of data, and its substantive history.[18]

As a hypothesis, this was used to illuminate some features of the recent sociology of power. It may well be that it has the wider implications which I have suggested in this paper. Substantive research may support the hypothesis. Notwithstanding the outcome of such broader-based enquiry and applicability, I would want to argue that the analysis presented in this paper might serve as a context for empirical social research which would enable us to transcend the nihilism of much recent sociological debate in which various dualistic paradigms (e.g. 'action' *v*. 'system'; 'positivist' *v*. 'phenomenological') have been opposed to each other as research strategies. Instead, I would want to propose them as different moments, in a temporal sense, in the development of a research problem. As such they are necessary and essential positions in critical debate. But they are not final berths.

Notes

1. Indexicality is a term widely used by ethnomethodologists, but which was initially formulated by Bar-Hillel (1954). To say that an expression is indexical is to say that it is relative to such contextual matters as who said it, and

in what kind of context it was said, where context 'indexes' or refers to such features of the expression as the occasion, place, time, etc., in which it occurred. It has been used in this way by ethnomethodologists such as Garfinkel (1967), Garfinkel and Sacks (1970), and Wieder (1974). More recently it has been used in phenomenological 'analysis' by Sandywell *et al.* (1975) to refer to the reliance of any text (spoken or written) upon the unspoken grounds of Being as the silent mystery of Language. Somewhat more concretely, I have attempted to use the concept to elicit some everyday practices of 'Power, Rule and Domination' (1975) in the empirical setting of a construction site. To say that the significance of a key text in the social sciences is in part posited on its indexicality is immediately to oppose Kuhn (1962), for whom key texts would be exemplary paradigms. I would argue that the contrary is the case for the social sciences. Marx, Weber and the other Grand Masters of the sociological litany owe their eminence, in part, to the contradictions which their texts engender, rather than to the range of indexical meaning that they disperse.

2. Pocock (1971, p. 23) suggests the historian's concern with the 'historically contingent truth' of the text:

> Political statements are such that they may convey more than one meaning and be of more than one order; they are made up of terms of many origins, bearing many possible implications . . . consider the significance of this for the historian. In the first place it seems to guarantee in a specifically political way and for specifically political reasons, the truth for his purposes of the general rule that a historical document can always be made to yield more information than it overtly conveys, more even than its maker intended it to convey: as when a charter reveals more about medieval society than his scribe intended to communicate or knew that he was communicating. The author of a political statement may intend to be ambiguous; but because the language and the range of its ambiguities are given him by society and exist in a context of use and meaning whose multivalency he cannot expect to control, his statements may convey meanings to others (especially after the processes of linguistic change have had time to proceed some way) outside of any range of ambiguity he may have intended. It is true that he could not have meant to convey any message which the language in his lifetime did not render it possible for him to have meant; it may be that he could not have meant anything which no contemporary hearer or reader could have understood him as meaning; but within these limits there is room for it to have happened to him (as happens to all of us) to mean more than he said or to say more than he meant.

3. Wittgenstein (1968, par. 664) uses the notion of a 'depth grammar' as a way of clarifying what might appear on the surface to be extremely muddled and puzzling. Chomsky's (1968; 1966) interest in 'deep' and 'surface' structure is far more technical. It would seem to point towards the universal possession of an innate grammatical competence for generating and transforming utterances. My use of the terms clearly derives from Wittgenstein (1968) and not Chomsky (1968; 1966).
4. Steiner (1975, pp. 8-9) notes the importance of what is not said with reference to the seemingly 'open' texts of Jane Austen:

> The urbanity of Miss Austen's diction is deceptive. No less than Henry James, she uses style to establish and delimit a coherent, powerfully appropriated terrain. The world of an Austen novel is radically linguistic:

> all reality is 'encoded' in a distinctive idiom. What lies outside the code lies outside Jane Austen's criteria of admissible imaginings or, to be more precise, outside the legitimate bounds of what she regarded as 'life in fiction'. Hence the exclusive functions of her vocabulary and grammar. Entire spheres of human existence – political, social, erotic, subconscious – are absent. At the height of political and industrial revolution, in a decade of formidable philosophic activity, Miss Austen composes novels almost extraterritorial to history. Yet their inference of time and locale is beautifully established. The world of *Sense and Sensibility* and of *Pride and Prejudice* is an astute 'version of pastoral', a mid- and late-eighteenth-century construct complicated, shifted slightly out of focus by a Regency point of view. No fictional landscape has ever been more strategic, more expressive, in a constant if undeclared mode, of a moral case. What is left out is, by that mere omission, acutely judged. From this derives the distinctive pressure on Jane Austen's language of the unspoken.

One could make similar observations on the equally artfully constructed 'fictional landscapes' of artists such as Constable, or indeed, of the producers of almost any text, particularly where it would seem to be 'naturalistic' (viz. Taylor, Walton and Young's (1973) critique of Matza).

5. A good example of this would be to think of the controversy which has raged over the extent of the subterranean Hegelianism of Marx's mature works, most notable in the attempts of the Althusserians to preserve the purity of the text of 'Capital' from Hegelian contamination. In part, the way in which this is done relates to the previous note. Althusser (1969) wants to make a 'symptomatic reading' of Marx. This will seek to construct 'the problematic, the unconsciousness' of the text. This, it is claimed, 'will allow us to establish the epistemological break that makes possible historical materialism as a science' (Althusser, 1969, p. 254).
6. Popper's (1970, pp. 56-7) defence of rationalism against Kuhn is pertinent here:

> I do not admit that at any moment we are prisoners caught in the framework of our theories; our expectations; our past experiences; our language. But we are prisoners in a Pickwickian sense: if we try, we can break out of our framework at any time. Admittedly, we shall find ourselves again in a framework, but it will be a better and roomier one; and we can at any moment break out of it again.
>
> The central point is that a critical discussion and a comparison of the various frameworks is always possible. It is just a dogma – a dangerous dogma – that the different frameworks are like mutually untranslatable languages. The fact is that even totally different languages (like English and Hopi, or Chinese) are not untranslatable, and that there are many Hopis or Chinese who have learnt to master English very well.
>
> The Myth of the Framework is, in our time, the central bulwark of irrationalism. My counter-thesis is that it simply exaggerates a difficulty into an impossibility. The difficulty of discussion between people brought up in different frameworks is to be admitted. But nothing is more fruitful than such a discussion; than the culture clash which has stimulated some of the greatest intellectual revolutions.

7. Particularly where the system is one of evaluation which takes the measure of other forms of life. Films such as 'Alphaville' or '1984' have dealt with this through the genre of science fiction, while a film like 'The Royal Hunt

for the Sun' has attempted to present the clash between different forms of life in both a dialectical and ethical appreciation of history; in this instance, Pizzaro's conquest of the Incas.

8. The sexual politics of the women's movement demonstrate this point in highly practical terms.
9. Clearly, the Reformation of Luther is a contradiction of this. Luther believed that 'the word of God, which teaches full freedom, should not and must not be fettered' (Luther, in Wolf, 1952, p. 345), and in consequence sought to eliminate all mediation between man and God, which would have implied the dismantling of God's temporal organisation, the Church, together with a concomitant rule and domination which comprised the church's earthly apparatus of coercion and administration. However, we should not forget that Luther was succeeded by Calvin, with the consequence that the former's radical project for the destruction of totalitarian earthly religious authority and the creation of congregational democracy was severely modified by Calvin's re-equipment of the church with the paraphernalia of practice organised according to the traditional principles of organisation: hierarchical control, co-ordination and communication.
10. Nihilism as a philosophical theme has been dealt with most thoroughly by Stanley Rosen (1969). Our treatments diverge considerably, particularly with respect to Wittgenstein (1968) (see Clegg, 1975; 1976).
11. Von Wright (1974, p. 4) discusses the root metaphors. Galtung (1967) does the best job that I know of in putting them into practice for sociology. Fletcher (1974) shows how sociology can get mis-shapen in the process.
12. Dahl (1958) can be seen as the almost final flowering of a mechanistic mode of thinking which derives directly from the impact of the Enlightenment on discourse such as that of classical mechanics. At a general level Matson (1964) pursues the lineage from classical mechanics to mechanistic science. Cassirer (1951) enquires into the philosophy of the Enlightenment generally. His second chapter was part of the background reading to this essay. Elsewhere, in a more general context, I have examined the traces of mechanism still persistent in debates on 'power' (Clegg, 1975, especially Chapter 2).
13. The idea of the 'possible society' derives from Wittgenstein (1968), via Blum (1971), and is discussed and used in Clegg (1975). The idea obviously has a considerable affinity with the notions discussed in notes 4 and 5.
14. Lukes wants to go further than this. He wants to be able to measure not only 'power-effects' but also the concept of 'interests' which Bachrach and Baratz express, albeit 'subjectively'. Lukes will talk about 'real interests', though, and, in so doing, attempt to resolve the following problem.

    We might want to say that power is sometimes exercised in an almost intangible way, in the manner in which certain issues in a certain arena are almost never raised to the point of contention. But how can we study something which never happens? How can we achieve a measure of absence, of nothingness? Lukes argues that this can be done by specifying the interests of the various parties which are engaged in the arena. This already presumes a certain discreteness as a property of social action which may well be lacking in empirical instances. It also limits analysis to groups which are already formed. However, if issues may not be, then why may groups not be as well?

    As an example of how Lukes thinks interests might be specified, and 'third dimensional' research be achieved, he cites Crenson's (1971) study of *The Un-politics of Air Pollution*. The cities involved were the lakeside cities of Gary and East Chicago, steel-making cities in the eastern United States. In the terms which Lukes takes from Dahl (1957), an A (US Steel), exercised power over a B (the city of Gary) because A acted in a manner which was against the interests of B. It did not do this in another city, C (East Chicago). The interests of the citizens, Crenson reasons, is in not being poisoned by air pollution. Therefore, not to oppose air pollution is not to raise an issue. It is to neglect one's real interests. This could be seen to be an exercise of power by an A over a B. In the A-C relationship, A did not exercise power over C. In this city, East Chicago, the citizens opposed air pollution as early as 1942 with local government legislation which it would have been within Gary's legal power to have enacted. Thus, East Chicago opposed US Steel, while Gary did not. Crenson holds that the explanation for this variance is that while Gary was a city dominated by one party and one company, East Chicago had a number of parties and steel companies. In Gary, one might say, the 'mobilisation of bias' was extremely active, which was not the case in the more plural East Chicago.

Crenson's research is excellent within its limitations. However, it is not suitable as a model for overcoming the issues which Lukes wants to confront. One cannot resolve epistemological issues with empirical solutions. At this stage of criticism in the discourse the resuscitation of John Stuart Mill (1842) in the guise of the empirical application of his second canon, the method of difference, will not resolve the issues. Crenson's application of the second canon, although ingenious, is not one which is immediately generalisable to very many research settings. This is because it is rarely that we deal with issues of interest which are as seemingly clear-cut as whether one prefers to live in healthy, or less healthy, conditions. (One might, for instance, prefer work now, rather than the risk of ill-health in the future, if one thought that ensuring the latter might risk the former. Many people enjoy the satisfaction that they derive from smoking themselves to death. One would think that their real interest was in the continuation of healthy life. On Crenson and Lukes' criteria this would seem not to be the case. Perhaps other issues and other interests cloud the seemingly perspicuous problematic of air pollution as well?) The interest which keeps obscuring such research may not be that which is under study so much as that through which it is studied. The problems and their empirical solutions are generated within an interest which is itself the problem. I do believe that it is possible to tackle these complicated issues in an empirical manner (as I have tried to in my own research into power (Clegg, 1975)), but that to do so, one has first to transcend the 'transcendental framework'. Transcending the transcendental framework is clearly a second-order activity. One might say that it is even a developmental process in the terms of a discourse. Habermas (1970) appears to argue this, according to Janet Wolff's (1975) account.

15. John H. Schaar (1970) makes it quite clear why one might no longer find it easy to discuss 'legitimate authority'.
16. Which finds its methodological advocacy in those scholars who recommend that one should study power 'reputationally', as for instance, Hunter (1953).
17. Or as I have put it elsewhere and in a slightly different context

> In attending to the various ways in which theorists have approached and used the concept of power, then, we are attending not only to their definitions and the critiques of these, but to the 'theorising power' which makes of such definitions and critiques orderly, recognisable and sociological phenomena. The air of authenticity which they wear as plausible scholarship is a manifestation of their mode of production. The actual writing merely re-presents and preserves the deeper possibility of how it is that they are at all possible. Their possibility as features of the sociological enterprise to be discussed, argued, debated and criticised is rooted in their methodical character. They result from the theorists'

engagement with method, and are only possible given the theorists' engagement with a tradition of theorising (Clegg, 1975, pp. 10-11).
18. What Marx termed 'praxis'.

References

Althusser, L. (1969). *For Marx,* translated by Ben Brewster. London: Allen Lane, The Penguin Press.

Bachrach, P. and Baratz, M.D. (1971). Two Faces of Power. In F.G. Castles, D.J. Murray and D.C. Potter (eds.), *Decisions, Organizations and Society*. Harmondsworth: Penguin, pp. 376-88. Originally published in *American Political Science Review, 56* (1962), 947-52.

Bar-Hillel, Y. (1954). Indexical Expressions. *Mind, 63*, 359-79.

Bauman, Z. (1976). *Toward a Critical Sociology: An Essay on Commonsense and Emancipation*. London: Routledge Direct Editions.

Blum, A.F. (1971). Theorising. In D.D. Douglas (ed.), *Understanding Everyday Life: Toward the Reconstruction of Sociological Knowledge*. London: Routledge and Kegan Paul.

Cassirer, E. (1951). *The Philosophy of the Enlightenment*. Boston: Beacon Press.

Chomsky, N. (1966). *Cartesian Linguistics*. New York: Harper and Row.

Chomsky, N. (1968). *Language and Mind*. New York: Harcourt, Brace and World.

Clegg, S. (1975). *Power, Rule and Domination: A Critical and Empirical Understanding of Power in Sociological Theory and Organizational Life*. London: Routledge and Kegan Paul.

Clegg, S. (1976). Power, Theorising and Nihilism. *Theory and Society, 3*, 65-87.

Commoner, B. (1972). *The Closing Circle: Confronting the Environmental Crisis*. London: Jonathan Cape.

Crenson, M.A. (1971). *The Un-Politics of Air Pollution: A Study of Non-Decision Making in the Cities*. Baltimore and London: The Johns Hopkins Press.

Dahl, R.A. (1957). The Concept of Power. *Behavioural Science, 2*, 201-15.

Derrida, J. (1967). *L'Ecriture et la difference*. Paris: Seuil.

Derrida, J. (1970). A Note to a Footnote in Being and Time. In F.J. Smith (ed.), *Phenomenology in Perspective*. The Hague: Martinus Nijhoff.

Donato, E. (1973). Structuralism: The Aftermath. *Sub-Stance, 7*, Fall, 9-26.

Durkheim, E. (1938). *The Rules of Sociological Method*. New York: The Free Press.

Eliot, T.S. (1952). *The Complete Poems and Plays*. New York: Harcourt Brace.

Fletcher, C. (1974). *Beneath the Surface: An Account of Three Styles of Sociological Research*. London: Routledge and Kegan Paul.

Foucault, M. (1970). *The Order of Things*. London: Tavistock.

Foucault, M. (1972). *The Archaeology of Knowledge*. London: Tavistock.

Garfinkel, H. (1967). *Studies in Ethnomethodology*. Englewood Cliffs, New Jersey: Prentice-Hall.

Garfinkel, H. and Sacks, H. (1970). On the Formal Structures of Practical Actions. In J.C. McKinney and E.A. Tiryakian (eds.), *Theoretical Sociology: Perspectives and Developments.* New York: Appleton-Century-Crofts.

Habermas, J. (1970). *Zur Logik den Sozialwissenschaften.* Frankfurt am Main: Suhrkamp Verlag.

Habermas, J. (1974). *Theory and Practice*. London: Heinemann.

Horkheimer, M. and Adorno, T. (1944). *Dialektik der Aufklarung*. New York: Social Studies Association.

Hunter, F. (1953). *Community Power Structure*. Chapel Hill: University of North Carolina Press.

Hunter, J.F.M. (1971). Forms of Life in Wittgenstein's Philosophical Investigations. In E.D. Klemke (ed.), *Essays on Wittgenstein*. London: University of Illinois Press.

Jay, M. (1973). *The Dialectical Imagination*. London: Heinemann.

Kuhn, T.S. (1962). *The Structure of Scientific Revolutions*, first edition. London: University of Chicago Press.

Levi-Strauss, C. (1969). *Tristes Tropiques*. Paris: Plon.

Lukes, S. (1974). *Power: A Radical View*. London: Macmillan.

Matson, F.W. (1964). *The Broken Image: Man, Science and Society*. New York: George Brazilier.

Mill, J.S. (1842). *System of Logic*. London.

Pocock, J.G.A. (1971). *Politics, Language and Time: Essays on Political Thought and History*. London: Methuen.

Popper, K.R. (1970). Normal Science and its Dangers. In Imre Lakatos and Allan Musgrave (eds.), *Criticism and the Growth of Knowledge*. Cambridge: Cambridge University Press.

Popper, K. (1972). *Objective Knowledge: An Evolutionary Approach*. London: Oxford University Press.

Popper, K.R. (1974). The Logic of the Social Sciences. In *The Positivist*

Dispute in German Sociology, translated by Glynn Adey and David Frisby, pp. 87-122. London: Heinemann.

Rosen, S. (1969). *Nihilism: A Philosophical Essay*. Yale University Press.

Ryan, A. (1972). 'Normal' Science or Political Ideology. In P. Laslett, W.G. Runciman and Q. Skinher (1972), *Philosophy, Politics and Society* (fourth series). Oxford: Blackwell.

Sandywell, B., Silverman, D., Roche, M., Filmer, P. and Phillipson, M. (1975). *Problems of Reflexivity and Dialectics in Sociological Inquiry: Language Theorising Difference*. London: Routledge Direct Edition.

Schaar, J.H. (1970). Legitimacy in the Modern State. In Philip Green and Stanford Levinson (eds.), *Power and Community: Dissenting Essays in Political Science*. New York: Pantheon Books.

Schutz, A. (1967). *The Phenomenology of the Social World*. Evanston: Northwestern University Press.

Simmel, G. (1969). The Dyad and the Triad. In L.A. Coser and B. Rosenberg, *Sociological Theory: A Book of Readings*, pp. 59-68. London: Macmillan.

Steiner, G. (1975). *After Babel: Aspects of Language and Translation*. London: Oxford University Press.

Taylor, I., Walton, P. and Young, J. (1973). *The New Criminology: For a Social Theory of Deviance*. London: Routledge and Kegan Paul.

Weber, M. (1964). *The Sociology of Religion*, translated by E. Fischoff with an introduction by T. Parsons. London: Methuen.

White, D.M. (1971). Power and Intention. *American Political Science Review, 65,* September, 749-59.

Wieder, D.L. (1974). Telling the Code. In R. Turner (ed.), *Ethnomethodology*. Harmondsworth: Penguin.

Winch, P. (1958). *The Idea of a Social Science*. London: Routledge and Kegan Paul.

Wittgenstein, L. (1968). *Philosophical Investigations*. Oxford: Blackwell.

Wolf, B.L. (1952). *Reformation Writings of Martin Luther*. London: Luterworth.

Wolff, J. (1975). Hermeneutics and the Critique of Ideology. *Sociological Review, 23,* 4, November 1975, 811-270.

Von Wright, G.H. (1971). *Explanation and Understanding*. London: Routledge and Kegan Paul.

5 ROLE-PLAYING AND ROLE PERFORMANCE IN SOCIAL PSYCHOLOGICAL RESEARCH[1]

Gerald P. Ginsburg

In a seminar at Oxford University early in 1976, the American social psychologist Leonard Berkowitz reported an interesting experiment which involved some deception of the participants. Chatting afterwards about the ethics of deception in experiments, Berkowitz expressed the view that in another five years or so, there won't be any more experimental social psychology as we know it today. Both individual universities and government agencies are developing guidelines which may well prohibit any and all deception of experimental participants, except under the most unusual circumstances. In view of this emerging development, it is worth considering the nature of deception research, what if anything would be lost by its demise, and experimental alternatives. In the framework of such considerations, this chapter will focus on a class of investigative procedures which has been recommended by some as an alternative or at least an important supplement to conventional, deceptive experimentation in social psychology: role-playing.

Background Context of Contemporary Role-Playing

The use of role-playing as a substitute for deception in experimental social psychology is a controversial issue. It has been simmering actively, especially in the United States, for a decade, ever since Kelman (1967) pointed out that deception had become a dominant research practice and queried whether we really had to lie and deceive in order to generate social psychological knowledge. However, role-playing has a fairly long history of use in psychology, other than as a substitute for deception, and a brief summary will provide a perspective from which to view the current controversy.

Role-playing has been used as an assessment technique for decades. During World War Two it was used in the United States for the selection of espionage and sabotage agents (OSS Staff, 1948). It also has been used in the assessment of more academic qualities, such as personality dimensions (see reviews by Mann, 1956; Leibowitz, 1968) and their expression in small groups (Borgatta, 1955). Currently, role-playing is being used for the systematic assessment of people's characteristic styles of interaction (McReynolds, deVoge, Osborne, Pither and Nordin,

1976) and in the assessment of deficits in social skills (Trower, Bryant and Argyle, 1977).

Role-playing also has been used as a therapeutic procedure. Among its earlier therapeutic applications was psychodrama (Moreno, 1946), and since then it has been used steadily in psychotherapy (Mann, 1956; Goldstein and Simonson, 1971) and in social skills training (Trower *et al.*, 1977). Furthermore, less well documented use of it has been made routinely to train people in sales, industrial relations, medicine and teaching, and in such man-machine systems as flight, weightlessness and driver simulations.

It is worth noting that all of these uses involve *active* role-playing, in which a person acts out a part in a scenario. A more passive form of role-playing has been recommended in recent years as a means for assessing the ethical quality of experiments, before the experiments actually are conducted (Berscheid, Baron, Dermer and Libman, 1973). None of these techniques has engendered much controversy in the technical literature.

There has been extensive use of role-playing in conventional experimental social psychology, too, which has not led to heated epistemological debate. For example, the Yale group used role-playing as a deliberate treatment condition in their studies of attitude and behavioural change (Janis and King, 1954; Janis and Mann, 1965). Also, Davis and his colleagues routinely use role-playing in their studies of jury decision processes (Davis, Kerr, Atkin and Meek, 1975); and we do the same in our laboratory studies of risk-taking in gambling (Blascovich, Ginsburg and Veach, 1975; Ginsburg, Blascovich and Howe, 1976). Another interesting and relatively non-controversial use of role-playing has emerged in the study of emotional expression and recognition (Davitz, 1964; Laird, 1974; Lanzetta, Cartwright-Smith and Kleck, 1976), in which experimental participants are asked to behave or appear as though they were experiencing a particular emotional state, or an augmented or subdued intensity of an emotional state.

These illustrative uses of role-playing have been subjected only to the usual, healthy scepticism of the empirical sciences, in which questions are raised about design artefacts and reliability of measures. However, a different and more heated sort of argument arose in 1967, when both Daryl Bem and Herbert Kelman took to task the very active and popular area of dissonance research. It is that argument which leads to the current controversy concerning role-playing and deception in the generation of social psychological knowledge.

Contemporary Controversy: Role-Playing versus Deception

In 1967, Bem published a paper in which he contended that internal psychodynamic mechanisms such as cognitive dissonance were not necessary to explain what essentially was sensible self-persuasion, in which a person accounts for what he has seen himself do, having been asked to account. The development of an 'interpersonal simulation' technique by Bem and the attacks upon it by others have been reviewed in lively detail elsewhere (Bem, 1972), and I need not cover it here.

Bem's argument challenged the conceptual heart of an immense array of experiments and beliefs; but Kelman's paper (1967) struck at its moral heart. Kelman pointed out that much of the research in social psychology in recent years had involved deception, often with outright lying and positive deceit. He questioned the morality of such actions, and he also questioned their wisdom. That is, he raised questions about both ethics and validity, although it is the ethical which evoked the strongest reactions and attracted the most attention. Kelman suggested that we might use role-playing as an alternative to deception, and it is that suggestion that provided a focus for the ensuing disagreements. It is worth examining the essential arguments of the protagonists in this debate, not for ethical reasons, but because of the truly basic epistemological and conceptual issues which the argument has brought to the fore.

Several people over the past decade have taken serious issue with the use of deception (Argyris, 1975; Forward, Canter and Kirsch, 1976; Gadlin and Ingle, 1975; Hamilton, 1976; Harré and Secord, 1972; Jourard, 1968; Kelman, 1967; Mixon, 1971, 1972, 1974a, 1974b, in press; Ring, 1967; Schultz, 1969), sometimes as part of a more general critique of the manipulative experimental approach *per se*. These writers as a group present at least three basic arguments against deception in the conduct of experiments. First, it is unethical. Second, it has undesirable epistemological consequences. For example, it requires, creates and tests a model of man who has unrealistically limited powers of thinking and of manipulating his environments and of comprehending his circumstances and taking consequent action; that is, the experimental subject is neither construed as nor allowed to act as an active agent with respect to the problem being studied. Yet, the entity which we are trying to understand, i.e. the person, *is* an active planning agent. Third, deception has undesirable methodological consequences. For example, word gets around rapidly in a student setting and it isn't long before all of the potential subjects presume that they will be deceived in any experiment. This in turn augments the inherent problems of response artefacts and the adoption of one or more roles by the subjects (Weber and Cook, 1972) which may interfere with both internal and external validity (Campbell, 1957). Most of the authors in the anti-deception group urge that the person be treated as a knowledgeable but not necessarily accurate informant who can participate with the investigator in the creation of our professional knowledge. They also display a recognition of the purpose of science – that is, to create adequate explanations and understandings – which is consistent with contemporary themes in the philosophy of science. The procedures recommended by this group include various forms of role-playing, self-disclosure and negotiation between investigator and informant.

The defenders of deception in social psychological experimentation (e.g. Aronson and Carlsmith, 1968; Freedman, 1969; Miller, 1972) also are highly critical of role-playing as a device for generating scientific knowledge. Along with some social psychologists who are critical of role-playing but do not defend deception (e.g. Rubin, 1973), these critics fault role-playing on several important grounds. First, role-playing is unreal with respect to the variable under study, in that the subject reports what he *would do,* and that is taken as though he did do it. Second, the behaviour displayed is not spontaneous, even in the more active forms of role-playing. Third, the verbal reports in role-playing are very susceptible to artefactual influence, such as social desirability. Finally, data are cited which imply that role-playing procedures are not sensitive to complex interactions, whereas deception designs are (Willis and Willis, 1970). Buttressing these essentially thematic arguments are data (reported by Homes and Bennett, 1974; and by West, Gunn and Chernicky, 1975) which show clear differences between the behaviour of deceived subjects and the behaviours predicted by role-playing subjects. In general, this group views science as involved in the discovery of natural truths, and they contend that role-playing simply cannot substitute for deception – a sad but unavoidable state of affairs. To hold otherwise, they argue, would constitute a retreat from empirical science to a psychology of intuition, speculation and consensus (Freedman, 1969).

Evaluation of the Criticisms of Role-Playing

A careful examination of the criticisms of role-playing reveals them to be largely unfounded. This will be demonstrated first by considering the purported lack of realism and spontaneity in role-playing studies; and then consideration will be given to the criteria in terms of which role-playing has been assessed by its critics.

Realism and Spontaneity

The target of most of the criticism of role-playing is what might be termed 'passive' role-playing. The investigator describes an experiment and asks the audience to predict the outcomes. Such a procedure does not produce spontaneous behaviour of the sort displayed in the experiment itself, and in that sense is neither 'real' nor 'spontaneous'. Nevertheless, the passive role-play procedure is useful under certain conditions and for certain purposes, provided it is modified so that each participant is asked to predict how he or some other concrete person would behave. Given such constraints, passive role-playing can be used to indicate what themes in an episode, such as an experiment, are likely to make a difference in the outcome. Bem has taken this position (1968) in some of the debates (e.g. Piliavin, Piliavin, Loewenton, McCauley and Hammond, 1969) concerning his interpersonal simulations. People are very sensitive to differences in the contents of the scripts.

The utility of passive role-playing will be illustrated later in this chapter, but there is another form of role-playing – *active* role-playing – which refutes the claims of unreality and lack of spontaneity. In active role-playing, the participants knowingly participate in the creation of an illusion by performing one or more parts in a scenario. Such a procedure may well generate spontaneous behaviour of the sort which would obtain in the natural setting being represented by the scenario, and with deep involvement on the parts of the participants. Three examples of such realism and spontaneity are described below.

In 1966, the Canadian Friends Service Committee published a most interesting report (Olsen and Christiansen, 1966). It described a Quaker exercise in non-violent resistance. One group of participants was assigned to defend Grindstone Island against attack, and to do so non-violently. Another group was given the assignment of attacking the island. Of course, everybody knew that it was a role-play exercise. Nevertheless, the exercise had to be stopped after 31 hours. A dozen people were bordering on shock. The defenders had behaved recklessly and unpredictably, and several had been judged to die – needlessly – by the referees. Those who were still 'alive' seemed dazed and incapable of further sustained and organised behaviour. It was a painful and revealing experience for all concerned; and it would be silly to claim that the exercise, clearly role-playing, did not involve spontaneity and reality.

Another example is the Stanford Prison Study, conducted by Zimbardo and his colleagues (Haney, Banks and Zimbardo, 1973). They wanted to show that prison brutality could be due to the social structure of the setting and was not necessarily due to personal characteristics, so they designed a role-playing study. They selected 24 college males through a newspaper advertisement, and assigned 12 to the prisoner role. All knew that they were to participate in a role-play study of prison life which was to continue for two weeks and for which they would be paid $15 a day. The prisoners were picked up in a police van, blindfolded, taken to the 'prison' in the basement of the Psychology building, stripped, skin searched, and put through the general prison intake routine. Violence and rebellion developed within two days, along with harassment and humiliation by the guards, who were able to destroy the group solidarity of the prisoners. One prisoner was released in 36 hours because of screaming, crying and disorganised thinking, and three others were released on the fourth day. Two of them showed severe emotional disturbances, and the other one had what was described as a psychosomatic rash over his whole body. The remaining prisoners became docile, passive and isolated, and they displayed considerable personal and social disintegration. Meantime, the guards became increasingly hostile and harassing. The experiment was terminated after six days. It was unquestionably powerful, even for the investigators: Zimbardo found himself being drawn into the swirling hostilities and tensions. Again, there seems little question about spontaneity.

On the other hand, serious questions have been raised about why the role-players behaved as they did, and issue has been taken with the assumption that the outcome reflected the operation of structural forces. Instead, the role-players may have been acting out their social stereotypes (Banuazizi and Mohavedi, 1975; Mohavedi and Banuazizi, 1975). Be that as it may, two points emerge: spontaneity of behaviour was evident; and the reasons for the behaviour are still hidden – or at least ambiguous. But the set of role-playing procedures offers greater promise for discerning the reasons for such behaviour than do conventional experimental techniques. The next example illustrates this latter point quite well.

Stanley Milgram (1963, 1974) conducted a series of studies of what he described as 'destructive obedience', in which the experimental subject was assigned to a teacher role and had to give a learner an electric shock each time the learner made a mistake. The learner was a confederate. The 'teacher' was instructed to give a stronger shock after each error, eventually reaching a purported and extremely dangerous 450 volts. To the surprise of everybody, about two-thirds of the subjects in the critical condition went all the way to 450 volts, despite objections, pleas and eventually awesome silence from the 'learner' in the adjoining room. Was this evidence of shockingly destructive obedience, equivalent to that of concentration camp guards? That is how the behaviour was interpreted, and the obvious discomfort of the 'teachers' – nervous giggling, lip-biting, clenched fists, profuse sweating – was interpreted as evidence of a severe conflict between obedience to authority and personal horror at the pain and possible harm being done to the 'learner'. The Milgram studies are widely presumed to reflect the sad inability of people to resist authoritative commands within appropriate institutional structures.

Mixon (1971, 1972) had doubts about certain elements of the interpretation of the Milgram series, and he also had misgivings about its ethics, so he undertook an ingenious sequence of role-playing studies, in which he used both passive and active procedures. By variations of the script that Milgram had used, Mixon was able to demonstrate and then to test a strong and plausible alternative to Milgram's interpretation. Specifically, Mixon interpreted his findings as demonstrating that Milgram's results rested heavily upon the apparent legitimacy of the authority of the experimenter and upon the limits of that legitimacy. An experimenter may have the right to instruct a subject to cause pain to another person in the conduct of research; but he does not have the right to direct one person to cause harm to another. Instructions which directed one person to cause harm (rather than pain) to another would be illegitimate.

Mixon argued that Milgram's subjects defied the experimenter when his commands were seen as illegitimate, obeyed him when his commands were seen as legitimate (and thus not causing harm to the confederate), and showed agitation, uncertainty and variation in behaviour when the legitimacy of the experimenter's orders was ambiguous. Mixon found much the same pattern in his active role-playing replications, including the agitation, and he was able to exercise considerable control by revising his scripts so as to alter the clarity of the legitimacy of the commands and thereby obtain 100 per cent compliance, 100 per cent defiance, or – as had Milgram – a mixture of about two-thirds compliance.

The three illustrations of active role-playing make it clear that the critics of role-playing have erred in conceiving of role-playing as necessarily passive and without spontaneity. Furthermore, the Mixon example goes further by demonstrating the precision of control that an investigator can gain by modifying the script of the role-play scenario. However, it should be noted that Mixon has not subjected his plausible understanding to critical test, nor has he identified the social rules by which judgements of the legitimacy of orders are guided. These qualifications notwithstanding, role-playing clearly has the potential for realism, spontaneity and involvement.

Criterion: The Deception Experiment

In the current controversy about role-playing, the question usually posed is whether role-playing procedures can substitute for deception in social psychological experimentation. The criterion by which answers to this question are evaluated is the deception experiment. Specifically, do role-playing replications generate results which match those of the original deception experiment? However, the deception experiment is an unsuitable criterion of social psychological knowledge, and for several reasons.

In the first place, deception experiments require secrecy and control for internal validity (Argyris, 1975), and they require naive subjects who will not respond to the experimenter as such but only to the intentionally manipulated variables (Aronson and Carlsmith, 1968). Yet, we know with little doubt that most of our experimental subjects are not naive, that they do react to the treatments and to the setting and the experimenter along dimensions other than the manipulation itself, that they pass the word around to each other about experiments, and that they are very unlikely to admit their lack of naiveté (Crowle, 1976; Glinski, Glinski and Slatin, 1970; Golding and Lichtenstein, 1970; Ring, 1967). Furthermore, we know that the knowledge of the subjects does affect the experimental outcomes, and often in complex and unpredictable ways (Silverman, Shulman and Wiesenthal, 1970; Stricker, Messick and Jackson, 1970; Weber and Cook, 1972). If we knew the meanings which the experimental setting and manipulations had for our subjects, we could reduce the demonstrable ambiguity (Weber and Cook, 1972) of the results.

Unfortunately, we can't discover the meanings of the manipulations or the setting because we can't enter into discourse with the subject – to do so would give him the opportunity to have an effect upon the experimenter or the design. Moreover, post-experimental interviews cannot yield unambiguous meanings because the meaning of an event derives from the whole act or episode of which it is a component. Therefore, an event is likely to have different meanings at the time it occurs in the midst of an experiment and after the completion of the experiment when the participant is asked about it. In general, meanings are not the sort of data we seek in deception frameworks because we do not construe our subjects as generating meanings upon which they take further action. Our subjects necessarily are construed as limited persons; that is, we conceive of them as though they had limited powers relative to people in everyday life (Forward, Canter and Kirsch, 1976).

Of course, we in fact *do* deal with meanings when we interpret our data. We use our own layman's knowledge of the culture to speculate about the meanings which experimental events hold for our subjects, and we base our interpretations on these speculations. So it isn't that we don't use meanings in our generation of knowledge; it simply is the case that instead of obtaining them systematically from the subjects, we speculate about them and select plausible ones ourselves. Commitment to a deceptive approach constrains us from discerning the very meanings which would allow unambiguous interpretation of our data.

Both Mixon (in press, a and b) and Foward *et al.* (1976) argue that there is an inherent and irresolvable dilemma in the deception design which logically prevents unambiguous inferences. We create a cover story in which a critical behaviour is defined as routine or incidental, but we have a private story which contains the real definition of that behaviour. The real definition construes the behaviour as one which the subject would avoid performing if he knew its real definition (e.g. pushing a shock lever may be defined privately by the experimenter and his colleagues as a heinous act of destructive obedience, while the experimenter defines it for the subject as a routine step in the experiment). That, of course, is why we set up deception studies. Notice the dilemma: we can draw an unambiguous inference about our phenomenon of interest only if the critical behaviour of the subject actually represents an instance of our private definition; but if it does represent such an instance, and the subject sees this, he will respond disingenuously. If the subject does not see the investigator's private meaning of the critical behaviour, then that behaviour may not be an instance of the private definition, and if the behaviour does not represent a clear instance of the private definition, how can we be said to have dealt with our variable of interest?

Hamilton (1976) extends this logically by pointing out that deceptions themselves are simulations. The experimenter role plays a cover story which he believes is functionally equivalent (for the participant) to the situation which the cover story is supposed to be. Thus, a deception experiment is not the same as a straightforward experiment, as in psychophysics, especially since the deception experimenter may explain the participant's behaviour with reference to his own definition of the situation rather than the participant's – and those two definitions are different, by deliberate intent.

Similarly, deceptive field experiments are simulations of the situation to which the contrived events are presumed to be functionally equivalent. For example, when a research assistant collapsed in a subway train (Piliavin and Piliavin, 1972; Piliavin, Rodin and Piliavin, 1969), he was role-playing. His behaviour was not analysed, but it is strongly implied in the published articles that the assistant's behaviour was thoroughly realistic and convincing to the other, naive passengers, who appeared to react spontaneously to it. Obviously, it is presumed that the research assistant participated so realistically that the actions of bystanders can be taken as reactions to the assistant as though he had *not* been role-playing. It is not known whether that presumption is justified, and it may be that the results are due to special features of the assistant's role performances. Therefore, interpretive ambiguity can be seen to exist even in deceptive field experiments; it is not restricted to deceptive laboratory studies.

Finally, both experimental subjects and experimenters appear to have a framework of role expectations and related rules which apply to experimental settings (Epstein, Suedfeld and Silverstein, 1973; Shulman and Berman, 1975), but their content is largely unknown. Again, our research orientation generally constrains us from attempting to determine them (Friedman, 1967; Harré and Secord, 1972). This is unfortunate, because it not only makes unclear the reasons for our experimental results; it also makes it difficult to specify the natural settings to which our results might apply since an important basis for generalisation is the comparability of the role/rule frameworks between the research setting and those settings to which we wish to generalise.

Summarising to this point, the critics of role-playing have displayed a misconception of role-playing as necessarily passive and without spontaneity. Also, they have used an inadequate criterion for assessing its utility – that is, the deception experiment. And they have asked the wrong question – namely, whether role-playing can substitute for deception. Deception experiments certainly have no absolute claim to truth or accuracy, and they appear to have certain inherent properties which preclude unambiguous inferences about social behaviour. The problem is not so much ethical as epistemological – deception procedures do not and cannot generate unambiguous information, either about the conditions under which behaviours occur or about the mechanisms which explain them. The next section offers several illustrations of the pitfalls which develop when one tries to assess role-playing as a substitute for deception.

Empirical Comparison of Role-Playing and Deception

A number of studies have attempted to compare role-playing and deception approaches to the generation of social psychological knowledge. Three fairly recent studies will serve to illustrate the difficulties in such attempts. All three studies reflect a naiveté concerning role-playing and the function of research in social psychological explanations.

Willis and Willis (1970)

This study has been cited as evidence of the inadequacy of role-playing as a substitute for deception (Miller, 1972). The study was a conformity experiment in which deception and role-playing were compared. In the conventional design, subjects judged the quality of a number of photographs, and then each was told how his partner had judged them. Furthermore, the subject was told how accurate his and his partner's judgements were, relative to judgements by experts, and he was given the opportunity to evaluate the photographs again. It was found that the partner's expertise had an important influence on the subject's judgements when the experiment was defined as a study of 'How people use additional information', but not if it was defined as a study of 'How people are influenced by each other'. Thus, an interaction effect was found in the conventional, deception design.

The role-playing procedure was passive. Participants were given a description of the experiment and were asked to predict how the deceived subjects would behave. The role-playing participants did not make the distinction between the two purposes of the experiment; they predicted that the deceived subjects would conform more to a more expert partner, regardless of the stated purpose of the study. Thus, the role-play replication did not produce the interaction effect.

Several aspects of this study are worth noting, in line with the discussion in the prior section. First, the role-play participants were asked how a deceived subject would act, not how they themselves would act, so they were not presented with a proper analogue of the deception experiment. They should have been asked to predict their own behaviours rather than to duplicate imagined deception subjects. Second, the role-players were given information about comparing role-playing and deception, thereby being given much more information than the deceived subjects. Both of these aspects are important and have to be taken into consideration in making comparisons (Horowitz and Rothschild, 1970; Darroch and Steiner, 1970; Mixon, 1971, 1972).

Finally, the outcome of the deception experiment itself is ambiguous. The results may have been due to the effects of suspiciousness, since more deceived subjects were suspicious when they were told that their partners were much more accurate than they were themselves. The greater suspiciousness could have interacted with the description of the purpose of the experiment as shown in Table 5.1.

Table 5.1

Definition of Experiment	Character to be Presented by Suspicious Subjects	Consequence
Information Processing	Demonstrate they are good at using new information	Use partner's judgement
Social Influence	Demonstrate they are not simple conformists	Reject partner's judgements

Therefore, the outcome could be due to the desire of suspicious subjects to present a certain character, a certain self, and not simply to the operation of conformity pressures to which the subjects responded in an un-self-conscious manner. This pattern is exactly the sort which Weber and Cook (1972) cited as a possibility if evaluation apprehension is aroused; and they warned that the results, although artefactual, are likely to be interpreted as the effects of independent variable manipulations.

The outcomes of the deception experiment are ambiguous, largely due to our ignorance of the meanings which the events held for people in each cell of the design. The deception experiment did not generate data which can be used as a criterion set. Also, the role-play design was not a direct analogue of the deception design. Thus, a comparison of the two designs is of little value.

Holmes and Bennett (1974)

In this study, the role-players were told that the experiment was a sham, a deception. They then were given the instructions that had been given to the subjects in the deception part of the experiment, informing them that they were going to receive electric shocks when a signal came on during the course of the experiment. The role-players also were told that anticipation of shocks generally leads to increased heart and breathing rates. The role players were able to duplicate the deception subjects' responses on an affect check-list, but they did not duplicate the increased heart and respiration rates of the deception subjects. This was taken as evidence that role-playing is a poor substitute for deception. However, the fact that the role-players did not show an increased respiration rate even though they had been told about it suggests that they were not adequately involved in the role-playing task. Respiration rate can be increased easily for short periods of time, but to do so requires a bit of acting, a willingness to look a bit silly, perhaps, and the role-players didn't do that. The success of a role-playing task depends upon the active participation of the role-players in the creation of an illusion (Mixon, 1974b); the fact that they didn't do so means that role-playing was not really tested. Once again, ignorance of the meanings which the various conditions held for the subjects makes internal comparisons ambiguous and the applicability of the results to other settings unascertainable. (Also, we have the problem of full knowledge again; cf. Horowitz and Rothschild, 1970.)

West, Gunn and Chernicky (1975)

These authors compared passive role-playing against a field deception procedure and found the role-playing lacking. The investigators were interested in whether people had been affected by Watergate, and especially whether they could be persuaded to engage in a burglary of company secrets. They also wanted to assess the sorts of accounts people would use to explain behaviour, either of oneself or of another person. It was expected that the deception subjects would explain their actions in terms of situational factors, while passive role-players would make greater reference to qualities of the person. The authors found that 45 per cent of the deceived subjects expressed willingness to participate in the burglary when it was described as being done for the Internal Revenue Service and the burglary team as being immune from prosecution. Introductory Psychology role-players had predicted 28 per cent, a dependably smaller amount. When the sponsor of the burglary was described as a competing firm, or as the IRS but without immunity, or just as the team itself trying to test its skill, agreement was low in actuality and was predicted to be low by the role-players. For the present purposes, we shall ignore the ethical issues in this study, and the authors' interest in attributions, and consider three points.

First, the role-playing task was constructed incorrectly. Role-players were asked, 'How many people out of 100 would agree to participate?' Such a question might imply 'How many would *do* it?' But we have no comparison for that question, because we don't know how many of the deceived subjects who agreed to participate under the immediate pressure of a private meeting with the burglary team actually would have gone on to perform the burglary. The role-players should have been asked, 'How many would go on to discuss the burglary at length with the experimenter and his confederate?' or '. . . with the burglary team?' Second, note that the question again deals with the base rate prediction rather than the prediction of a concrete instance.

Third, the critical situation for the deceived subject occurred when he found himself in a private meeting with two men who proposed a burglary and presented themselves as experts in such activity. The subject was under great compliance pressure – not to perform the burglary, but to agree to perform it and to participate in the ensuing discussion. It seems reasonable to presume that he was performing a role in that strange setting, and whether he would have continued his line of actions to the completion of a burglary episode is enigmatic.

Therefore, the criterion performance of the study may itself have been an instance of active role-playing, which may or may not have been transformed through further stages to an actual burglary. Again, we see that internal comparisons are ambiguous because we don't know the meanings of the conditions for the subjects; and applicability of the results to natural settings of interest – such as Watergate – simply is not ascertainable.

So, an examination of studies which pitted role-playing against deception makes clear that we can't learn very much from those comparisons, except in the negative: viz., deception cannot be used as a criterion procedure. Furthermore, it is clear that subjects and experimenters perform within certain roles, and their behaviours are guided by rules. Unfortunately, the details of these role/rule frameworks are largely unknown. On the other hand, role-playing can be used to facilitate the identification of role/rule frameworks. In fact, careful consideration of role-playing procedures will make it evident that they provide us with a wide range of tools for enhancing our understandings of human behaviour. Role-playing is not a panacea for all of our investigative and conceptual problems, but neither is any of the other procedures by which we generate the knowledge of our field; and role-playing procedures, if used correctly, do afford us great control over the episode we wish to study. The next section deals directly with these issues.

Role-Playing: Its Nature and Potential

At first glance, the essential feature of role-playing is pretence. Both the audience and the performer know that the performer is pretending, and the knowledge that each knows that the performance as a pretence is shared by all concerned. This feature appears to distinguish role-play performances from real-life behaviour. However, the distinction is not nearly so clear or simple. As will be seen, pretence is not limited to role-playing. The nature of role-playing, as an investigative technique in social psychology, is complex, and it must be understood within the larger context of the objectives of social psychological research.

Objectives and Strategies in Social Psychological Research

The objective of science is to create understandings, to generate accurate and effective explanations (Toulmin, 1961). Prediction and control are means by which we advance and assess our understandings, but it is the understandings which are our ultimate objective. Theories are the extended statements of our understandings, and they are preceded by the recognition of some non-random pattern which needs explanation (Harré, 1976a). There are times when we only have a hunch about the existence of a non-random pattern, and it is necessary to conduct research to establish its existence and form – what might be called critical description (Harré and Secord, 1972). Then, as Harré (1976a) points out, further research is undertaken to establish the range of conditions under which the phenomenon obtains. The most creative step is the construction of an analogue of the presumed mechanism which generates the now identified phenomenon under the range of conditions within which the phenomenon has been observed to occur. That analogue, or model, usually must be compatible with the known instances of the phenomenon, and it must not be incompatible with the knowledge of the times. That is, the model generally must be both adequate and plausible. Subsequent research, and perhaps advances in related technologies, may lead to the establishment of the actual existence of the things or processes hypothesised by the model, and of their causal production of the observed, non-random patterns. At that time, the theory no longer involves a model, but a description of the thing itself. The acceptance and applicability of the theory is basically dependent upon its plausibility, its compatibility with what is considered to be obviously real in the current era. Beliefs about reality change over time, both within scientific communities and across large cultures – we now accept the world as round, despite the fact that nobody falls off – and even our most firmly established scientific laws are potentially evanescent, dependent upon the metaphysics of the period (Harré, 1976a, p. 39). Schlenker (1974) also argues that laws and theories 'are man-made abstractions and interpretations of the world'

(p. 12) and that scientific laws are statements about patterns. If someone breaks a scientific law, it can only be because the 'law' was inadequate. Thus, as is becoming increasingly clear even to contemporary social psychologists, scientific activity does not involve the discovery of 'natural laws', but the discovery of non-random patterns and the creation of models which explain those patterns in a manner compatible with fact.

Harré (1976a) also points out that models can be used to represent, perhaps in simplified or idealised form, the subject-matter on which the model is based. An example might be a drawing of the human circulatory system, based upon knowledge of human cardiovascular anatomy. However, the more directly creative use of models is analogical: the unknown mechanism which generates an observed phenomenon is modelled after some subject-matter (entity, process) which is known and well understood. The behavioural and social sciences are replete with past and current examples: the telephone switchboard and mass action models of brain activity; the dramaturgical models of human social activity; the talkative and rational lay scientist as a contemporary model for attribution behaviours; the middle-class, college-educated person, sensitive to logical inconsistencies, as the cognitive dissonance model of human thinking and acting; and a wide variety of engineering systems as the models for human memory and information-processing.

It is essential to note that models not only are used in explanation, but they guide the activities of those who use them. This is true for scientists in their use of scientific models, and for persons in general in their use of beliefs about why people do things and what causes what. In this context, it is worth noting that role-playing scenarios, of both active and passive forms, are models of the structure of a given situation and the potentials for comprehensible action within it. This has been suggested by Mixon (in press, b) and we will return to it later, after considering the objectives of social psychological research *per se*.

Several features of social psychological research are worthy of special attention. First, we usually are interested in understanding situated actions but in being able to generalise to settings other than the one in which data were gathered. In studies involving infrahuman species, with the exception of ethology, it often is presumed that an animal's performance in the experiment reflects some internal process of legitimate interest. The process may be physiological or psychological. The experimental performances of the animal are not used to generalise to other settings as much as they are used to reveal some internal process. Unfortunately, in social psychology we cannot claim that the psychological and social processes that we discover in the laboratory are general processes because the behaviours which imply the processes usually are *feignable* (Mixon, in press, a). That is, it is within the capacities of the person to perform an action or not, as he chooses. We usually are interested in behaviours which *do* vary from one occasion or setting to another; we try to identify the controlling conditions or contingencies, and we worry about 'person-by-situation interactions'. Social psychological research usually yields generalisations to *behaviours-in-settings*, and not to a general model of the organism which stands in some functional relationship to the organism itself, as is the case with most information-processing and physiological models.

Second, the behaviours of interest to us usually occur within sets of roles and are guided by rules, although the rules do not completely determine the behaviours. The guiding rules pertain both to instrumental activities necessary for the successful completion of the act, and to the presentation of character or face (Harré, 1976b). Third, the behaviours, or actions, occur as components of delineable episodes (Argyle, in press; Harré and Secord, 1972), and they derive their meanings in large part from those episodes as the episodes unfold or develop.

Fourth, the understanding of much human behaviour requires an understanding of the meanings which episodes and their component actions have for the participants (Mixon, in press, a; Shotter and Gregory, 1976). This point was illustrated in the earlier discussion of the inherent ambiguity of deception experiments. That ambiguity stems in part from not knowing and not being able to determine the meanings which episodes and actions hold for the experimental subjects. This feature is more broadly applicable than it might appear at first glance. James Jenkins (1974), after two decades of memory research from an associationistic perspective, has found it necessary to reject that perspective in order to account for an accumulation of initially unexpected findings. People recall the events they have experienced, not the 'stimuli to which they have been exposed' (p. 788). They recognise sentences never before seen if the sentences reasonably accurately describe events which had been described by other sentences which they had seen. It is the meanings of the events which are important. If the event is a sentence which a person heard, the quality of that event is given by the 'total meaning of the sentence in that context' (p. 787). People construct events within the framework of their contexts of occurrence, and the recollection of events also is a constructive process.

This is not to say that people are always able to identify changes in their actions or the conditions under which those changes in actions took place; in fact, there is considerable evidence that they can't (Nisbett and Wilson, 1976). That does not mean that the conditions under which changes in their actions occurred were not meaningful; it simply means that the context of action had been altered. Of course, the human species is susceptible to automatic effects of biologically relevant environmental events; but the vast majority of human behaviour requires for its understanding an understanding of meanings.

In summary, social psychological research involves the construction of models, just as does research in other sciences. However, most of the human actions which social psychologists wish to understand are situated actions which occur within role/rule frameworks, are embedded in meaningful contexts, and are feignable – within the capacity of the person to perform or not, as he chooses. These features set the context for further analysis of role-playing as an investigative procedure.

Passive Role-Playing

In this procedure a person is presented with a description or other portrayal (e.g. a videotape) of an action setting and asked what he or someone else would do in that setting, usually at some critical point in time. He is not asked to perform the action, and the actor whose action he is to guess may be himself or some other person. The amount and specificity of information given to the judge or guesser can vary widely. As a rule, the experimental focus has been only on the outcome of the episode (e.g. the proportion of people who guessed that a true subject in the setting would perform action X).

As noted earlier, it is the passive procedure which has been the target of much of the criticism of role-playing (Freedman, 1969; Miller, 1972). However, Mixon (in press, b) has argued that passive role-play descriptions should be construed as verbal models, and should be assessed as such. The problem is to distinguish good from bad models, and this can be accomplished by testing the accuracy with which a model simulates that which it was designed to simulate. For example, in the study by West *et al.* (1975) cited earlier, the simulation subjects were given a description of the burglary planning scenario in which the naive deception subjects found themselves.

That description was supposed to be a verbal model of the action episode within which the naive subjects found it necessary to agree or not agree to pursue further the idea of conducting a burglary. It was presumed by West *et al.* that there was a reasonably clear moral proscription, or rule, in the action setting – specifically, one should not engage in burglaries, even with purported government sanction. This presumption served as an interpretive baseline for the authors, and they apparently built it into the description given to their simulation subjects, whose judgements did not match the actions of the naive, deceived subjects. As Mixon (1972, 1976b) has pointed out for the verbal description which Milgram gave to students and colleagues of his destructive obedience studies (Milgram, 1963, 1974), the simulation description probably described the deceptive action episode from the experimenter's perspective. Therefore, the verbal model presented to the simulation subjects was inaccurate; it did not model what it had been designed to model, and it could throw little light on the modelled phenomenon. It could have been revised, time and again, until the judgements of the simulation subjects matched the actions of the deceived subjects. In fact, that is exactly what should have been done, if the authors wished to evaluate the implicit baseline which served as their basis for interpreting the actions of the naive subjects. That implicit baseline was based on the premise that the action situation in which the naive subjects found themselves contained the proscriptive rule that one should not engage in burglaries, even for government agencies. The passive role-playing procedure could – and should – have been used to test that implicit baseline. The same was true of Milgram's interpretation of his data, later tested and found wanting by Mixon's use of various passive role-playing descriptions which served as verbal models (see Mixon, 1976b, for an extended discussion of this issue).

Passive role-playing procedures are best used to assess our understandings of some event, especially events which are enigmatic. Scripts or descriptions of a setting can be constructed and modified until the desired outcome is achieved. The changing judgements of the testers of the model (the simulation subjects), in relation to changes in the script or description, will reveal which aspects of the description were informing their judgements. The model need not be a verbal one, but may be an action episode on stage or film or videotape (for example, see Darley, 1976). The major value is to generate an understanding of the situated episode within which an action of interest is embedded, and in terms of which it must be understood.

If a simulation does not replicate the original experiment, the fault lies with the experimenter, not the method. The simulation subjects typically are similar to the naive subjects in the original experiment, so the action to be simulated is not beyond the behavioural capacities of the simulation subjects. The actual behaviours involved in the simulation are not invalid in principle; both novelists and experimenters are able to give written descriptions of what people will do quite effectively, and there is no reason to believe that simulation subjects cannot write descriptions or predictions of the target behaviour. Therefore, the difficulty must lie in the information given to the simulation subjects, both in the description written by the experimenter and in the testing setting constructed by him for the subjects.

Active Role-Playing

Active role-playing procedures also may be construed as models. The experimenter creates a scenario and directs its performance, and thereby generates a simulation of some situation in which he is interested. The scenario is performed in real time by performers who agree, along with the experimenter and the audience, to participate in the creation of an illusion. The illusion is created for the players *by* the players, within the framework of the script, and the illusion is the model of the setting or episode being simulated. The character being performed by the actor may represent the actor himself or some other person. As with passive role-playing, the active procedure allows the investigator to assess his understanding of some event or situation by manipulating his script so as to yield outcomes which match or deviate in deliberate fashion from those of the situation being modelled. However, the active procedure also allows us to assess our understandings of the processes by which the outcomes are achieved, since the scenario is played out in real time.

For example, an experimenter may modify the sorts of character being presented by an actor, such as angry or pleasant, and assess the effects on the kinds of outcomes which the actor produces. Or the experimenter may alter the sorts of other characters with which an actor must interact, and assess the effects on both the character developed by the actor and/or the outcomes produced by the actor. The experimenter may establish certain rules in terms of which a simulated jury must decide guilt or innocence, and then observe the process by which the final jury decision is produced.

Active role-playing and passive role-playing are similar, then, in that each is a model, and each reflects our understandings of that which the model is designed to simulate. Each can be assessed, as noted above, in terms of the degree to which the model simulates that which it was designed to simulate. However, the two procedures do differ in the form of their simulations. The passive procedure uses a verbal description as its model of the simulated episode or setting, while the active procedure uses active performances by willing participants as the model. There is no *a priori* reason to expect the two model forms to produce equivalent simulations of a social setting or episode, without considerable effort and trial by the investigator. Moreover, the active procedure places much more emphasis on the construction of meanings and actions by the subject than does the passive procedure (Forward *et al.*, 1976), although both procedures involve the subject in testing the authenticity of the simulation.

Variations in Role-Playing

The range of role-playing variations is very wide. As already noted, one can set up active or passive versions, involving action or verbal models, respectively. Moreover, role-playing offers an extremely wide latitude in specification of the role/rule structure of the setting or episode being simulated. It allows variations in the rate at which the episode unfolds, the substantive detail of the setting and even the degree of completion of the episode. This is all accomplished by the script that the investigator constructs.

The script can be structured in such detail that the role-players have no freedom, except for the expression of character. Or they simply can be told to perform as if they were in the natural setting of interest, with minimal additional instructions. For example, in our gambling studies of shifts in risk-taking (Blascovich, Ginsburg and Veach, 1975; Ginsburg, Glascovich and Howe, 1976), we ask our participants to '. . . play as though you were playing with your own money . . .' and '. . . try to win as much as you can . . .' Smith (1975) also has used loosely specified scenarios to generate a more elaborate set of attitude change strategies than is contained in the consistency and dissonance theories still popular in experimental social psychology.

Furthermore, a given episode can be played and replayed innumerable times, each with a deliberate modification in the script. This can be continued until the behaviour of interest emerges (Mixon, 1972). The script then can be changed to test the effects of particular themes or variables on the development of the episode. And it is worth noting that we can observe the development or emergence of the episode in real time – as well as repeatedly. It also is important to note that the control allowed by script modification is potentially quite precise; and this provides for a high degree of internal validity – necessary for the unambiguous interpretation of data (Campbell, 1957).

Moreover, our control over the script means that we can construct a role/rule framework for a scenario which matches what we believe to be the important roles and rules of the natural episodes in which we are interested. The comparability of role/rule frameworks bears directly on the accuracy with which the model simulates its object, and close comparability should facilitate the external validity of an investigation. This is an important point, and will be elaborated upon in the next section of the chapter.

A scenario can cover long or short time periods; and it can be played out in the natural setting of the episode, or in some other setting which is supposed to represent it, such as a stage or a laboratory.

An audience also can be used profitably. The audience could witness a scenario in one or more of its versions and then answer questions about the meaning and sensibility of the scenario, and also about its sensitivity or insightfulness, thereby providing a range of understandings made plausible by the staged display of features which the investigator felt were important. Darley's (1976) use of videotape scenarios illustrates such an application. He devised two scenarios of a fight scene to tap the audience's conception of legitimate counter-aggression.

Role-playing procedures can be used to *test* one's ideas, too, as well as to explore and generate ideas. For example, once an investigator believes he understands why the actions of interest do and don't occur, he can set up two scenarios, in both of which the opportunity to perform the critical action exists, but the script must neither require nor preclude the performance of that critical action. Each scenario should be run many times with different role-players, analogous to experimental trials. If the investigator's understanding is adequate, all actors in one scenario will perform the critical action, and none will perform it in the other. Mixon (in press, a) discusses this at some length and calls it the 'All-or-None' strategy. Also, as Forward *et al*. (1976) point out, the usual parametric approach of conventional experimental design can be applied, with random assignment of subjects to conditions (scenarios) and deliberate alterations of scenarios and of performance settings.

The 'All-or-None' approach constitutes a test of the investigator's understanding, and in a critical fashion. It forces the investigator to synthesise the episode which he claims to understand. Harré has reminded us (1976a, p. 40) that the crowning achievement in organic chemistry and biochemistry is the synthesis of those compounds which the chemists feel they have come to understand through analysis. He considers the sort of method developed by Mixon to be a start towards the 'replication of reality'.

Thus, the range of role-playing variations indeed is very wide. One can set up active role-playing or passive role-playing, and the character being played can be specified or left unspecified. The script or description can vary immensely in detail; and the scenario being played out can run for short or long periods of time, allowing acts within the episode to unfold naturally or by direction. Furthermore, the scenario can be played out in the natural setting or some other setting which is supposed to represent it, such as a stage or a laboratory; and the procedures can be used both to generate and to test our understandings.

Role-Playing, Role Performance and Role/Rule Frameworks

Any behaviour occurs in a context (Argyle, 1975); therefore, that behaviour should be studied in the type of episode in which its natural occurrence was noted, or a reasonable facsimile of that episode. This means that considerable observation and scholarship may be necessary before we develop some idea of the role/rule structure of the episode. The current work by Marsh (1976) illustrates just such an anthropological field approach. He was interested in the apparently meaningless violence and hooliganism of the adolescent and young adult spectators at football matches. After two years of personal observation, interviews with spectators and police, and extensive use of long-distance videotaping, Marsh was able to demonstrate the existence of considerable structure and meaning in the behaviour of the spectators. He identified a complex role/rule framework which specifies the actions and the performance styles for various roles, and for advancement from one role to another.

Once we gain some idea of the structure of the setting or episode, we can devise a role-playing scenario of it, incorporating those structural features which we believe are important. The scenario of the episode would be revised until the behaviour of interest becomes sensible as a meaningful unit with it. This would provide us with a reasonably strong understanding of the behaviour as part of our constructed episode, but we still would have to use our judgement, our observational skills, and our scholarly talents to assess its comparability to the natural episodes of interest to us. However, because we have made clear the role/rule structure of our scenario, and because that structure was based in part upon what we discerned as the structure of the natural episode, our reflection back to the natural episode is much less problematic than is the case with deception experiments. In them, the role/rule frameworks are ambiguous and perhaps unknowable, although the evidence is strong that they do exist. An essential conceptual theme of the chapter is that much of the human behaviour of interest to social psychologists is typical rather than atypical, wilful and feignable rather than simplistically caused, and guided (but not fully determined) by rules which are differentially applicable to different roles in a situation. Furthermore, the human person is seen as an active and planning agent who performs many of his actions knowingly, but in a context of meanings. Therefore, much of human action *is* rule-guided role performances.

Active role-players perform within a role/rule framework that is largely known or knowable to the investigator, while subjects within deception experiments perform within role/rule frameworks generally *un*known to the experimenter. Given the orienting bias of the preceding paragraph, behaviour in natural settings also constitutes role performances guided by sets of appropriate rules. Therefore, the study of social behaviours – all of which occur within role/rule frameworks – might best be conducted under circumstances in which those frameworks are knowable than under circumstances in which they are not.

Sceptics might argue that even if the importance of role/rule frameworks were granted, and even if the orienting bias articulated above were granted, active role-playing still would be critically different from human actions situated in natural settings. After all, role-playing in its active form involves pretence on the part of the performer and audience; the outcomes of the actions are not final and irreversible; and the actor does not presume that the character he is displaying is taken by the audience as a true instance of him. However, the outcomes of most natural episodes are free of finality, too; and pretence – by all parties – is not restricted to role-playing, but is rather common in every-day affairs. And in some role-play procedures, the character displayed by the actor is presumed to be a true instance of him. This is especially true in the use of role-playing for psychological assessment, but it also may occur in research uses. So role-played performances and actions in natural settings are not different categorical types. Instead, as argued earlier, role-playing of both active and passive types constitute models of social settings or episodes. As such, they can be useful in both the generation of our understandings of those episodes or settings and the testing of our understandings.

On the other hand, it is important to recognise that most uses of role-playing will not enhance our understanding of a specific person. Instead, role-playing most often will illuminate the role/rule context within which actions of interest occur and within which those actions are meaningful. In order to understand actions of interest, we must understand the context in which they occur. Role-playing models will prove most useful as simulations of the role/rule contexts of action.

The deliberate investigative use of active and passive role-playing as a modelling procedure is new. Some conceptual analyses of considerable merit have been published (Forward *et al.*, 1976; Hamilton, 1976; Mixon, 1971, 1972, in press a,b), and more are sure to emerge; but there is a dearth of conceptually based methodological work which evaluates the various role-playing variations as research tools. The purpose of this chapter has been to review the issues regarding role-playing as an investigative procedure in social psychology, and to cast role-playing within the general context of modelling the role/rule frameworks within which human actions occur. The purpose has not been to offer a new conceptualisation or methodological innovations. A cautionary methodological comment is in order. Role-playing is an investigative procedure which can be used to generate scientific knowledge. However, to be used in that way, the traditional requirements of replicability and intersubjective unequivocality must be met. Research designs must not be confounded, must be internally valid, and must be capable of reasonable and rational extension to the natural settings of interest. The usual criteria of inter-coder or inter-judge reliability must be met, when applicable; and the interpretation of meanings must make use of a written code system within which the categories are exhaustive and mutually exclusive (Muehl, 1961). I stress this point because it would be easy to fall prey to the temptation of the single, insightful investigator who knows his interpretation is correct and convinces the world of it by his most persuasive arguments. We should keep in mind Boring's (1963) admonition to mistrust our own capacity for forming unbiased inferences and to insist on controls for protecting our conclusions from our predilections (p. 251). Furthermore, role-playing should be seen as a complement to conventional experiments, survey research, field observations, and even the analysis of documentary material and biographies. That is, it should be seen as an important addition to our investigative armamentarium, not as a replacement.

In closing, I hope I have laid to rest the strong but generally indefensible criticisms of role-playing procedures in experimental social psychology, and have stimulated some thought about the plausible utility of those procedures. They certainly can be used to facilitate our understanding of human behaviour and – if one wishes – human experience. And that is all that any of our investigative procedures allows, for the enigmatic nature of the meaning of events and settings within which we act precludes unambiguous extension from the setting of investigation to other settings of interest, and even interferes with internal validity. The recent argument by Greenwald (1975) to the effect that dissonance and self-perception theories cannot be disconfirmed conceptually probably can be extended to much of social psychology – since in most of our theories we require personal reactions by the person to the stimuli, and that introduces an inherent uncertainty. The various role-playing procedures can help to reduce that uncertainty, although not eliminate it.

Note

1. This paper is based in part on a talk given at the British Psychological Society Workshop on New Methods in Social Psychological Research, held at the University of Oxford in November 1975. The paper has been improved by the helpful comments of Michael Argyle, Glynis Breakwell, Mansur Lalljee, Don Mixon and Paul Secord.

References

Alexander, C.N. and Knight, G.W. (1971). Situated identities and social psychological experimentation. *Sociometry, 34*, 65-82.

Aronson, E. and Carlsmith, J.M. (1968). Experimentation in social psychology. In G. Lindsey and E. Aronson (eds.), *Handbook of Social Psychology* (revised edition), Vol. II. Reading, Mass.: Addison-Wesley, 1968.

Argyle, M. (1975). Do personality traits exist? *New Behaviour*, 31 July, 176-9.

Argyle, M. (in press). Sequences in social behaviour as a function of the situation. In G.P. Ginsburg (ed.), *Emerging Strategies in Social Psychological Research*. London: Wiley.

Argyris, C. (1975). Dangers in applying results from experimental social psychology. *American Psychologist, 30,* 469-85.

Banuazizi, A. and Mohavedi, S. (1975). Interpersonal dynamics in a simulated prison: A methodological analysis. *American Psychologist, 30,* 152-60.

Barclay, A.M. (1971). Information as a defensive control of sexual arousal. *Journal of Personality and Social Psychology, 17,* 244-9.

Bem, D.J. (1967). Self-perception: An alternative interpretation of cognitive dissonance phenomena. *Psychological Review, 74,* 183-200.

Bem, D.J. (1968). The epistemological status of interpersonal simulations: A reply to Jones, Linder, Kiesler, Zanna and Brehm. *Journal of Experimental Social Psychology*, *4*, 270-4.

Bem, D.J. (1972). Self-perception theory. In L. Berkowitz (ed.), *Advances in Experimental Social Psychology*, 6, pp. 2-62. New York: Academic Press.

Berscheid, E., Baron, R.S., Dermer, M. and Libman, M. (1973) Anticipating informed consent: An empirical approach. *American Psychology, 29,* 913-25.

Blascovich, J., Ginsburg, G.P. and Veach, T.L. (1975). A pluralistic explanation of choice shifts on the risk dimension. *Journal of Personality and Social Psychology, 31,* 422-9.

Borgatta, E.F. (1955). The analysis of social interaction: Actual, role-playing and projective. *Journal of Abnormal and Social Psychology, 51,* 394-405.

Boring, E.G. (1963). *History, Psychology and Science: Selected Papers*. New York: Wiley.

Campbell, D.T. (1957). Factors relevant to the validity of experiments in social settings. *Psychological Bulletin, 54,* 297-312.

Crowle, A.J. (1976). The deceptive language of the laboratory. In R. Harré (ed.), *Life Sentences*, pp. 160-74. London: Wiley.

Darley, J.M. (1976). A naive psychological analysis of counteraggression. Unpublished manuscript, Department of Psychology, Princeton University.

Darroch, R.K. and Steiner, I.D. (1970). Role-playing: An alternative to laboratory research? *Journal of Personality, 38,* 302-11.

Davis, J.H., Kerr, N.L., Atkin, R.H. and Meek, D. (1975). The decision processes of 6- and 12-person mock juries assigned unanimous and two-thirds majority rules. *Journal of Personality and Social Psychology, 32,* 1-14.

Davitz, J.R. (1964). *The Communication of Emotional Meaning*. New York: McGraw-Hill.

Epstein, Y.M., Suedfeld, P. and Silverstein, S.J. (1973). The experimental contract: Subjects' expectations of and reactions to some behaviours of experimenters. *American Psychologist, 28,* 212-21.

Forward, J., Canter, R. and Kirsch, N. (1976). Role-enactment and deception methodologies: Alternative paradigms? *American Psychologist, 31,* 595-604.

Freedman, J.L. (1969). Role playing: Psychology by consensus. *Journal of Personality and Social Psychology, 13,* 107-14.

Friedman, N. (1967). *The Social Nature of Psychological Research: The Psychological Experiment as a Social Interaction*. New York: Basic Books.

Gadlin, H. and Ingle, G. (1975). Through the one-way mirror: The limits of experimental self-reflection. *American Psychologist, 30,* 1003-9.

Ginsburg, G.P., Blascovich, J.J. and Howe, R.C. (1976). Risk taking in the presence of others. In W. Eadington and Coburn (eds.), *Gambling and Society*, pp. 336-46. Springfield, Ill.: Charles C. Thomas.

Glinski, R.J., Glinski, B.C. and Slatin, G.T. (1970). Non-naivety contamination in conformity experiments: Sources, effects and implications for control. *Journal of Personality and Social Psychology, 16,* 478-85.

Golding, S.L. and Lichtenstein, E. (1970). Confession of awareness and prior knowledge of deception as a function of interview set and approval motivation. *Journal of Personality and Social Psychology, 14,* 213-23.

Goldstein, A.P. and Simonson, N.R. (1971). Social psychological approaches to psychotherapy research. In A.E. Bergin and S.L. Garfield (eds.), *Handbook of Psychotherapy and Behavior Change*, pp. 154-95. New York: Wiley.

Greenwald, A.G. (1975). On the inconclusiveness of 'crucial' tests of dissonance versus self-perception theories. *Journal of Experimental Social Psychology, 11,* 490-9.

Hamilton, V.L. (1976). Role play and deception: A re-examination of the controversy. *Journal for the Theory of Social Behaviour, 6,* 233-50.

Haney, C., Banks, W.C. and Zimbardo, P.G. (1973). Interpersonal dynamics in a simulated prison. *International Journal of Criminology and Penology, 1,* 69-97.

Harré, R. (1976a). The constructive role of models. In L. Collins, *The Use of Models in the Social Sciences*, pp. 16-43. London: Tavistock Publications.

Harré, R. (1976b). Rules in the explanation of social behaviour. In P. Collett (ed.), *Social Rules and Social Behaviour*. Oxford: Basil Blackwell.

Harré, R. and Secord, P.F. (1972). *The Explanation of Social Behavior*. Totowa, New Jersey: Rowman and Littlefield.

Holmes, D.S. and Bennett, D.H. (1974). Experiments to answer questions raised by the use of deception in psychological research: I. Role playing as an alternative to deception; II. Effectiveness of debriefing after deception; III. Effect of informed consent on deception. *Journal of Personality and Social Psychology, 29,* 358-67.

Horowitz, I.A. and Rothschild, B.H. (1970). Conformity as a function of deception and role playing. *Journal of Personality and Social Psychology, 14,* 224-6.

Janis, I.L. and King, B.T. (1954). The influence of role playing on opinion change. *Journal of Abnormal and Social Psychology, 48,* 211-18.

Janis, I.L. and Mann, L. (1965). Effectiveness of emotional role-playing in modifying smoking habits and attitudes. *Journal of Experimental Research in Personality, 1,* 84-90.

Jenkins, J.J. (1974). Remember that old theory of memory? Well, forget it! *American Psychologist, 29,* 785-95.

Jourard, S.M. (1968). *Disclosing Man to Himself.* Princeton: Van Nostrand.

Kelman, H. Human use of human subjects: The problem of deception in social psychological experiments. *Psychological Bulletin, 67,* 1-11.

Laird, J.D. (1974). Self-attribution of emotion: The effects of expressive behavior on the quality of emotional experience. *Journal of Personality and Social Psychology, 29,* 475-86.

Lanzetta, J.T., Cartwright-Smith, J. and Kleck, R.E. (1976). Effects of nonverbal dissimulation on emotional experience and autonomic arousal. *Journal of Personality and Social Psychology, 33,* 354-70.

Leibowitz, G. (1968). Comparison of self-report and behavioral techniques of assessing aggression. *Journal of Consulting and Clinical Psychology, 32,* 21-5.

Mann, J.H. (1956). Experimental evaluations of role playing. *Psychological Bulletin, 53,* 227-34.

Marsh, P. (1976). Careers for boys: Nutters, hooligans and hardcases. *New Society*, 13 May.

McReynolds, P., deVoge, S., Osborne, S.K., Pither, B. and Nordin, K. (1976). *Manual for the IMPRO-I (Improvisation Test for Individuals).* Reno, Nevada: Psychological Service Center, University of Nevada, Reno.

Menges, R.J. (1973). Openness and honesty versus coercion and deception in psychological research. *American Psychologist, 28,* 1030-4.

Milgram, S. (1963). Behavioral study of obedience. *Journal of Abnormal and Social Psychology, 67,* 371-8.

Milgram, S. (1974). *Obedience to Authority*. New York: Harper and Row.

Miller, A.G. (1972). Role Playing: An alternative to deception?: A review of the evidence. *American Psychologist, 27,* 623-36.

Mixon, D. (1971). Behaviour analysis treating subjects as actors rather than organisms. *Journal for the Theory of Social Behaviour, 1,* 19-32.

Mixon, D. (1972). Instead of deception. *Journal for the Theory of Social Behaviour, 2,* 145-74.

Mixon, D. (1974a). If you won't deceive, what can you do? In N. Armistead (ed.), *Reconstructing Social Psychology,* pp. 72-85. Baltimore, Maryland: Penguin Books.

Mixon, D. (1974b). Why pretend to deceive? Paper presented at the annual meeting of the American Psychological Association, New Orleans, Louisiana, 3 September.

Mixon, D. (in press a). Studying feignable behavior. *Representative Research in Social Psychology*.

Mixon, D. (in press b). Understanding shocking and puzzling conduct. In G.P. Ginsburg (ed.), *Emerging Strategies in Social Psychological Research*. London: Wiley.

Mohavedi, S. and Banuazizi, A. (1975). Rejoinder to comments. *American Psychologist, 30,* 1016-18.

Moreno, J.L. (1946). *Psychodrama*. New York: Beacon.

Muehl, D. (1961). *Manual For Coders*. Ann Arbor, Michigan: Institute for Social Research,University of Michigan.

Nisbett, R.E. and Wilson, T.D. (1976). Telling more than we can know: Self-perception and the representativeness heuristic. Unpublished manuscript. Department of Psychology, University of Michigan.

Olson, T. and Christiansen, G. (1966). *The Grindstone Experiment: Thirty-One Hours*. Toronto: Canadian Friends Service Committee.

OSS Assessment Staff. (1948). *The Assessment of Men*. New York: Rinehart.

Piliavian, J.A. and Piliavin, I.M. (1972). Effect of blood on reactions to a victim. *Journal of Personality and Social Psychology, 23,* 353-61.

Piliavin, J.A., Piliavin, I.M., Loewenton, E.P., McCauley, C. and Hammond, P. (1969). On observers' reproductions of dissonance effects: the right answers for the wrong reasons? *Journal of Personality and Social Psychology, 13,* 98-106.

Piliavin, I.M., Rodin, J. and Piliavin, J.A. (1969). Good samaritanism: An underground phenomenon. *Journal of Personality and Social Psychology, 13,* 289-99.

Ring, K. (1967). Experimental social psychology: Some sober questions about some frivolous values. *Journal of Experimental Social Psychology, 3,* 113-23.

Rosenberg, P.P. (1952). An experimental analysis of psychodrama. Unpublished Ph.D. dissertation, Radcliffe College. (Cited by Mann, 1956).

Rubin, Z. (1973). Designing honest experiments. *American Psychologist,*

28, 445-8.

Schlenker, B.R. (1974). Social psychology and science. *Journal of Personality and Social Psychology, 29,* 1-15.

Schultz, D.P. (1969). The human subject in psychological research. *Psychological Bulletin, 72,* 214-28.

Shotter, J. and Gregory, S. (1976). On first gaining the idea of oneself as a person. In R. Harré (ed.), *Life Sentences,* pp. 1-9. London: Wiley.

Shulman, A.D. and Berman, H.J. (1975). Role expectations about subjects and experimenters in psychological research. *Journal of Personality and Social Psychology, 32,* 368-80.

Silverman, I., Shulman, A.D. and Wiesenthal, D.L. (1970). Effects of deceiving and debriefing subjects on performance in later experiments. *Journal of Personality and Social Psychology, 14,* 203-12.

Smith, J.L. (1975). A games analysis for attitude change: Use of Role-enactment situations for model development. *Journal for the Theory of Social Behaviour, 5,* 63-79.

Stricker, L.J., Messick, S. and Jackson, D.N. (1970). Conformity, anticonformity and independence: Their dimensionality and generality. *Journal of Personality and Social Psychology, 16,* 494-507.

Toulmin, S. (1961). *Foresight and Understanding.* London: Hutchinson.

Trower, P., Bryant, B. and Argyle, M. (1977). *Social Skills and Mental Health.* London: Methuen.

Weber, S.J. and Cook, T.D. (1972). Subject effects in laboratory research: An examination of subject roles, demand characteristics, and valid inference. *Psychological Bulletin, 77,* 273-95.

West, S.G., Gunn, S.P. and Chernicky, P. (1975). Ubiquitous Watergate: An attributional analysis. *Journal of Personality and Social Psychology, 32,* 55-65.

Willis, R.H. and Willis, Y.A. (1970). Role playing versus deception: An experimental comparison. *Journal of Personality and Social Psychology, 16,* 472-7.

6 INTERVIEWING: THE SOCIAL PHENOMENOLOGY OF A RESEARCH INSTRUMENT

Michael Brenner

1 Introduction

Methodologists of the research interview stress the desirability of socially sterile conditions in the interview situation. This entails, as Deutscher (1972) has put it, that:

> neither the interviewer nor the instrument should act in any way upon the situation. The question, ideally, should be so put and so worded as to be unaffected by contextual contaminations. The interviewer must be an inert agent who exerts no influence on response by tone, expression, stance, or statement. The question must be unloaded in that it does not hint in any way that one response is more desirable or more correct than any other response. It must be placed in the sequence of the instrument in such a way that the subject's response is not affected by previous queries or by his own previous responses (p. 325).

Of course, this is only the normative ideal of research interviewing. In practice there are numerous difficulties inherent in the social organisation of the interview which make universal claims for measurement by means of interviewing quite untenable. This has been acknowledged for some time (see Hyman *et al.*, 1954).

First, there is the problem of social interaction with the people under study. The interview constitutes an interpersonal encounter. Hence, attempts at measurement in interviewing take the form of fleeting social relationships which resemble those of everyday life. Just as everyday social encounters involve situational definitions which can be problematic for participants, so the process of social interaction in the interview depends on the conceptualisations and constructions evolved by the interviewer and respondent.

Second, there is the problem of communication, or more precisely, the problem of the adequate understanding of the linguistic forms of expression used by interviewer and respondent. During the interview, interviewer and respondent are immediately faced with the task of having to penetrate and to understand the meanings exchanged. But there may be severe limitations to effective communication and understanding. Respondents may talk ungrammatically and their talk may not be sharp in terms of meaning and cannot be sharpened, either by the interviewer or the respondent; and interviewers may not be able to fully clarify problems arising from misunderstanding of questions. The problems of the interview arise from its very nature: it is bound up with social interaction and the communication of meaning in language. This means that methodologists can only make reasonable claims for measurement by means of interviewing if the interview is fully understood as a device created by the researcher and enacted by interviewer and respondent to reveal patterns of social knowledge. One might assume, therefore, that methodologists would have had invested considerable effort in trying to identify, and to systematically research, the social interactional and communicative quality of interviewing encounters. But, by and large, they have not.

This chapter has been written in an attempt to partially remedy this situation. On the following pages, the research interview is conceptualised and phenomenologically explored as an instance of complex social interaction. Some empirical evidence stemming from research on interviewing by the author is included to substantiate the analytical views expressed.

2 The Social Interaction Paradigm

McCall and Simmons (1966) have pointed out many of the complexities involved in thinking of social relationships in terms of social interaction. They start from the definition that social interaction cannot be resolved into a single function of one participant influencing the other, but instead must be expressed as a joint function, as a mutual influence. Inherent in this definition are a number of important features of social interaction which deserve some elaboration. It is possible to differentiate interactions according to the *tasks* involved. Interaction can only be a joint accomplishment of participants if a task structure, or a situation of interaction, be it explicit in the form of a plan for interaction or implicit in the form of intention, has been, to some extent, agreed about. It is the task which provides the boundary to an interaction. Or, in other words, everyday life can be seen as an ongoing stream of interactions separated by task boundaries.

The realisation of tasks in social interaction involves a dramaturgical format, that is, the enactment of *roles* leading to effective task performance. The realisation of tasks also requires a ceremonial format, that is, *rules* are attributed, or imputed, by participants to a situation of action in order that roles may be legitimately enacted. Finally, in the ideal case, the performance of tasks in interaction will allow participants self-expression and self-fulfilment. That is, task performance can be the mere rule-structured enactment of roles, but often also becomes the vehicle for the support of identity.

It is important to realise that these features of interaction combine in many ways. Weinstein and Deutschberger (1964) point out that, given a task,

> the problem for each participant is to choose a line of action adequate to his purposes (whatever they may be, and whether or not they accord with the purposes of the others) while still keeping the others bound in the relationship – that is to say, not terminate the interaction unsatisfactorily. Ego and alter must co-operate if either is to achieve his own imperative, even if these imperatives are not in themselves entirely compatible.

From this account, two issues emerge. The first relates to the *stability* of interactions. Participants tacitly attribute to each other the proposition that any person acts as a socially competent and responsible individual. They trust in each other that each participant will know the standards by which his performance will be evaluated as proper or improper, as any participant knows the standards. This makes co-operation in interaction possible, because unco-operativeness can meaningfully be construed as unreasonable by participants, and hence be sanctioned. The second issue relates to the *dynamics* of interaction. Participants also know that the standards of adequate performance often do not have sharp boundaries, being underidentified, so to speak, and that they can be negotiated. This makes it possible for interactants to operate selfishly, while still appearing co-operative. Stability in interaction can be endangered if the enactment of proper roles does not lead to self-fulfilment, or if the task itself becomes irrelevant to participants. Hence, interaction can be characterised as the realisation of a task by means of the enactment of roles according to rules thought to be relevant to a situation of action, and criteria of self-expression and identity, and also as a bargaining situation. That is, negotiation can take place about whether a task is equally relevant to all participants, whether roles comply with rules properly and whether the task-relevant roles allow sufficient self-expression. In the light of this argument, stability in interaction must be seen as a temporary contract between participants that they will engage in a task with a specific role and rule structure. Of course, such contracts are hardly ever binding in a strict sense. This makes stability a transient phenomenon in many instances: 'The bargain may not stand, for as others elaborate their lines of action, the actor may find it unrealistic and proceed to negotiate a new one with himself on the basis of a raised or lowered set of aspirations' (Weinstein and Deutschberger, 1964, p. 453).

An important source of orderliness in interactions arises from the fact that the enactment of roles complies with rules relevant to a specific situation of interaction. Harré and Secord (1972) have provided a useful general identification of the concept of rule:

> Rules guide action through the actor being aware of the rule and of what it prescribes, so that he can be said to know what to do in the appropriate circumstances by virtue of his knowledge of the rule, and the explanation of his knowing what to do lies in his knowing the rule and being able to recognise the occasions for its application (p. 181).

It is important to note that Harré and Secord's identification of rule does not necessarily imply that actors know explicitly the rules involved in the realisation of conduct. Their identification of rule involves *awareness*, on the part of the actor, of the rules appropriate to actions and situations of action. This means, for example, that people know whether their conduct, during a dinner party, complies with the rules appropriate to that event, but they will not necessarily know the full set of etiquette rules appropriate to a dinner party themselves. Conduct is planned, realised and expected on the grounds of taken-for-granted, tacit knowledge of the rules involved in a situation of interaction. Or in other words, tacit knowledge of the rules allows participants to express and expect appropriate *strategies* for action. The fact that people can only assume of each other tacit knowledge of the rules involved in conduct, but not necessarily knowledge of the rules themselves, gives rise to problems as regards the general possibility of writing out the rules actually realised, or followed, in interactions.

Given that people may, on their own grounds, attribute rule-following conduct to each other, rather than assume that that conduct has been quasi-mechanically *generated* according to rules, it follows that the particular rules which different people attribute to the *same* conduct can differ. People's beliefs about the nature, the necessity and the applicability of rules can differ, and their understanding and knowledge of the rules that are supposed to govern their actions may also differ. Also, people may be able to attribute orderliness to conduct, but they may not be able to say what, precisely, the rules are on which they base their attributions.

In interaction, we can assume that the orderliness of conduct will be judged by participants by attributing, where applicable, to the enactment of roles, the propriety of basically *four* layers of rules. It is important to note here that we do not assume that participants have *explicit* knowledge of layers of rules; they have, in most instances, only tacit knowledge. These layers of rules may be elaborated thus:

(1) There is the layer of formal-legal rules such as law, official morality and codes of ethics. The totality of interactions initiated in a society complies with this layer of rules, at least in most instances.

(2) Any interaction complies with a layer of etiquette rules specific to a particular social culture or class or group. Such rules govern polite interaction among persons when they are in public or private places.

(3) Interactions may be governed by a layer of relational rules. These are generated on idiosyncratic grounds in long-term social relationships among co-workers, friends or lovers. Relational rules may redefine the extent to which formal-legal rules and rules of etiquette are made valid in interactions, since participants have constructed their own private rules of what is right and proper. Thus, formal-legal and etiquette rules can be relaxed in encounters on the grounds of rules derived from long-term relationships (see Denzin, 1970, p. 133).

(4) There is the layer of rules specific for the task of interaction: playing a game of chess, being involved in an interview, or adequate reasoning in a mathematical argument.

In ordinary social interaction, the task rules will always be surrounded by constraints deriving from interpersonal attributions of formal-legal, etiquette and, sometimes, relational rules to conduct. Usually, task rules will have to comply with formal-legal and etiquette rules, that is, the interaction will take place within the boundaries drawn by the latter rule layers. But participants may attribute their own relational standards to an interaction situation and may, hence, interpret the propriety of the actions of other participants using idiosyncratic criteria. That is, instability in interaction, trouble, can be brought about by construing the enactment of a role as improper on relational grounds, although this may not break any other layer of rules. Similarly, a rule-breaking performance may be tolerated or excused and, hence, remedied on relational grounds. From this, it follows, in more general terms, that the propriety of actions can be negotiated within various layers of rules, and determined by identifying the relevant layers of rules. Or in other words, the same action may have various meanings according to which layer of rules is attributed to that action. For example, if a husband hits his wife, she may construe the assault as a formal-legal offence, or may find it excusable on relational grounds, or take revenge within some local agonistic framework.

Let us summarise the discussion so far. The following points concerning some crucial elements of the interaction repertoire people must utilise in encounters have emerged:

(1) Social interaction originates from the interpersonal construction of a task. Then, lines of action can be developed.

(2) Any social interaction is a highly orderly accomplishment. Participants have to enact relevant roles which comply with various layers of rules relevant to specific situations of action in order to maintain meaningful interaction.

(3) Participants must co-operate to achieve personal goals. In the case of trouble, problems concerning the propriety of conduct can only be sorted out according to the co-operative nature of interaction, that is, according to the mutual acknowledgement of participants that conduct must comply with rules specific to that encounter, whatever it may be decided the encounter actually is.

(4) Due to rule-following in interaction and its co-operative quality, bargaining, or negotiation, becomes possible. In a case where a participant feels that his imperatives of action are not acknowledged, or are apparently misconstrued, by other participants, he can negotiate the situation within the degrees of freedom permitted by the other participants, that is, within the limits of the rules attributed by other participants to the interaction situation.

(5) According to changes in the task definition of an encounter, mutual role and rule attributions and perceptions might change. Hence, in any ordinary interaction participants must be prepared for unanticipated turning-points which often require redefinition of the plans, means and conditions of interaction. Hence, what becomes a task in ordinary social interaction is open to reconstruction by

the participants, as are also definitions of self, roles and rules.

(6) In the ideal encounter, the task is enacted by participants in such a way as to achieve the fulfilment of self-expression and identity, to express models of self to participants and to comply competently with the role-performances required by the particular interaction tasks.

3 The Social Structure of the Interview

There are some phenomenological attributes of the interview which are of basic importance. In the case of a household interview, the situation of interaction between interviewer and respondent is usually that of strangers meeting on the respondent's territory. The relationship has been initiated by the interviewer and the respondent has voluntarily agreed to co-operate. The task of the encounter is strictly defined. This means that the interviewer *must* stick to the rules which surround the task in order to appear credible throughout the interview, while the respondent is invited to follow the task order inherent in the relationship.

Given the quality of the interview as an interaction between strangers on the respondent's territory, initiated by the interviewer for research purposes, the compliance of the interview conduct with the following layers of rules has to be ensured:

(1) The interview has to conform to 'respondents' rights', that is, to certain legal, moral and ethical standards. In the introductory phase of the interview, a number of points have to be made explicit to the respondent. The name of the organisation (on whose behalf the survey is being undertaken) has to be mentioned. The interviewer has to explain the sampling procedure, that is, he has to give an explanation of how the respondent came to be selected for interview. The purpose of the survey has to be identified. The interviewer has to stress the confidential nature of the enquiry, that is, the information provided by the respondent is to be treated as confidential under all circumstances, his identity will not be disclosed to anyone outside the research agency, and perhaps not even there, and reports based on information supplied by the respondent are to be presented in such a way that the identity of the respondent cannot be discovered. The interviewer has to indicate that the interview is voluntary and that the respondent has the right to refuse to answer questions. The interviewer must give some

indication of the length of the interview. Finally, he must reveal his identity by showing his authorisation card (see Atkinson, 1971, p. 33).

(2) The interview will be conducted within rules of etiquette. That is, the interviewer will perform his task politely and with special care to ensure full respondent co-operation, while assuming that the respondent will use the formal courtesy that applies to interaction among strangers.

(3) The interview will be conducted within task rules. The rule for the respondent is that he may/should provide full answers. The task rule set for the interviewer is more comprehensive. As regards *his conduct*, the interviewer must take care that nothing in his words or manner implies criticism, surprise, approval or disapproval, either of the questions or the respondent's answers, or other happenings during the interview. As regards asking the questions, the interviewer must read out questions exactly as they are worded. He must read slowly, but meaningfully. He must ask the questions in the order in which they are presented in the questionnaire. He must ask every question that applies to the respondent. He must repeat questions which are misunderstood or misinterpreted. He must keep track of the changes which he makes deliberately, if necessary, or inadvertently, in the questionnaire. As regards the *conduct of the respondent*, interviewing will often involve the handling of difficult situations when the respondent tries to inject an extraneous task into the interview, for example, he may start arguing with the interviewer about the propriety of questions. Then, the interviewer must try to bring the respondent back to his essential task objective in the interview, that is, to provide full answers. For example, by a variety of actions the respondent can be reminded that he is doing a good job if he answers the questions fully. Positive feedback plays an important role here. As regards incomplete or inadequate answers, the interviewer must probe. Probes will require the respondent to clarify an answer sufficiently or, at least, they will lead to an attempt at clarification.

(4) The interviewer has to be prepared for respondents to use their own relational standards to assess the interviewing relationship. That is, at any time, the respondent may produce actions, on idiosyncratic grounds, which can make the conduct of the interview difficult for the interviewer.

Given this rule structure of the interview, the following role formats can be proposed:

(1) As regards the interviewer, his actions will be bound to a fairly depersonalised role performance because he has, primarily, to conform to the layers of rules that comply with the task. That is, to avoid trouble he cannot inject his own relational standards into the interview.

(2) As regards the respondent, he is much freer in his role enactments than is the interviewer. At any time, he can enlarge on the definition of the situation as interview by reading the interview also as an interesting and satisfying encounter, as a chance to express his dislikes, disappointments and ideas. Also he can read the interviewer's performance within his own relational standards as an improper fulfilment of the interaction contract on various grounds. He can doubt the propriety and the sense of the questions as well as the style of questioning. He can challenge the interviewer as a person on a variety of grounds, for example, by doubting the interviewer's competence. Finally, he can use idiosyncratic ways of enacting his task role.

In principle, social interaction in the interview is, at any point in the interview, contingent upon the agreed-about task structure of the interview. In cases where trouble arises, that is, when a participant's action is seen as an illegitimate performance by others, this can be sorted out by demonstrating the appropriateness of that action to the originally agreed-about structure of the task. This is not so in everyday-life encounters, because participants can meaningfully deny that any task structure has been agreed about at all. But of course, it can happen in interviews that the agreed-about task structure of the encounter can be read as having-become-illegitimate, or can be construed as having-dissolved, by the respondent. In such a case, there is only one specific trouble resolution strategy open to the interviewer, which is contingent upon the task structure of the encounter as seen and enacted by the interviewer. This trouble resolution strategy will take the following form: the interviewer will account for his behaviour, on various layers of rules, as appropriate and will encourage the respondent to take up his task role again, that is, to provide answers specific to questions. The respondent can then carry on doubting the propriety of the interviewing performance, but only within reasonable limits. That is, if the respondent becomes completely dissatisfied with the interview, the interview has to be terminated. Otherwise, after sorting out the argument, the interview will be carried on.

It is important to note here that trouble of this kind can be initiated by the respondent at any time and on many, often highly idiosyncratic, grounds during the interview. This means that the interviewer will frequently experience stability of interaction in the interview as being a temporary achievement only. Whenever trouble is created by the respondent, the interviewer has to remedy the situation, that is, to reconstruct the encounter as an interviewing task. In the extreme case, he will have to enlarge on the formal-legal propriety of the interview, while he may also point out, politely, that his actions are task-relevant or task-routine. From this argument, it follows that the interaction strategies used by interviewer and respondent on various layers of rules can often be dissimilar and may sometimes be asymmetrical or even antagonistic. For example, when the interviewer appeals to the respondent's tacit knowledge of the task rules, the respondent may meaningfully deny that he ever accepted, fully, the propriety of these rules.

Often, the interview will take place in the presence of participant-observers or observer-participants. That is, the interviewer-respondent interaction can be complicated by the presence of, typically, other family members. This presence may just be distracting or cause interruption, as is the case with children. But sometimes, bystanders can size up their undefined roles as participants and can begin to enact various specific roles during the interview. They may help to provide answers. They may gatekeep or censor answers. Sometimes they may start interfering with the conduct of the interview in undesirable ways, hence making the interviewer's performance seem illegitimate. If the latter kind of trouble arises, the interviewer must rely on his repertoire of trouble-resolution strategies, but in some instances, he may appeal to the respondent to decide whether his performance is improper or not, because in the interview the respondent is made an expert-partner. While the interviewer appears as an expert in asking questions, the respondent is made, by the task, an expert in providing appropriate answers. In this sense, bystanders can appear both to the interviewer and the respondent as strangers to the interviewing encounter, intruding illegitimately into an otherwise correct performance. This is illustrated by the following example:

I: And tell me which description best fits your present family situation. Could you give me the letter?

R: Mmhm, hang on (pause) G.

I: G.
R: Mmhm.
Respondent's wife interferes: What's that then?
R (angry voice): Oh it's nothing, nothing, er, that it could never interest you.
W: Mmhm.

So far we have looked at the interview in terms of orderly synchronic social interaction. But of course, interviews are not just conceptualised as interactions, they are designed to bring to the surface patterns of knowledge submerged in the respondent's consciousness. That is, the respondent's answers are never heard by the interviewer solely in themselves, as performative actions, but as representing, or pointing to, some reality to which the respondent can gain cognitive access. Hence, the respondent's answers must not only be evaluated by the interviewer in terms of adequate communicative performance, but must also be interpreted in terms of the reference they make to the reality denoted or connoted by them. The referent of an answer may be a fact, a belief about what the facts are, feelings, standards of action, present or past action, or conscious reasons for beliefs, feelings, policies or actions (see Selltiz *et al.*, 1964, pp. 243-53).

In hearing the respondent's answers then, the appearance of utterances is judged by the interviewer in two ways. First, as a performance relevant, or irrelevant, to the interviewing task, and second, as giving glimpses of the patterns of reality which purportedly underlie them. In the first case, the interviewer evaluates answers in terms of orderly task performance, while in the latter, he must grasp the meanings inherent in the respondent's talk. Probing, typically, takes place according to the two dimensions of answers. An answer may be proper in terms of task performance, but may also be read as meaningless, confused, unclear or ambiguous. Here, the interviewer must probe towards the meaning of an answer. This comes out in the following example:

I: Now in the general election, are you more likely to vote for a particular person or a particular party?
R: Party. Conservative if you er, want to know what the party is.
I: Mmhm, amm, and why is that?
R: The same thing except in the local it's best personally and in the country I think it's best for the country in the general election, like, it's just, it works the same way, like.
I: Sorry?

R: In the local election because I think it follows my views in the local election but it's the same for them, in the national election as expressed in the country.

I: Fine.

But an answer may be meaningful yet improper in terms of task performance. This happens, for example, if the respondent gives a clear account which does not relate to the question objective. Then the interviewer must probe towards an answer appropriate to the task in question.

To summarise, each interview is structured as an orderly social relationship to reveal the meanings that respondents attribute to patterns of reality. It is important to note here that the meanings revealed are strictly contingent upon the forms of interaction the interview takes. It is the social organisation of the interview which sets boundaries for the meanings to emerge. The interview must be seen, in this sense, as providing a structured social framework within which meanings may be systematically revealed, but also as a structure which gate-keeps and filters meanings. From this argument, it follows that answers cannot be interpreted at face value, independent of the context of interaction in which they constituted performative actions, but must be interpreted at the level of the sense which those utterances have to the participants during the interview interaction.

The relevance of this conceptualisation of answers in the interview to a theory of the validity of survey data cannot be overestimated. It has been noted that the meaning of a topic may vary according to the layers of rules attributed to that topic. Hence, respondents may give answers on any layer of rules they find appropriate. For example, in the case of social desirability, respondents formulate answers, not on the grounds of their own relational standards, but on the grounds of etiquette or formal-legal rules, hence avoiding embarrassment. Or, in more general terms, whenever a respondent finds a question uncomfortable or difficult, he may answer on any layer of rules which he takes to be appropriate to that question. In the extreme case, the respondent may communicate nothing about himself, but still communicate efficiently as required by the interview task. But in the latter case, we have to admit, all answers will be invalid.

In the example below, this strategy becomes apparent. The respondent finds it difficult to provide an answer on relational grounds, but then escapes into an etiquette-bound meaning of the issue in question:

I: Er, what do you mean when you call someone a close friend?

R: Well, your your question an, your question answered that didn't it? Your question, er answered my answer.
I: Yes.
R: Gave you my answer there. The question itself.
I: Anything else?
R: No (pause).
I: umm
R: It could be anybody you could confide in.
I: Yes.
R: Knowing that they won't repeat anything to any, er, any other person unless you, er, gave them *carte blanche* to do so, like, you know, if you was talking privately to anybody. Anything personal.
I: Fine.

The possible invalidity of responses can often not be detected, due to the lack of concurrent validity criteria. But as we have seen, it is not necessary to take responses at face value. A study of the interaction in the interview will reveal the extent to which an answer has been affected by layers of rules, and hence the extent to which an answer can be taken as validly pointing to an underlying reality.

4 Layers of Rules in the Interview

There are broadly three types of interactive performances during an ordinary research interview: the interaction related to closed questions, the interaction related to open questions and the interaction related to topics during the interview which are not prescribed by the interview task, that is, reading out the questions and recording the answers. In the case of unproblematic performance, the interview is enacted by participants in the form of a string of question-answer sequences, punctuated by etiquette-bound statements concerning the openings and closings of sequences and concerning feedback and transitions. The layers of rules involved here relate primarily to the task with limited reference to etiquette.

But each type of performance can have specific problems which arise from the fact that the respondent may use layers of rules other than those of task and etiquette to evaluate the interview. As regards closed questions, the respondent may find the precoded answers inappropriate. He might find them inapplicable to his personal situation, or not exhaustive enough or not sufficiently detailed to allow an answer. Or he may find a question itself unclear or ambiguous. In these cases, the interviewer will rely on specific task and etiquette rules and will clarify and probe in such a way that either a precoded response can be arrived at, in a non-directive manner, or not. In the case of open questions, the respondent may find a question unanswerable, or he may answer but with an irrelevant or inadequate answer. Again, the interviewer will clarify and probe carefully until a sufficient answer has been accomplished. As regards talk not identified by interviewing procedures, and this often means queries related to the legitimacy of the situation, the interviewer will have to remedy the situation and lead the respondent back into his task role.

In cases where problems arise during the interview, the interviewer is trained to use strategies that will enable him to successfully prevent the disclosure of his personal self which might influence the respondent in undesirable ways, and to disclose only his professional role. This apparently leaves the interviewer in a weak position as far as interaction strategies are concerned because he has to remedy trouble constructed by the respondent by depersonalised means. The interviewer cannot use his own relational standards, because this would be incompatible with the task of being a non-judgemental and unprejudiced observer. This means that the interviewer has to remedy trouble in a somewhat paradoxical way. He must sort out the problem to the satisfaction of the respondent, but without admitting himself fully to the substance of the reason for the trouble. He may legitimate the situation within formal-legal, etiquette and task standards. If this is not possible, he has to give in to the idiosyncratic constructions of the respondent, that is, to not hear them. The interviewer is particularly vulnerable if he is attacked as a person during the encounter, because the interviewer does not appear in this role in the task script. Here, the respondent can exert most of his power. This becomes clear in the following dialogue:

R: May I ask you have you got any idea what your career's going to be?
I: Um, yes, OK, er, I'm doing this part-time. I already work for the health service.
R: Full-time?
I: Er, yes, I work full-time for the health service.
R: Non-productive, er, is it?
I: Um
R: Non-productive employment?
I: Well, what I produce is information.
R: Ah
I: So it's
R: It's non-productive really.

I: Right, now (attempts next question).

Clearly, the apparent powerlessness of the interviewer results from the fact that he cannot use his own relational standards to meet the respondent's challenges. He is caught in the rigid task role required by criteria of measurement. This is in contrast to the information interview where the interviewer can act on personal, sometimes highly idiosyncratic, grounds.

The asymmetry in interaction strategies between interviewer and respondent also becomes clear if one looks at the order in which layers of rules can appear in relation to each other. For the interviewer, there is only one possible sequential order of rule layers: his enactment of the task rules must comply with etiquette rules and both must comply with formal-legal rules appropriate to the interview. For the respondent, there are two basic sequential orders of rule layers in the interview. In the ideal interview, the respondent will enact his relational standards within his task role. That is, his relational rules will comply with the task rules which are grounded in etiquette and formal-legal rules. In this case, the interview is unproblematic, because interviewer and respondent are equally engaged in the fulfilment of the task requirements. But the respondent may deviate from his task role, and this is done by his using his relational standards to override all other rule layers. That is, all task-relevant layers of rules become contingent on idiosyncratic attributions. This usually means that the respondent's performance does not relate easily or straightforwardly to a question-objective or other requirements of the interview task. The interviewer then has to re-establish the task format as required by a particular question, as in the following example:

I: OK, here's the third question. Thinking of people, including relatives, whom you consider to be really good friends, that is people you feel free to talk with about personal things, about how many such friends would you say you have?

R: Ah, let's see now (pause) two, three, four, er, then again. I mean I don't talk to them all about the same areas (uses fingers to count) er four, er five, eerh (sigh), mm, yes, they, er, I suppose you, it's like the er things on a dart-board, er (pause).

I: Well, can you give me a number please?

R: Well, say five.

Clearly, the respondent's idiosyncratic perception of the question leaves the interviewer in a fairly helpless situation. He cannot stop the respondent acting out his relational standards. He can only probe, hence indicating to the respondent the proper task requirements. But it is left to the respondent to find the question answerable and to take up the task again.

A more dramatic case of relational rules overriding other layers of rules arises when the respondent, or a bystander, questions the propriety of the interview or the interviewer's performance. Hence, the interviewer has to legitimate his conduct. In the following example, the respondent's wife starts questioning the legitimacy of the situation. Luckily for the interviewer, the respondent supports his efforts in remedying the situation:

W: What's the reason for all this then?
I: This is to give us training, er.
R: It's training.
W: Well, how is it training *you*, you.
I: Well.
W: It's all very personal what you have been asking.
I: It's given me experience of undertaking er, an interview with people, we're being trained how to er conduct interviews and it's no use us being taught in the classrooms.
R: Yes.
I: We have to get out and actually feel what it's like.
R: With strangers really.
I: and have the experience, it's it's the practical aspect.
R: Yes.
W: But I thought you said there was going to be nothing personal, but everything you've asked Mr Smith has been about his personal views.
R: Ah, it's not personal. Ah there's nothing, yes, it's personal in the in that sense but it's not personal on your sex life or anything like that. Put it that way.

The row continues, but already at this point the strategies that can be used by participants in interviewing interaction become clear. The respondent parties can meaningfully attribute their own relational standards to the interview. They can take it personally, but the interviewer cannot. He must show that he does not intrude into the privacy of the respondent party. In this case, this is done by the respondent. He submits the meaning of 'personal' to a semantic analysis and points out that the interviewer asks personal questions on the layers of rules relevant to his performance and does not violate these standards.

5 Conclusion

The analysis concerning the social organisation of the research interview presented in this paper is very limited, being so by virtue of the phenomenological style of presentation chosen. But the instances of interview talk discussed here have at least illustrated the point that responses are moulded, and affected, by a complex structure of interaction which is quite difficult to conceptualise. Some evidence has been produced for the hypothesis that responses, irrespective of their research value, appear as orderly acts in the stream of interaction that makes up the interview in desirable and undesirable ways. In this sense, the semantic value of a response is bound to its status as an act of rule expression which itself is tied to the structural conditions of interaction inherent in interviewing encounters.

If this view of the interview is valid, it seems sensible to conceptualise the measurement theory of the interview in terms of the actual micro-social processes that inevitably determine the elicitation of responses. This would be in contrast to current interview methodology which primarily recommends the socially sterile procedures for interviewing which suggest, paradoxically, as evident in Deutscher's (1972) account quoted in the introduction, that we should make the interviewer act *without acting*, as if the interviewer could ever *not* influence the situation of action in the interview by means of his own performance.

References

Atkinson, J. (1971). *A Handbook for Interviewers.* London: Her Majesty's Stationery Office.

Denzin, N.K. (1970). *The Research Act: A Theoretical Introduction to Sociological Methods.* Chicago: Aldine.

Deutscher, I. (1972). Public and Private Opinions: Social Situations and Multiple Realities. In S.Z. Nagi and R.G. Corwin (eds.), *The Social Contexts of Research.* London: Wiley.

Harré, R. and Secord, P.F. (1972). *The Explanation of Social Behaviour.* Oxford: Blackwell.

Hyman, H.H. *et al.* (1954). *Interviewing in Social Research.* Chicago: University of Chicago Press.

McCall, G.J. and Simmons, J.L. (1966). *Identities and Interactions.* New York: Free Press.

Sellitz, C. *et al.* (1964). *Research Methods in Social Relations.* New York: Holt, Rinehart and Winston.

Weinstein, E.A. and Deutschberger, P. (1964). Tasks, Bargains and Identities in Social Interaction. *Social Forces, 42,* 451-6.

7 MEANING – WHO NEEDS IT?[1]

Herbert Menzel

Introduction

What is the proper place in sociological discourse of the meanings which the actions studied by sociologists have to the actors who perform them? The dispute over this question has gained new virulence in recent years, but it would be false to claim that it has ever been absent from sociology. There has never been a time when some one point of view dominated the field to the extent of silencing other viewpoints, although one or another viewpoint might gain relative ascendancy for a period.

At the present time, the set of viewpoints is much too diverse to be ordered along a single continuum, but its range may be illustrated by the following two. One is the view that references to actors' meanings, and to other 'notions inside actors' heads', have no place in proper scientific discourse at all, except perhaps as a sort of shorthand notation for clearly understood behavioural equivalents. This seems to be the view of B.F. Skinner (1971), for example. At the extreme opposite is the view that ascertaining and elucidating actors' meanings (variously specified as justifications, rules, or actors' intentions) is not only legitimate but exhausts the possibilities of 'explaining' social action. It is as far as a sociologist can go, it is the denouement of the sociologist's search. This seems to be the view of Louch (1969) and Winch (1958).[2]

Most sociologists who are articulate on this subject today, however, adopt a kind of two-phase position: the phenomena which the social researcher studies must first be delineated, classified, and, perhaps, 'understood', according to the meaning they have for the actors involved. Only after the phenomena have been packaged in this way are their occurrences and their transformations to be 'explained' in terms which are meaningful to the analyst and his public; these 'objective' terms do not necessarily make further reference to meanings to the actors, except perhaps in so far as they have clearly understood equivalents of an 'objective' nature.

So much is common to the views of authors otherwise as diverse as Weber, Kaplan, Schutz and Parsons. Of course, they differ in the precise interpretation of these statements.

At any rate, today most sociologists once again recognise that one must respect the meanings which actions have to their actors, if one is to formulate worthwhile explanations of social phenomena.

In the short first part of this chapter, I will echo this recognition, and will develop some specifying points by means of two illustrative cases.

But how is one to go about paying the necessary respect to actors' meanings? At just what point is the determination of actors' meanings to enter the sociologist's search for explanations? In the second part of the chapter I will call attention to certain obstacles which stand in the way of following precepts which are often enunciated in response to this query.

These obstacles – in brief summary – are:

(1) Actions, more often than not, have multiple meanings. The same behaviour is likely to have various meanings to the several interaction partners involved, and quite frequently even to one and the same actor.

(2) It is not always the most fruitful strategy to focus the explanation of the occurrence of an action around the meanings it has to its actors. Such an invariant course would in fact deflect our attention from certain kinds of explanation which most of us find vital, at least in some important instances.

(3) Certain research problems would be precluded if one always insisted on adhering to actors' definitions of their own acts.

In the third and fourth parts of the chapter I hope at least to point out certain directions in which, I believe, solutions to this dilemma are to be sought.

1 The Importance of Actors' Meanings to Sociological Explanations

I will report two vignettes in order to develop my points under this heading. I call the first one *Altruism on the Bowery*. The Bowery is a street in New York, where drunks and derelicts hang out; and 'altruism' is a subject that my colleague Ronald Kessler and I became interested in some time ago. Altruism, as you can imagine, is hard to find on the streets of New York City, where people will often pass by those in obvious need of help.

On a certain afternoon I was walking along the Bowery, when I saw a man lying on the sidewalk some distance away. His clothes were dirty and torn, an empty whisky bottle lay near his hand, and he seemed to be unconscious. Another dishevelled man, not too steady himself, was squatting next to him, looked into his face, said some words, and pulled the lying man's jacket up around him. It was the first time I had seen one drunk help another in that neighbourhood, and I said to myself: 'There is still some solidarity left in the Lumpenproletariat. There is altruism in the streets! Wait till I tell Ron Kessler that I saw it with my own eyes!'

Just then another man, dirty and dishevelled like the first two, but a little steadier on his feet, came up from the other side and started to yell at the good Samaritan. It was not until he yelled a second time that I understood his words: 'Get out of the man's pocket! Get out of the man's pocket!' One drunk robbing another who is unconscious is what *he* saw with *his* own eyes.

This story points up the following lessons:

(1) The meaning of a piece of behaviour to its performer is often far from obvious; even an eyewitness who 'sees' a given act performed may be wrong.

(2) Being keyed in to the subculture is vital to alert one to alternative meanings, and to their observable signs.

(3) Once alerted, easily observable earmarks for differentiating different kinds of acts (e.g. altruistic from non-altruistic) can often be found.

(4) Imputing the wrong meanings to acts, in instances like this one, would make nonsense out of any subsequent attempts to explain the occurrence of the acts by relating them to other 'facts'.

My next story is called *Shakespeare in the Neighbourhood*. In 1964, a mobile theatre was organised in New York City. It went from neighbourhood to neighbourhood, set up its stage in a local park or school playground, and performed Shakespeare's *Midsummernight's Dream* for two or three nights in each of these places. The neighbourhoods chosen were mostly working-class districts, with a largely black and Puerto Rican population.

Two sociologists, then at the Bureau of Applied Social Research of Columbia University, were engaged to evaluate the enterprise, and they tell many interesting things in the short book that resulted (Faust and Kadushin, 1965). Although many people showed pleasure in these performances, there were negative reactions as well, some quite disturbing (p. 45):

> In earlier times, and still surviving in some parts of Europe, audiences expressed their opinions of the actors by throwing various objects at them. That custom was revived by the audiences of the Mobile Theater. The objects ranged from jelly beans, spitwads, and paper clips shot from rubber bands to peaches, eggs, rocks [and] firecrackers . . .
>
> Observations . . . identified the culprits as teen-agers and . . . boys. . . . the incidents were spontaneous in each neighborhood . . . There is no evidence that the perpetrators in one neighborhood were even aware that similar incidents had occured earlier in other neighborhoods.

At this point both the sociologists and the sponsors of the plays asked themselves what this behaviour meant, and developed a series of alternate hypotheses, each of which would have different action implications.

> Were the teen-agers criticizing the artistic level of the performance? Although this is the meaning of the 'European custom' to which the authors allude, it seemed unlikely here.
>
> Were they objecting to the felt 'irrelevance' of Elizabethan drama to their life situations? If so, perhaps different plays should be shown, or Shakespearean plays recast so as to bring out their contemporary relevance.
>
> Were they reacting to a feeling of not being welcome? Perhaps advanced publicity for the plays needed to be distributed more widely, or in Spanish as well as English; or perhaps ushers at the play needed to be more tactful.
>
> Or were they protesting felt racial discrimination in the staffing of the enterprise? Perhaps one should go further in recruiting racial and ethnic minorities for the casts of these performances.
>
> Or did the protesters, perhaps, resent the patronizing attitude with which the elite from downtown appeared to bring the blessings of culture to the benighted poor? This would, perhaps, call for linking the affair up with local grass-roots initiatives.

The answer to the puzzle was obtained in one of those 'unplanned' ways for which wisely designed social research must always make room. The researchers held 'discussions in Canarsie with boys who admitted to having thrown things' (Faust and Kadushin, 1965, pp. 46-7).

> They were contacted in the performance area during the show and, once assured that they would not be identified, were willing to discuss (and brag about) their actions. The principal complaint these boys had against the Mobile Theater was that it usurped their 'territory', a school playground, without their permission . . . Many neighborhoods have no place other than the school playground where a large number of boys can congregate . . . and . . . make a lot of noise . . .
>
> . . . The playground is therefore the focus and, in their opinion, the property of these gangs. When the Mobile Theater arrived, they felt unjustly dispossessed and deprived of what they considered their rights.
>
> The boys had industriously made holes in the wire fences surrounding the playgrounds . . . to provide . . . entrance at night. [When the theater arrived, it] closed up . . . the fence holes . . . This was of course viewed by the boys in Carnarsie as further encroachment, since they regarded the holes as their 'property' . . .

In other words, the boys defined the situation as one of an invasion of their property and an infringement of their rights, and the meaning of their rock-throwing was an attempt to drive the invaders from their territory.

What lessons does this story add to those of the previous one?

(1) Sometimes a separate, deliberate undertaking to unearth the meaning of acts is necessary. In this example it is unlikely that a sound check-list of observable indicators could be developed, which would make it possible to distinguish 'protests against turf invasion' from 'protests against Elizabethan irrelevance', etc., in the act of observation.

(2) Sometimes understanding the meaning of the act and explaining its occurrence are almost identical. Once the meaning of 'turf invasion' had been recognised, there were almost no puzzles in filling in the remainder of the explanation, and therefore there were almost no puzzles in deciding what to do about it.

The authors' recommended (pp. 51-2) as follows:

> The theater should have an experienced youth worker on its staff, who would concentrate on contacting and winning over the neighborhood gangs some time before the theater was to arrive in each

> neighborhood . . . They should talk to the boys at the playground, attempt to win their consent to the performance and . . . they should try to recruit the boys' help in setting up the show, and acting as ushers. In addition, some parts of the playground should be left free for the boys to use, at least during the day; and arrangements should be made for the boys to have another place available on performance nights. The theater should not close up any of the holes in the fences, but should, instead, recruit some of the boys to stand guard at these places.

2 Ambiguities and Contradictions in the Appeal to Actors' Meanings

I need not further elaborate the importance of the meaning of events and actions to the actors involved; this importance is well-recognised in sociology today. It is much less clear just how the social researcher is to live up to this recognition, and just what it implies for actual research steps. Relevant precepts can, to be sure, be found in many places. In one wording or another they call upon the sociologist:

– to speak of what people do in terms of meaningful 'acts' rather than in terms of spatio-temporally defined 'behaviour',
– to determine the meanings of actions by patient and empathetic observation, taking care not to let his own definition of the situation intrude;
– to ascertain what actions mean to their actors uninfluenced by alleged explanations of their occurrence by outside forces;
– in fact, to postpone any attempt at an explanation of the occurrence of actions until their meanings to their actors have been ascertained;
– to give the meanings, once ascertained, the central place in any explanation.

We might call these the doctrines of the importance, the objectivity, the autonomy, the temporal priority, and the explanatory centrality of actors' meanings.

In the following pages, I will point out certain ambiguities and shortcomings of these doctrines. The first of the ambiguities stems from the multiplicity of meanings of most behaviour.

(a)Multiple Meanings of the Same Behaviour

Many writers have pointed out that it is more sensible, more fruitful, and certainly more natural to conceive of the phenomena that social scientists are interested in as 'actions' rather than as 'behaviour'; where 'in "action" is included all human behavior when and insofar as the acting individual attaches a subjective meaning to it' (Weber, 1947). I take this to mean, approximately, that one should (and normally does) not classify together sets of behaviour which are similar in physico-temporal or in physiological terms, but rather those pieces of human conduct, no matter of what physiological behaviours they may be composed, to which a similar symbolically expressible intention on the actor's part can be ascribed.

Thus, if one sees a certain movement of the left arm of one person among many assembled in a room, it would be possible to describe the phenomenon physically as 'Mr Jones' left arm rose by 8 inches,' or, more behaviourally, as 'Mr Jones raised his left arm,' but it would probably be more sensible to say that 'Mr Jones asked for the floor,' and thus to regard it as the 'same' action as if he had held up a card in his right arm, or had stood up and said 'Mr Chairman!' or had gone through any one of several other behavioural performances which are recognised as 'asking for the floor'.

I concur that it is usually, and perhaps always, more sensible to conceptualise phenomena of human conduct as 'actions' rather than 'behaviours'. I also agree that there is not very much human behaviour which is not part of some action or other. Nevertheless the directive 'speak of what happens as acts rather than behaviour' leaves the matter in a very ambiguous state. This is so because any one behaviour is likely to constitute more than one act. This is most easily made clear by an illustration. For this purpose I invite the reader to consider the following vignette, keeping in mind as the central question, '*What was Mr Smith doing behind the lawn mower*?'

Mr Smith lives in a house in the suburbs. On a certain Saturday morning we can see him pushing a machine around on the grass: it is a lawn-mower. What is he doing? Most of us would agree that he is 'mowing the lawn', meaning thereby not only that the grass gets shorter as he walks over it with his machine, but also that Mr Smith set out to mow the lawn; that is why he is pushing the machine around; he wouldn't do it if his grass were made of Astroturf. And such a belief of ours would almost never be wrong, perhaps with rare exceptions in cases of somnambulism or of the imitative behaviour of a feeble-minded person.

Aha, so that's what Mr Smith is doing, that is the meaning which converts behaviour into act: he is mowing his lawn. But having registered this fact, have we really finished our task of deciding what act is involved, of interpreting, of 'understanding' what he is doing, of determining if the performance is 'intentional'?

No, we have not finished, for while it is (almost unquestionably) true that Mr Smith is mowing his lawn, there are a number of other things which he is also doing by the same behaviour:

he is beautifying his garden;
he is exercising his muscles;
he is avoiding his wife;
he is conforming to the expectations of his neighbours;
he is keeping up property values in Scarsdale;
and he is angering his new neighbour, Mr Ifabrumliz, who prefers to sleep late, and feels that Smith's mowing is a criticism of his, Ifabrumliz', unkempt lawn.

There is no question that all these things are happening, and that they are happening as a result of Mr Smith's pushing the lawn-mower around. Not only is his grass getting shorter but his biceps are getting harder, he is out of earshot of his wife, his garden is becoming more beautiful, his neighbours will nod approval, real-estate values rise and Mr Ifabrumliz' ulcer starts burning. All of these things are happening, but it is not at all clear whether each of these things was intended by Mr Smith – maybe it was, maybe it was not.[3]

So far I have restricted myself to the meanings that the mower-pushing behaviour may have to Mr Smith himself. But most acts which are of interest to sociologists are links in chains of interaction, and are likely to have diverse meanings to the several interaction partners. Take Neighbour Ifabrumliz: his ulcer burns, his hostility to Smith increases, when Smith mows the lawn, because he is being criticised, he is being put down, by Smith's behaviour: that is the meaning Smith's behaviour has to Ifabrumliz. His ulcer burns and his anger rises quite independently of whether that was also the meaning the behaviour had to Smith.

What, then, shall we say was *the* nature of the act that we observed? It was a 'lawn-mowing', for sure; but was it, in addition, gymnastic exercise? Was it wife-avoiding? Was it an act of conformity? Was it putting down the neighbour Ifabrumliz? Since it may have been one, or several, or all of these, it seems pointless to me to ask which was 'the' meaning of the act, as though there could be only one; and it seems false to me to somehow regard the job as done when one meaning has been identified. For knowing that the behaviour did mean any one of these does not foreclose the possibility that the same behaviour had one or more of the other meanings as well.

Even after a meaning has been identified, one still must decide whether it is necessary to determine if the given behaviour does not also have certain other meanings – does not also constitute certain other acts. And one must still decide around which of the several meanings of the act (if any) to pursue one's further enquiries and build one's explanations.

It seems to me that one must consider the purpose of an investigation in order to make these decisions; they cannot be derived from the observations alone. Consider again the example of Mr Smith and his lawn-mower. Whether 'getting away from the wife' is involved is, perhaps, important if one wants to know why Mr Smith mows his lawns at the particular times he does; whether or not 'exercising his muscles' is involved would be relevant if one were interested in the effects of introducing power-mowers. And if one's research interest happens to be in the sources of tensions in surburban neighbourhoods into which a new ethnic group has recently begun to move, the meanings of each resident's behaviour to his neighbours might be more relevant than the meanings of that behaviour to the actor himself.

These observations can be summarised in the following four points:

(1) Most streams of behaviour can be carved up, or assigned meanings, and hence conceptualised as 'acts', in more than one way, and more than one of those may very well be valid simultaneously.[4]

(2) Therefore it is fallacious to insist on determining 'the' meaning of an act, as though there necessarily were one which is somehow the most fundamental or the most real one. Even though it may often be possible to indicate one meaning as the minimum meaning that the behaviour certainly has (such as 'he's mowing the lawn' in the example given), there is no reason to believe that that meaning is the one that has the greatest explanatory value, or supplies in any sense the true motive power. (In the example, 'conformity' or 'getting away from the wife', if valid, are likely to have more explanatory power than 'mowing the lawn').

(3) Hence, it cannot be said that the job of interpreting an act is done when one has identified one meaning of it, or the one meaning one is pleased to designate as the 'true' one. Other meanings may be applicable as well, and whether or not their applicability is relevant will depend on the purpose of the investigation.[5]

(4) For some purposes, what is more crucial is not the meaning of a behaviour stream to the actor, but rather to specifiable interaction partners. In many instances, the different meanings which an act has for several interaction partners must all be taken into account.

A fifth point may be added:

(5) There is a great deal more unintended action going on than would appear from the correct observation that very little human conduct is not the component of *some* intended act; for it may nevertheless also be the component of one or more forms of conduct which are unintended. (In the example, Mr Smith surely maintained property values, gained the approval of his Anglo-Saxon neighbours, and angered his new ethnic neighbours, but it is a moot question whether he did each of these intentionally.)[6]

(*b*) *Actors' Meanings as Sources of Bias*

So far, we have been concerned with how the meanings of acts and situations to their actors are to be ascertained. Because of the multiplicity of these meanings, we have found difficulty with the recommendation to ascertain these meanings by observations uncontaminated by the researcher's own definition of the situation.

Now we must consider how central a place is to be given to actors' meanings, however ascertained, in the formulation of sociological explanations. Should these meanings be accorded the central place in all sociological explanations, as is often demanded in the current literature? Although I believe that it is sound general practice to be guided by these meanings in one's search for the explanation of the occurrence of actions, I believe that it would be a mistake to be guided by these considerations exclusively and invariably. To do so would deflect one's attention from a whole range of potential explanations which few sociologists would want to see excluded from consideration.

Once again I find it easiest to make my case by means of an example. Suppose we would like to know how American atrocities in Vietnam came about – how it was, for example, that women and children were shot by American soldiers who, a few months earlier, had been reasonably well-behaved, decent citizens of their home towns.

What was the Meaning of Mi-Lai? One way to search for an answer to this question would be to concentrate on the meanings that these acts had for the soldiers involved. This might perhaps be done by interviewing them in depth, listening to their conversations after the battle, psycho-analysing them, or closely observing the contexts of situations and of other acts surrounding each of the deeds. No matter how these meanings were ascertained, I believe one would find them to be composed of elements like the following:

> I was acting in self-defence. Or, at any rate, in order to head off threats to my own life. Besides, I had to defend my team, and head off threats to my buddies' lives. You can't take chances with those people. They will even hide grenades in their skirts. If you don't get them first, they'll get you. And you can't tell the Viet Cong from the peasants – they are too sneaky for that. Even women will shoot at you when you are not watching. If you make allowances for women and children, you end up blown to bits. I've seen it happen. Besides, life is cheap to those people: you can see it by the crazy way they will attack us, when we are so much better armed. And besides, I was doing what everybody was doing.

I submit that these would not be mere surface rationalisations, but the sincerely held beliefs of these soldiers. More than that – they are true: the soldiers *have* seen comrades blown up by grenades that had been hidden under peasant women's skirts; they *really* can't tell the Viet Cong apart from the people; and everybody *was* doing it.

Concentration on these meanings and definitions of situations may well lead to some fruitful insights. But it would leave out of account – it would, indeed, deflect us from even considering – possible explanations along the following lines:

> American troops in Vietnam are doing the work of an occupying power on foreign soil; the presence of the occupying power is seen as illegitimate probably by the majority of the people, but certainly by a sizeable portion of that part of the Vietnamese population which is politically conscious and activated. That politically activated part of the population is very numerous; the Viet Cong cannot be told apart from the people because they *are* the people; and it is not possible under such circumstances to maintain an occupying force on foreign soil without atrocities, i.e. without breaking one's own rules of 'clean' warfare. Once the decision to maintain an occupying force in such circumstances is made, atrocities must follow by a relentless logic. It is not even so much that the generals

will decide on atrocities for strategic reasons, as that soldiers will resort to them in situations of perceived self-defence, and that field commanders will resort to them under the pressures they feel coming from below in the concrete situations.

Such an explanation, by the way, need not at all deny that the meanings alluded to earlier were sincerely held, and corresponded to the way in which the situation was experienced by these soldiers. The meanings attributed to the soldiers, and even explanations built around them, need not be invalid, in order for alternate (social-structural) explanations to be valid simultaneously. And for many problems, probably including the one of American atrocities in Vietnam, it may be precisely social-structural explanations which, if valid, could help orient us towards effective action in our own lives.

Many readers may, of course, doubt that a valid explanation of the occurrence of American atrocities in Vietnam can be found along such social-structural lines; and such an explanation would, indeed, require much more empirical and theoretical grounding than can be given here.

But unless one is willing to rule out explanations of this kind – social-structural explanations – from sociology altogether, one must not insist that explanations must invariably use actors' meanings as their core; for such a precept would not even allow structural explanations to come up for consideration.

It might be objected that the problem in the above example results not from concentrating on *meanings* to actors, but from concentrating on the *wrong actors*: the soldiers in Vietnam, one might say, were mere pawns in the undertaking; the decisions were made in the White House and the Pentagon, and we should have investigated the meaning of these decisions to the likes of Westmoreland, Nixon, Rusk and Johnson.

But we could not have decided to do this without a rule for deciding which actors' meanings to pursue, and that rule could not itself be based on meanings to 'the' actors; it would have to be in 'objective' terms. Furthermore, even the meaning of the relevant decisions to, say, the Joint Chiefs of Staff would hardly point to the 'structural' explanations suggested above, but would rather be in terms like the following:

we are minimising the loss of American lives;

we are holding ground against an enemy who will not wage war fairly;

we are achieving peace with honour.

On this point, I would like to quote from a review by Victor Navasky (1972) of David Halberstam's book, *The Best and the Brightest* (1972), which 'sets out to discover why America got involved in the worst and messiest war in our history', in spite of having high in the counsels of government 'the best and the brightest' of Americans.

> . . . the book's main and most remarkable contribution [says Navasky] is to introduce us in depth to the architects of America's involvement in Vietnam – not only the McNamaras and Rusks, but also the Rosencrantz's and Guildensterns of the Federal bureaucracy . . . His portraits are superb . . . We see the . . . characters in action, from a distance, up close, and occasionally even from inside their heads . . . . Anyone who would understand the decision-making process during these years cannot do without analyses of this sort.
>
> But again one must ask whether focusing on 'the players' in the game doesn't tend to downgrade the possibility that they are primarily instruments of the so-called war system rather than determiners of the war.
>
> Why are we in Vietnam? [Navasky asks again] In portraying the decision-making process as a struggle between the humanists and the rationalists . . . Halberstam has been faithful to, if critical of, the perspective of his subjects, and to that extent his inquiry may lack optimal historical imagination.
>
> It may be, ironically, that to get a book as rich in inside information, insight, and occasional wisdom as this one, requires someone who lives in the penumbra of 'the best and the brightest,' who has access to their confidence . . . and that the beneficial limits of such a collaboration are [to adopt] the same shared assumptions which make it possible.

I conclude that in the search for explanations, a concentration on actors' meanings is sometimes indispensable, usually helpful, sometimes not helpful, and occasionally misleading.

(*c*) *Whose Problems are Research Problems?*

There is another lesson to be learned from the vignette about atrocities in Vietnam. So far we have concentrated on the role of actors' meanings in the explanation of the occurrence of these acts. We must now consider their role in the identification of the acts to be explained. Just what is to be included under the term 'atrocities'? When we seek to answer this question by reference to the meanings of acts to their actors, following the doctrine that researchers must not impose their meanings on the actions studied, we come to a disturbing realisation: the acts we are interested in did not have the meaning of 'atrocities' to any of the actors involved, under any of the interpretations cited in the earlier paragraphs. Nobody, neither foot soldier, nor field commander, nor Joint Chief, nor President, ever said, 'Let's go out and do some atrocities.' Only in retrospect, long after the acts, did some of the participating soldiers come to see their own past acts as atrocities.

And yet I believe that we are fully justified in phrasing *our* research problem as seeking an explanation for the occurrence of atrocities. Consider the alternatives. One alternative is to be guided by the actors' definitions of their own acts, and hence to regard these acts variously as acts of self-defence, of platoon solidarity, or of loss-minimising military tactics. But this strict constructionist insistence on actors' meanings will not do, for we would still have to select out *certain* acts of self-defence, *certain* acts of platoon solidarity, or *certain* forms of military tactics as the phenomena to be explained – and what would differentiate them would be precisely their character of 'atrocities'. And yet they would not have this character in the eyes of their perpetrators.

There is yet another alternative. It would seek to avoid terms of controversial applicability, like 'atrocities', by substituting for them more operational equivalents, on the application of which everyone could, presumably, agree, such as 'killing babies', 'burning down straw huts', and the like. But this would be a false and impoverishing scientism, for we must seek explanations which will encompass any new 'atrocities' that the genius of modern warfare may invent tomorrow, and which could not be included in any finite list of operational equivalents we could draw up today. In that sense, the specification of the meaning of general terms must always remain open-ended, must always end with the implied phrase '. . . and things like that', where the *tertium comparationis* of 'like' is, in principle, unstatable.

But if it is 'atrocities' we are researching, and if they do not have the meaning of atrocities to their perpetrators, to whom do they have that meaning? To us. Who is 'us'? It is you, dear reader, and I; it is all the parties to any ongoing dialogue about the formulation of a research problem; it is 'us' the researchers, together with the audiences for whom we write, and the publics whose 'problematic' experiences prompt our investigations. These problem-experiencing groups (researchers, publics and audiences) may or may not include the actors to be investigated; they may or may not share the actors' definitions of the situation. Yet it is not only legitimate, it is vital, that research problems be conceptualised in terms of the meanings to the problem-experiencers, even when they do not coincide with the meanings to the actors involved.

I hope to make this claim more convincing by the examination of yet another illustrative narrative. This vignette will, at the same time, display more fully the mutual dependence of research purposes and the imputation of meanings to acts.

This story takes place near the top of a hill on a Friday afternoon. Although it is unseasonably dark for that time of day, we can make out a number of men squatting on the ground, moving their arms about and shouting in an apparently gay mood. Moving closer, we realise that they are taking turns picking up small objects from the ground, and throwing the objects down again; all this is interspersed with conversations and shouts. The small objects prove to be cube-shaped. The shouts contain frequent references to the numbers 7 and 11. What kind of action is going on here?

With some knowledge of the culture, we interpret: they are rolling dice, they are shooting craps, they are gambling.

For many possible sociological interests, this would be the appropriate characterisation of these acts. We might, for example, be interested in studying the relationship of gambling behaviour to religious doctrines, or the diffusion of particular games among different ethnic groups.

Or we might rise to a slightly more abstract level and say: 'Aha! Leisure Behaviour', and incorporate this datum in our study of the role of leisure behaviour in reinforcing the segregation of social classes and of ethnic groups. Or we might focus on the intra-group processes here, seeing, perhaps, if one person wins more often than the others, and if his name is 'Doc'.

On the other hand, we might look around a little more and see various pieces of clothing on the ground and notice that these are being handed to members of the gambling group in accordance with the fall of the dice; and listening to bits of conversation, we might recognise another act in the same behaviour: they are not only gambling, they are not only passing their leisure; they are dividing up the loot after a robbery. And this would be an appropriate way of conceptualising the act if we are, for example, studying honour among thieves, the norms governing the distribution of spoils, rules of fair allocation of property rights, or the like.

But now we find out more, by paying closer attention, and by interviewing bystanders who were on the scene longer than we. It turns out that the person to whom the loot had belonged was not merely robbed:

he is being killed, he was, in fact, tortured, tried and convicted as a radical agitator: he is right now dying a slow death; and the gamblers whom we were observing are soldiers.

Upon noticing this, our designation of the act constituted by the same behaviour will shift once again, but this time it will shift more profoundly than before. Now we will say, this is persecution, this is oppression, and the soldiers, who are so cheerfully gambling away the belongings of the victim of persecution, are callous, are cruel, are dancing on the graves of the oppressed.

Diffusion of behaviour patterns; ethnic segregation in leisure behaviour; dominance in small groups; norms concerning property rights; suppression of deviance from dominant ideologies: is there any doubt that each of these is a legitimate domain for sociological enquiry? Is there any doubt that the behaviour described above deserves consideration as a specimen of each of these processes? Yet each of these successively stated research purposes required a re-designing of the action being studied: the same stream of behaviour was successively assigned the meanings of 'gambling', of 'leisure behaviour', of 'deference to a group leader', of 'dividing up the loot from a robbery', and of 'dancing on the graves of the oppressed'.

Did the behaviour have all of these meanings to the soldiers who carried it out? They would probably agree that it was gambling and leisure behaviour, though hardly that it constituted deference to a group leader. They would probably agree that it was dividing up the yield of a job, thought it is questionable whether they would call it 'loot', and the job a 'robbery'. They surely would reject the labels 'oppression' and 'dancing on the grave of the oppressed'.

Unless we are ready to surrender our right to study phenomena in these terms, we manifestly cannot rely on any 'true meaning to actors' as the criterion of choice among such possible interpretations. It is we who must choose, it is we who must decide among these interpretations of the act – we, who together are seeking an understanding of this frightening behaviour. We cannot rely on the actors to make the choice for us; for they – quite literally – know not what they do: *non enim sciunt quid faciunt.*

In summary, reflection on these examples leads to the recognition that any research problem will necessarily have to be phrased, initially, in the terms in which it is experienced as a problem – by whom? By those of us who experience it as a problem. This means us the researchers, together with any actual or intended publics, audiences, served populations, or clients whose puzzlement, scientific curiosity, practical need to know, or critical consciousness provides the motivation for undertaking our research.

This set may or may not include the actors to be studied, and the meanings which acts and situations have to us may or may not coincide with the meanings of the same phenomena to the actors involved. Nevertheless, it is up to us to formulate problems for research, in the first instance, in terms that are meaningful to *us*; and our eventual solutions will have to be re-translatable into such terms. During the intervening search for explanations, to be sure, we are well advised to take into account what things mean to the actors whom we are studying.

3 Steps Towards a Resolution

I will now try to re-state the chief lessons learned in the above discussion in more succinct terms, adding new qualifications where necessary. In the fourth section of the chapter, I will examine the potential for ascertaining the meaning of acts independently of their explanations. Together these points will, I believe, constitute a necessary set of emendations to the doctrines of the objectivity, autonomy, temporal priority and explanatory centrality of actors' meanings in sociological enquiry.

(a) One Must Specify 'To Whom?' when Asking What Acts and Situations Mean

Acts and situations do not have meanings to only one set of actors, but to diverse sets of interaction partners, to other interested parties, and to investigators and the publics which they represent. Hence it is never sufficient to speak of 'meanings' without specifying 'to whom'.

(b) Researchers Must Make Choices and Take Responsibility in the Assignment of Meanings to Acts

Even for a given actor, a behaviour or a situation is likely to have more than one meaning. For this and the above-stated reasons, the meaning of an act is seldom dictated unambiguously by what we can observe, by the testimony of actors, or by other 'data'; in most instances, the determination of the meaning of an act requires a heavy dose of researcher input.

The researcher who wishes to respect the meanings of acts in his theorising faces several tasks of choosing. He must choose the particular partners to an interaction to whose meanings he will give central place. Each time a meaning has been assigned to an act, he must choose whether to search for further meanings. Among the several meanings which will have been identified, he must choose the ones around which to focus his further enquiries and around which to build his explanation.

How are we, as investigators, to make these choices? Our research purposes will go a long way in determining them. Our theoretical framework, the factors which we regard as changeable and manipulable, the intended range of time, place and circumstance of the understanding we seek in a given enquiry, will all play a role. The empirical adequacy and explanatory power of the understanding ultimately achieved will be criteria in the long run.

This is hardly the place to set forth how a researcher's theory work is to be done.

But this much is clear: these choices cannot themselves be based on actors' meanings and definitions of situations, since the appropriate identification of meanings and definitions is precisely what is at issue. It plainly will not do to appeal to the actors in question, or to 'the phenomena on their own terms', to make these choices for us. It is, at best, an illusion to believe that one can simply 'study the phenomena of everyday life on their own terms, . . . make use only of methods of observation and analysis that retain the integrity of the phenomena' (Douglas, 1970, p. 16) without considerable input on the researcher's part.

(c) One Must Distinguish Problem-Formulating Discourse From Explanatory Discourse

Before going any further, I find it necessary to make a distinction among types of sociological discourse; no single set of guidelines can define the place of actors' meaning in sociological discourse of all types.

In particular, one must distinguish discourse which delineates problems for investigation from discourse which furnishes explanations for the problems. (Compare the discussion of theoretical-explanatory concepts in Kaplan, 1964, pp. 54-62.)

(d) Problem Formulations Must Respect the Meaning of Acts to Us, the Enquirers

Many, possibly most, problems for sociological research have their origin in puzzlements which are experienced in terms which make reference to act meanings:

– When will Bowery derelicts show altruism to one another?
– How can the destructiveness of neighbourhood youngsters against

Shakespearean theatre be reduced?
– How come Americans commit atrocities in Vietnam?

It is in these terms that the problems are first experienced as problems, and it is in these terms that they motivate the undertaking of sociological enquiry. Whatever scientific terms they may be translated into will have to remain responsive to these experienced problems, and any scientific solution will have to be retranslatable into such terms, if our motivating curiosity is to be satisfied.

In thise sense it is quite correct to say that 'the phenomena to be studied must be the phenomena as experienced in everyday life' (Douglas, 1970, p. 16). But if, at this point, we raise the question 'in *whose* everyday life?' or – as phrased earlier – 'meaning to whom?', then a little reflection shows that the act meanings which are most vital in the formulation of problems for research are the meanings of the acts in question to us, the enquirers, i.e. to those to whom the problem is a problem.

It is what *we* experience as 'altruism' that we want accounted for; what impresses *us* as destructive that we want reduced, what *we* think of as atrocities that bewilders us and calls for an explanation.

These are the research tasks to be pursued, even if the behaviour in question does not have the same meanings to its actors. I believe that this claim, which I developed in greater detail in my discussion of 'atrocities' in section 2 (c), is in line with the impact of the following statement, although possibly not with the intentions of its author:

> All of sociology is directed either to increasing our understanding of everyday life, or, more practically, to improving our everyday lives . . . Sociology . . . necessarily begins and ends with the understanding of everyday life (Douglas, 1970, p. 3).

I concur fully, but would supply emphasis as follows:

> All of sociology is directed either to increasing *our* understanding of everyday life, or more practically, to improving *our* everyday lives . . . Sociology . . . necessarily begins and ends with *our* understanding of everyday life.

That is to say, *my* sociological work is directed to increase *my* understanding and to improve *my* life; the sociology whose nature is the subject of the current dialogue between you, dear reader, and me, must be directed to increase *our* knowledge and to improve *our* lives; and the sociology which we share and intend to share with a community of other scholars, of readers, of social critics, of clients, and of activists must be directed to their understanding and their lives and, in the best of circumstances, to increasing their and our common understanding and to improving their and our communal lives.[7]

(e) Explanations Should Respect the Meanings of Acts to Their Actors, but Need Not Invariably be Centred Around these Meanings

I have already argued this matter in section 2 (b). In order to clarify certain points, I return once more to the analysis of the legionnaires throwing dice for the belongings left behind by their victim. In the earlier discussion, I attended to the meaning to be assigned to this behaviour in delineating a problem for investigation. Now I would like to turn to possible explanations of such a problem.

Once we agree that, for our purposes, the observed behaviour constitutes 'dancing on the graves of the oppressed', we may become interested in various questions of explanation.

One of them is: how is it possible for human beings to behave in this way? Various alternate hypotheses suggest themselves, each proposing a different meaning of the act. For example:

(1) The soldiers are psychopaths, cleverly selected by the authorities for this disgusting job; then this is, to them, just another bit of routine behaviour;

(2) they have been given drugs to dull their awareness and their willpower; then the act was, to them, a mistake – perhaps a tragic mistake;

(3) they have been brainwashed to believe that the victim was the member of a subhuman and pernicious race; then the act was, to them, justice – although genocide to us.

Up to this point, we are still talking about what the act meant to the actors, consciously. On the other hand, the explanation of the cheerful gambling may lie elsewhere:

(4) Perhaps these soldiers have been forced to participate in an act which they themselves regard as cruel persecution; they are now in a deep crisis of conscience, and their raucous gambling is a desperate attempt at denial, a flight into unreality, a last psychological

defence against breakdown.

And perhaps:

(5) the whole scene is taking place inside a concentration camp, in which the 'soldiers' who today do the dirty work for the persecutors are themselves inmates whose turn to be annihilated will come tomorrow; and the rolling of the dice is their grasping at a last straw of joy.

When we call the behaviour a last psychological defence against breakdown, or the last grasping at a straw of joy, we are no longer talking about a meaning of the act of which its perpetrators were aware. We are, rather, talking about a meaning which makes the act explainable to us, in spite of whatever meaning it may have to the actors. Nevertheless we still 'explain' the behaviour by attributing to it a psychological function – albeit an unconscious one – in the actors' life. And when, finally, we explain American atrocities in Vietnam by the situational pressures and strategic necessities which inhere in a military occupation in the face of a politically aroused, hostile population, neither meanings to the actors nor functions in the actors' psyche play a central role in our explanation.

If we allow that explanations like these can have legitimate status in sociology, then we are agreed that sociological explanations are *not necessarily* explanations via the meanings of the acts to the actors involved, nor by the definitions which these actors give to the situations in which the acts take place. Just when explanations of various kinds are appropriate must be determined from the nature of research goals, and from empirical information. It cannot be stated *a priori.*[8]

(f) Explanations Which Make No Reference To Actors' Meanings Do Not Seem Promising, But They Cannot Be Outlawed a priori

To say, as I did above, that actors' meanings do not necessarily occupy the central place in sociological explanations, is not to say that sociological explanations can avoid reference to these meanings altogether. Even the illustrations which I used in the preceding section do make *some* reference to actors' beliefs, attitudes, values, intentions, motives, and definitions of situations. Is this an inevitable feature of all legitimate sociological explanations?

It is, of course, possible to *define* sociology as the science of certain meaningful acts. Just this is, in fact, endorsed by most sociological writers on the subject – by such 'mainstream' authors as Max Weber,

George Herbert Mead, Talcott Parsons, and Abraham Kaplan, as well as by phenomenological and existentialist sociologists. All these writers insist that it is behaviour conceptualised in terms of actors' meanings that is the business of sociology.

It is not quite clear if they mean thereby to designate the problems which sociology is to explain, or the explanations which sociology is to offer.

While it is possible to define sociology either as the science which seeks to explain meaningful acts, or as the science which seeks to explain behaviour by reference to its meanings to the actors involved, it is important to realise that neither of these definitions entails the other. In fact, when strictly interpreted, they conflict. For it is unlikely, and can certainly not be affirmed *a priori*, that only appeals to actors' meanings and definitions of situations can contribute to the explanation of the occurrence of meaningful acts, nor that such appeals would explain nothing but behaviour formulated in terms of acts having these very meanings. The history of many scientific disciplines and specialities shows a transition from one of these kinds of definitions of the field to the other. They start out as sciences of certain subject matters, and they end up as sciences of whatever can be explained by the theories which they have developed. Chemistry once was the science of substances and later that of irreversible processes; currently it is the science of whatever can be explained by means of the notions of valences, molecular structure, and the chemical bond. Genetics started out as the science of family resemblances in the plant and animal kingdom, but has become the science of only those family resemblances, and other phenomena, which can be accounted for by Mendelian ratios and constellations of genes.

It would seem to be in line with these trends to define sociology as the science of whatever can be explained by a certain set of theoretical concepts. Should these concepts be actors' meanings, motives and intentions? I would propose that these should be among the defining theoretical concepts, but for reasons already stated I would find it unwise to insist upon giving them the central place in every explanation before it is admitted as a sociological one.

If, on the other hand, we define sociology in terms of its problem domain, and restrict that domain to meaningful acts, then we cannot *a priori* rule out that the occurrence of these acts may not, in part, be explained by factors as 'meaningless' as heredity, climate, geographic barriers, or endocrine incompatibilities, to say nothing of patterns of human behaviour defined in such terms as density of populations, turnover of contacts, frequency of encounters, or the like, which make very little reference to any actors' meanings. Hence I see no *a priori* reason that compels us to outlaw explanations which make no reference to actors' meanings.

Personally, I believe that explanations without reference to meanings are seldom likely to succeed. Most of the attempts to construct explanations of this sort which I have seen strike me as unpromising and tortuous. But one of them might succeed some day. I am not ready to bar anyone from attempting them; I am not ready to condemn anyone for having attempted them. While I might regard such efforts as unpromising, misplaced and even foolish, I see no reason for regarding them as sinful. I do not see that such attempts deny the humanity of those studied, nor that they make the observer of the scene, as one writer put it, 'alien to it, uncomprehending, and without sympathy, [looking] through the microscope or the telescope as through a keyhole, peering, and peeping' (Maslow, 1966, p. 49).

4 Meaning Imputations and Explanations: Priority and Independence

I began this chapter by acknowledging the great importance of respect for actors' meanings in sociological enquiry. I then examined certain oft-repeated methodological precepts, which are intended to do justice to this importance, and pointed out certain ambiguities and shortcomings. This led me to call for the tempering of these precepts in certain ways. I emphasised that the researcher inevitably has choices to make when he seeks to determine what acts and situations mean, and I recommended that he make these choices in such a way as to maximise service to the explanatory goals of his enquiry.

This may seem dangerously close to violating yet other oft-repeated methodological principles: to determine the meanings of acts prior to any search for an explanation of their occurrence – and certainly independently of such explanations. I must now confront this issue directly, but would first like to state my position on certain relevant matters more fully.

I take it that what we try to achieve by our scientific activities is the understanding of certain experiences. More specifically, it is the kind of understanding that will give us a better handle on problems and opportunities that present themselves to us in our lives. They may be problems and opportunities of action, of decision, of critique, or of curiosity – scientific or otherwise; but they are, at any rate, experienced as problems and opportunities in our lives even outside the particular scientific activity which they motivate.

The kind of understanding we try to achieve by our social-science activities as a whole is one that will give us a better handle on the problems and opportunities of our extra-scientific lives. The kind of understanding which we try to achieve in any particular scientific investigation or programme is one that will give us a better handle on the problems and opportunities which we face when we are not engaged in the particular research.

In the recent words of a sociologist – a strong advocate of putting actors' meanings at the centre of sociological discourse:

> . . . all scientific knowledge itself must be seen as grounded in its usefulness . . . ultimately, scientific thought like any other thought, is grounded in our purposes and hence, in its usefulness to us . . . Scientific knowledge, then must be seen as useful knowledge . . . The fundamental challenge of the sociological endeavor today must be to develop useful knowledge of the complex gamut of everyday life . . . (Douglas, 1970, pp. 26-7 and 43).

It seems to me to follow from this that the reason for using actors' meanings and definitions of situations in our explanations – the whole reason for doing so – is the expectation that our explanations will then result in a richer yield of lessons usable in our lives and expressible in the language of our problem-formulating discourse.

We might therefore want to set down the following methodological rule: 'Reject ways of imputing meanings to actors that do not yield successful explanations; use those imputations that do yield successful explanations.' But can we really choose our meaning-imputations simply on the basis of the success they lend to our explanations? Are we not rather constrained to impute to the actors we study only meanings which we know to be correct – meanings which they really hold? It is this question which resolves itself into the issue whether the correctness of the meanings which we impute to actors is to be established independently of, and prior to, the correctness of the explanations in which these meanings are to play a part.

Are There Any Direct Procedures for Establishing Meanings?

In what follows I will call the explanations which are the desired end product of a particular scientific investigation the 'object explanations'. To establish a meaning imputation merely by the success of object explanations in which it plays a part is to do so by an indirect inference. Are there any other, more direct, procedures for determining what acts and situations mean to actors?

At first sight, it appears obvious that more direct procedures for imputing meanings, and for validating these imputations, are available, since we seem to use such ways all the time. For one thing, there are numerous situations both in our scientific and extra-scientific lives, where we feel sufficiently familiar with the current symbols and cues to 'know' what actions mean to their actors, simply by attending to the actions themselves, or to the actors' accompanying speech or other expressions, without any special techniques. Even when doubts do arise about the correctness of some of these imputations, we appeal to arguments that do not require any special devices – 'He told me so,' 'I overheard him say so to this friend,' 'We all feel that way in such situations,' etc. Over wide ranges of situations we get along pretty well this way; i.e. the decisions we reach in our own actions on the basis of these imputations work out pretty well.

Second, social scientists have introduced a multitude of deliberate devices for ascertaining actors' meanings and definitions of situations. Surely there must be valid procedures somewhere among the depth interviews, the participant observations, the projective tests, the 'familiarity obtained through the investigator's own experience . . . history, literature, biography, and ethnography' (Phillips, 1971, p. 129), the semantic differentials, the psycho-analytic interviews, the eliciting of actors' self-reports, the attitude scales, the content analyses of speech and symbols, the 'sympathetic understanding and intuition by means of which the observer can view cultural phenomena from within, (Tiryakian, 1965, p. 678), the participant 'imaginings of the imagination of others' (Greer, 1969, pp. 167-8), the participation in the symbolic world of those being studied (Phillips, 1971, p. 129), the ethnomethodologists' experimental disturbance of normative expectations, and so on.

Nevertheless doubt might be expressed about the proposition that these ways of ascertaining and validating actors' meanings are independent of the validation of the object explanations into which these meaning-imputations are to be incorporated. This doubt would rest on the view that all these allegedly 'more direct methods' are themselves made up of imputations and inferences whose accuracy cannot be tested in any other way than through the success of some explanations and predictions to which they give rise.

But even if the view in the last sentence is accurate (and I think it is), it does not justify the doubt. For one must not overlook the fact that these determinations and tests, even if they are, perhaps, inferential in their turn, are nevertheless separate from the inferences which constitute the 'object explanations' of any particular study. They are separate, and can be separately verified, in the following sense:

(a) the more direct procedures can be performed prior to the testing of the object explanation, and even prior to its construction;

(b) the more direct procedures may be found valid even though the object explanation is (subsequently) found to be false;

(c) once validated, the meaning imputations produced by the more direct procedures can be used again and again, in quite diverse object explanations;

(d) we often have reason to have more confidence in the more direct procedures than we do in the available procedures for verifying the object explanations.

I conclude that it is usually possible to determine actors' meanings, independently of, and prior to, the testing of a particular object explanation in which they are to be incorporated.

However, while it is possible, it is often difficult. It may require great efforts and long periods of time.[9] Sometimes the price to pay is so high that it is, for all practical purposes, impossible to use the more direct methods. There is little doubt that the more direct procedures for imputing meanings and testing these imputations should be used as long as it is not unduly difficult to do so; as long, that is, as the anticipated gain in the quality of the resulting object explanations exceeds the loss from the required effort and from the resulting postponement of the object research.

The Gain from the More Direct Procedures

What is the nature of this gain in object-explanation quality that can result from the use of the more direct procedures for imputing meanings, and for testing these imputations? In fact, why should there be any gain at all?

Why should one bother with such allegedly more direct ways of determining correct meaning imputations, if it is true that the whole purpose of these imputations is to improve the success of the object explanations? Is it not enough to find out whether the object explanations work? After all, that is all we are asking our meaning-imputations to accomplish.

Although this argument has some merit, there are several interrelated reasons for applying separate procedures for determining correct meaning-imputations, whenever practicable:

(1) If we take seriously the meaning-imputations produced in connection with the object explanation of any one phenomenon, then these imputed meanings will always have implications for the explanation or prediction of many other phenomena as well. It would be desirable to select meaning-imputations in such a way that these surplus implications would work out as well.

(2) The procedures used for verifying an object explanation – which is typically a complex network of assumptions and propositions – are often very imperfect. As a result, our confidence in the validity of any one object explanation, although positive, is not very high.

(3) Even a verified object explanation does not definitively 'prove' the correctness of the meaning-imputations embodied in it, because of the well known 'problem of induction'.

The combined result of (1) – (3) is that the same meaning-imputation, or at least the same procedure for imputing meanings, has to be tested out in a large number of diverse object explanations, before it would merit our confidence as correct.[10, 11]

(4) We often have more confidence in some of the more direct procedures than in the procedures for verifying object explanations. Sometimes this is so, because such procedures as participant observation often carry their own convincing power, rooted as they are in immediate experience and long familiarity with the activity-world in question (cf. Phillips, 1971, p. 136). At other times our greater confidence rests on the more worked-out and established scientific procedures, such as certain projective techniques, or the semantic differential.

(5) It is often less time-consuming to use the more direct procedures than to test an object explanation; especially, than to test a sufficient number of diverse object explanations to give adequate 'indirect' confidence in the correctness of the meaning-imputations, as described above.

As a combined result of (4) and (5), the more direct procedures also enable us to pre-select correct meaning imputations, and thus to pre-select for eventual verifying only those object explanations which have the highest likelihood of being found valid.

Must More Direct Procedures Invariably Be Insisted Upon?

It is for these reasons that I believe that the establishment of the 'correct' meaning imputations should be undertaken independently of, and prior to, the testing of any particular object explanation, whenever this can be done with satisfactory confidence and at a reasonable cost.

The moot question is whether independent and prior determination of meanings must *invariably* be insisted upon, no matter what the price in effort and delay. This question is crucial, because if the answer is 'yes', it will often mean not only the postponement of a particular research enterprise, but the long-term postponement of entire realms of investigation and, in some instances, the permanent cancellation of investigations into certain subjects.

It is here that I part company with those who give an affirmative answer in such words as the following (my emphasis):

> If we accept the proposition that the *first* task of the sociologist is to discover the rules employed by the actor for managing his daily affairs, the reader may well [ask] . . .: Does this mean that we cannot engage in social research until this task has been accomplished? The answer is a qualified 'yes' (Cicourel, 1964, p. 52).

> Thus, the exploration of the general principles according to which man in daily life organizes his experiences . . . is the *first* task of the methodology of the social sciences (Schutz, 1954; 1963, p. 242).

> . . . the study of action would *have to* be made from the position of the actor . . . one would *have to* see the operating situation as the actor sees it, . . . ascertain their meaning in terms of the meaning they have for the actor . . . and would *have to* see his world from his standpoint (Blumer, 1966, p. 542).

> Macro-analysts ought . . . to be . . . starting with an analysis of the lower-level-orderings found in everyday life and proceeding to an analysis of higher levels of social ordering *only when* they have solved the problems of the lower levels (Douglas, 1970, p. 8).

> Elucidating the logic of intention is prior, as a methodological problem, to determining truth or falsity in terms of particular criteria for distinguishing, let us say . . . fact and superstition (Natanson, 1972, p. 1237).

I do not object to doing any of these things. My objections are only to the *'must'*, *'first'*, *'have to'*, and *'only when'* in these statements.

I part company because insisting on the more direct methods of imputing meanings makes sense only as long as it is true that this procedure results in more confidence in the correctness of the meaning-imputations, and in a wiser investment of our research efforts. This is typically the case when we deal with ways of life with which we are familiar, or can become familiar, or with procedures which have already been tried and tested sufficiently widely to earn our confidence.

But when we deal with cultures so foreign to us, with social strata with which we are so lacking in familiarity, with aspects of 'meanings' so subtle and so deep in the person's psyche, or with other matters so constituted that we lack confidence in the 'more direct procedures' that are already available, despair of a tolerably expeditious way of devising such procedures; and find ourselves fretting for years and even decades over what things 'really' mean to the persons studied; then it is better to fall back on the more indirect procedure of letting the testing of object-explanations be simultaneously the testing of the meaning-imputations incorporated in them. For in such circumstances, even the testing of a number of diverse object explanations sufficient to constitute a tolerably acceptable test of the meaning imputations involved will be more expeditious than waiting until more direct adequate methods are available.

To insist, under such circumstances, that one must first be sure of 'meanings' before one can proceed to explanations and their testing, rests on a fallacious understanding of the process of scientific explanation and verification. Even where the procedures which I have called the 'more direct' ones are available, where we *do* have ready confidence in them, this confidence rests on nothing but the experience (or belief) that the meanings which are imputed according to these procedures lead to explanations, predictions, expectations and action implications which work.

It is chimerical to think that inferences can ever be 'true' in any other sense, that they can be verified in separation from all statements about the object world to which they give rise.

Notes

1. Earlier versions of this text were presented in lectures at the University of Amsterdam, the Vienna Institute for Advanced Study, and the University of Montreal, beginning in December 1972. I wish to thank Drs Derek Phillips, Jürgen Pelikan, Collette Carisse and Michael Brûlé for these opportunities.

2. Compare also Giddens, 1976, pp. 44-5, for an exposition of Louch's and Winch's formulation.
3. At this point, I do not want to go into the very interesting question of how we would determine whether each of these was Mr Smith's intention. I only want to mention in passing that we may sometimes answer 'yes' without necessarily implying that he was aware of it. If, for example, Smith invariably went out to mow the lawn just when his wife came home, we might suspect that he is, perhaps unconsciously, doing it 'in order to get away from his wife,' even if he should quite sincerely deny it.
4. Giddens (1976, p. 80) castigates 'philosophers [who] presume that the question "What is he doing?" has a unitary answer . . . a man may be said to be "bringing down a metal implement on wood", "chopping logs", "doing his job", "having fun", etc. . . . the philosopher then . . . looks to show that only some are "correct" or "valid" act-identifications . . . But all of these characterisations can be quite correct descriptions of what is going on: although, depending upon the context in which the query is formulated, only certain of them will be "appropriate".'
5. 'That which is being asked for in the question "What is happening?" is relative to . . . the interests that stimulate the enquiry . . .' (Giddens, 1976, p. 80).
6. Cf. Giddens (1976, pp. 74 and 77): 'There are, of course . . . many things that people do . . . which they do not do intentionally . . . A person who switches on the light "to illuminate the room", perhaps also "alerts a prowler". Alerting the prowler is something the person did, although not something he intended to do.'
7. One proviso: Although the above describes what our sociological enterprise as a whole must aim at, any one particular investigation or programme may have a narrower goal, only indirectly linked to the above broad goals. After all, the problem which motivates us to undertake a particular investigation may 'already' be a theoretical one, presenting itself to the problem-experiencer – in this case, a social scientist – in scientific rather than common-sense terms.
8. According to one point of view, explanations via actors' meanings, intentions and definitions of situations are never appropriate; such notions do not have any legitimate status in scientific discourse at all. My defence of the use of such terms in empirical science, which I do not wish to elaborate here, would be similar to that given some time ago by such writers as Carl K. Hempel (1952), Edward Tolman (1951), Lee Cronbach (1971) and Abraham Kaplan (1964), under such slogans as 'hypothetical constructs', 'intervening variables', 'theoretical terms', and 'construct validity'. The justification of the use of these notions of so-called unobservables always lies in the increments which their use is believed to lend to our power to explain relationships among phenomena that we *do* experience, or that *can* be 'observed', as it is usually put. I would, however, give the matter a somewhat more relativistic and open-ended interpretation, by replacing the phrase 'statements about observables' with something like 'statements whose mode of verification is not moot in the given community of discourse', or, more particularly, 'statements whose mode of verification does not depend on assent to the explanations about to be developed or tested'.
9. There is no shortage of literature pointing out these difficulties, and the shaky assumptions by means of which they are often glossed over.
10. In the context of any particular object explanation, 'correctness of meaning-imputation procedure' means, essentially, that one has grounds for believing that subsequent object explanations, which rest on meanings imputed by the same procedures, will also be found to work.

11. This is the essence of the procedure currently called 'construct validation' (Cronbach, 1971), but the core idea goes back to Weber. Nevertheless, it does not seem to cut much ice with Peter Winch, nor with Derek Phillips:

> I want to question Weber's implied suggestion that Verstehen . . . needs supplementing by a different method altogether, namely the collection of statistics. Against this, I want to insist that if a proffered interpretation is wrong, statistics, though they may suggest that that is so, are not the decisive and ultimate court of appeal for the validity of sociological interpretations in the way Weber suggests. What is then needed is a better interpretation, not something different in kind. The compatibility of an interpretation with the statistics does not prove its validity . . . what is ultimately required is a philosophical argument . . . (Winch, 1958, p. 113).

Phillips says similarly:

> Weber . . . believed that the appropriate procedure for verifying one or another interpretation was to establish statistical regularities, based on the collection of empirical data. Statistical laws or regularities, however, have nothing to do with the correctness of an interpretation. (Phillips, 1973, pp. 120-1).

One would at least expect that claims like Weber's would be seriously debated, instead of being rejected out of hand as absurd, especially in view of the ample literature on construct validation and on the related, though narrower, notion of validating 'intervening variables' ('interpolated variables' would be more accurate) by the patterns of association among so-called observables (see, for example, chapters by Marx and Spence in Marx, 1963; Willer, 1967, Ch. 5; Stephens, 1968, Ch. 5; Lazarsfeld, 1972; and especially Cronbach, 1971).

References

Blumer, Herbert (1966). Sociological Implications of the Thought of George Herbert Mead. *American Journal of Sociology, 71,* 535-44.

Cronbach, Lee J. (1971). Test Validation, In R.L. Thorndike (ed.), *Education Measurement,* 2nd ed., *American Council on Education,* pp. 443-507.

Cicourel, Aaron V. (1964). *Method and Measurement in Sociology*. New York: Free Press.

Douglas, Jack D. (1970). Understanding Everyday Life. In Jack D. Douglas (ed.), *Understanding Everyday Life.* Chicago: Aldine.

Faust, Richard and Kadushin, Charles (1965). *Shakespeare in the Neighbourhood.* New York: The Twentieth Century Fund.

Giddens, Anthony (1976). *New Rules of Sociological Method*. New York: Basic Books.

Greer, Scott (1969). *The Logic of Social Inquiry*. Chicago: Aldine.

Halberstam, David (1973). *The Best and the Brightest.* London: Barrie and Jenkins.

Hempel, Carl (1952). Foundations of Concept Formation in Empirical Science. Chicago: University of Chicago Press.

Kaplan, Abraham (1964). *The Conduct of Inquiry*. San Francisco: Chandler.

Lazarsfeld, Paul F. (1972). Notes on the History of Concept Formation, in his *Qualitative Analysis.* Boston: Allyn and Bacon.

Louch, A.R. (1969). *Explanation and Human Action.* Berkeley, California: University of California Press.

Marx, Melvin H. (ed.) (1963). *Theories in Contemporary Psychology.* New York: Macmillan.
Maslow, Abraham (1966). *The Psychology of Science.* New York: Harper and Row.
Natanson, Maurice (1972). Book review of Alan Ryan's *Philosophy of the Social Sciences* in *American Journal of Sociology, 77,* 1237-8.
Navasky, Richard (1972). Review of Halberstam's *The Best and the Brightest* in *New York Times* book review.
Phillips, Derek (1971). *Knowledge from What?* Chicago: Rand McNally.
Phillips, Derek (1973). *Abandoning Method.* San Francisco: Jossey-Bass.
Schutz, Alfred (1954). Concept and Theory Formation in the Social Sciences. In Maurice Natanson (ed.), *Philosophy of the Social Sciences: a Reader.* New York: Random House, 1963.
Skinner, B.F. (1971). *Beyond Freedom and Dignity.* New York: Alfred E. Knopf.
Stephens, William N. (1968). *Hypotheses and Evidence.* New York: Crowell.
Tiryakian, Edward A. (1965). Existential Phenomenology, *American Sociological Review, 30,* 674-8.
Tolman, Edward C. (1951). Psychology versus Immediate Experience and Operational Behaviorism and Current Trends in Psychology. In his *Collected Papers in Psychology.* Berkeley, California: University of California Press.
Weber, Max (1947). *The Theory of Social and Economic Organization.* New York: Oxford University Press.
Willer, David (1967). *Scientific Sociology.* Englewood Cliffs, New Jersey: Prentice-Hall.
Winch, Peter (1958). *The Idea of a Social Science.* New York: Humanities Press.

8 THE STRUCTURALIST ANALYSIS OF COMMUNICATION: AN EXAMPLE OF PROBLEM-CENTRED METHODOLOGY

David D. Clarke

The writers of general textbooks in the sciences and social sciences would often have us believe that enquiry proceeds from problems to solutions, or from issues to the choice of methods to investigate them. In practice the reverse is all too often true. Research methods and expertise are produced like commodities in need of a market, and the researcher finds himself looking for new applications for his special knowledge of statistics, or experimental design or computer programming, just as the manufacturer may have to search out new markets for his chosen range of products. Too much time, effort and money have to go into the establishment of research facilities and teams, for their chosen *modus operandi* to be overturned as each new problem arises. Consequently a specialisation develops in many subjects according to methods rather than topics, which is in part a desirable and efficient division of labour. Other consequences are less desirable. Important problems may be neglected for want of a convenient method, and those problems which are tackled may have to be modified and distorted to fit the demands of the analytic procedure.

A problem-centred methodology is an attempt to escape from these difficulties by giving the problem itself pride of place in the research procedure and invoking particular research techniques as the need arises. Clearly this can only be exemplified with respect to particular problems. For the time being I shall concentrate on one issue which is central to my own research, although the principles which apply here may also be suitable elsewhere. The issue is that of how we may best detect and describe the structure of communication and relationship between people.

The structure in question is predominantly diachronic. That is to say it consists of the orderly or non-random arrangement of communicative events or signals in the domain of time. At its simplest, such a structure would consist of a set of events, with a time-order relation defined upon them. More complex descriptions of the structure might include other relations such as functional equivalence between items (which, being a transitive, reflexive and symmetric relation, would necessarily divide the universe of events into a number of mutually exclusive equivalence classes) and special relations such as 'performed-by-the-same-actor-as' which has the effect of defining the roles of persons in an interaction consisting only of events.

Let us suppose that the capacity of people to produce and understand novel social interactions is a kind of competence, not unlike linguistic competence (Chomsky, 1965). It could be envisaged as having three basic components. The first is a repertoire of signals (facial expressions, utterances, styles of dress, tones of voice, and so on) which would be the counterpart of a lexicon. The second is a facility or procedure for imposing a constraint on the repertoire so that sensible combinations of signals can be produced and recognised.

Clearly this communicative system, like language itself, is not so constructed as to allow any combination of elements to be used. If it were we would not have such common recourse to concepts like deviancy, madness and nonsense. The constraining facility on the repertoire may be conceived of as a kind of syntax of action. The third component is a constraint on the relation between activity structures and their interpretations. This is required if communication is to be achieved effectively, since it enables the actor to represent meanings in his activities systematically, so that the observer or interlocutor can recover the meaning from the activities. This might be called the semantic component.

It is most important to note that the inclusion of these three components in the model of communicative competence does not imply that they can usefully be regarded as independent or even distinct. It is merely to suggest that the union of the concepts and processes associated with each needs to be considered, without in any way implying that the intersections are small or unimportant.

Let us concentrate, for the sake of convenience, on the second component, the syntax, and pose the question, 'How may a grammar of interaction be devised?' Several possible methods come to mind. The most obvious (and least promising) is that of experimentation. It might seem that the natural way to examine the context and circumstances in which different signals can meaningfully occur would be to manipulate circumstances and observe the ensuing communication. However there are serious difficulties with this approach. The important circumstances in which people frame their communication cannot be readily manipulated. Poverty, privacy, affection, grief, achievement, ill-health, and all the other factors which substantially influence the content and style of people's relationships cannot be altered arbitrarily just to see what happens. It would neither be practicable nor ethical to attempt it. Deception experiments may offer the means to make these circumstances appear to change, but they too are fraught with numerous and now familiar difficulties (Harré and Secord, 1972).

'Sampling studies' do not fit the bill either. A true experiment in which one variable is manipulated and another observed should not be confused with studies in which particular subjects or situations are chosen for their value on an 'independent variable', such as sex, which is neither variable nor manipulable. Such a confusion would do violence to the justificatory logic behind experimental discovery procedures.

The structure of spontaneous behaviour has other properties which make experimental studies difficult. Stimulus and response, or cause and effect cannot be easily identified. The behaviour stream is not constructed by organisms who return one response for each stimulus, so much as people who gather information, store it, hoard, process, forget, distort, compare, and synthesise it, before embarking on organised courses of activity whose relation with 'stimuli' may be impossible to identify. The need for any experimental manipulation may render the technique unsuitable, since real communication situations are often private and closed in the sense that any intrusion would turn them into something quite different.

Three broad research strategies seem to be more suitable for this problem than experiments. One is the (unobtrusive) recording of communication situations and detailed statistical and ethological analysis of the resulting records. Naturally, when the material is as complex as human communication an ethology is required which goes beyond the positivist preoccupation with observable displays of movement and sound, so as to incorporate the necessary representation of meaning and context.

A second strategy involves the collection and synthesis of the fragmentary though surprisingly sound judgements the native actor can make of structure, meaning and propriety. This is to use the native's intuitions of sense and nonsense just as a linguist might use the native speaker's intuitive recognition of sentences as data to demarcate the set of morpheme strings which are well formed.

The third research strategy is even more like the practices of generative linguists. It entails the production (by means of whatever insights are available) of a series of hypothetical generative operations which constitute an organised grammar, not unlike any other iconic model, (Harré, 1976). It is then an empirical matter to determine the extent to which the grammar meets the imposed criteria of adequacy, which in this case might be to reproduce all speech-act sequences which are sensible dialogues.

It would be a mistake to assume that these three strategies represent mutually exclusive policies between which a choice must be made. All three have their part to play, and should be integrated in any given structural study. However, the emphasis given to each must depend on the source and nature of the information available.

In the case of conversation analysis the last approach may well be the most promising as the conversation analyst has much the problem, and much the same information available at the outset, as the linguist. We all have an accurate, though fragmentary knowledge of the orderliness of our own social milieu. The problem is to frame a coherence theory which will locate all these insights in a single generative system. Because of this striking resemblance with the linguists' situation I shall only elaborate on this quasi-linguistic strategy for conversation analysis here. Those who would like to pursue the details of ethological studies of sequences should consult Dawkins (1976), Slater (1973), Hutt & Hutt (1970), Altman (1965), or van der Kloot (1975) for examples.

Further examples of strategy two, the elicitation and synthesis of subjects' judgements may be found in Clarke (1975a, 1975b, 1976, in press a and b).

The problems of writing a behaviour grammar are not unlike those of making a map. The objective is to take a list of the possible behaviour sequences which can occur, and then induce an organisational diagram for the generative process. That might be likened to the task of producing the map of a set of places and their interconnections from a list of possible journeys. This idea lends itself to the use of graph theory in which each behaviour (or place) is a node and each transition (or route) an arc. Such representations have been popular with analysts of behaviour sequences but they can be misleading. The graph in Figure 8.1 is a fair representation of the strings

ABD
ACD
ABCD
ACBD etc.

and may be easily constructed from those strings. However the graph in Figure 8.2 is not a fair representation of the strings

ABC and
DBE

although it is derived in the same way from these two strings, which are in this case the only 'sentences' in the 'language'. The reason being that the graph only represents first-order transitions, that is transitions between immediately adjacent events. As a consequence the map or generative diagram shown cannot be prevented from producing

D B C and
A B E

Figure 8.1:

An Adequate Graphical Representation of the First Example 'Language'

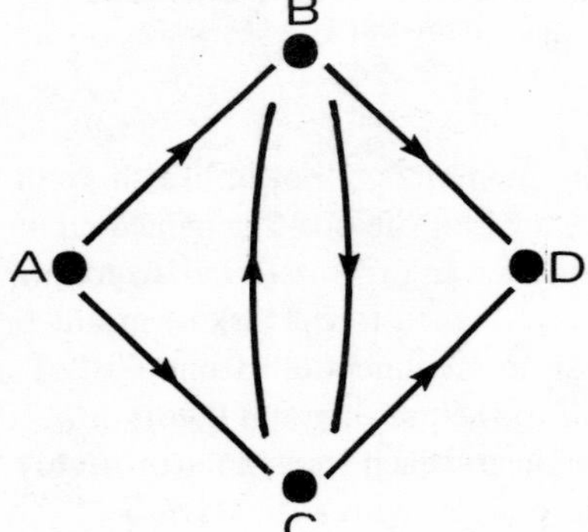

Figure 8.2:

An Inadequate Graphical Representation of the Second Example 'Language'

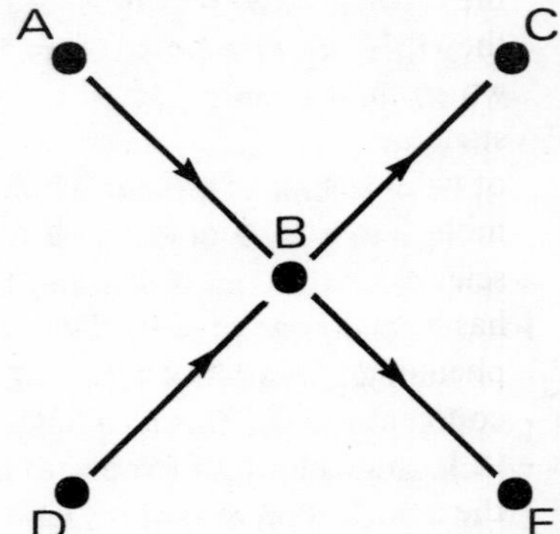

which are illegal. Having entered state B the system has no way of relating an exit path to an entry path. This, however, runs counter to the obvious nature of a social interaction where the likely sequiturs to a certain move do depend critically upon its antecedents.

A question, for example, will draw different replies depending on whether it was asked as a second attempt following a refusal to reply or whether it was asked for the first time.

It seems, then, that a simple graph or matrix of event-to-event transitions is likely to be inadequate as a behaviour grammar, and our discovery procedure should be geared to something more suitable.

Let us consider the kind of knowledge to be produced by the discovery procedure and the kind of knowledge which is available at the outset. The knowledge to be produced may be described in the terms of Clarke (in press, a). Here a distinction was made between three levels of behavioural description, the first, second and third orders of structure. The second (or evident) order was taken to represent the familiar regularities of behaviour which we all recognise, such as the propriety of a remark or the well-formedness of a sentence. The first order is the level of explanation by reduction, at which one asks the question 'How?' or 'By what process?' This might include the detailed analysis of the substructure of a remark, with all its fine-grained and largely unattended nuances of posture, gesture and facial expression, or the fine phonological structure of a sentence. The third order is suggested by the existence of the first. If it is possible to take the evident order and dismantle it in search of explanations, it should also be possible to synthesise the rather fragmentary information it contains and ask what is the coherent whole, of which the second order is itself the parts. How for example can our fragmentary knowledge of social life be turned into a coherent generative biography or syntax, which will demonstrably integrate and reproduce the individual second order facts which are so familiar?

A discovery procedure based on this conception of first, second and third order is shown in Figure 8.3.

The information available at the outset is our tacit knowledge of social order. Just as the native speaker can tell whether a string of morphemes is a sentence, so too the native actor can say when an interaction is well formed, but in neither case can they say how such judgements are made, or provide an explicit procedure for making them. In other words the knowledge is there but in tacit form. The purpose of the discovery procedure is to elicit the knowledge and then systematically check and refine it.

The first problem is that of gaining access to the tacit knowledge or competence of the actor. It manifests itself in three ways. It is the resource for producing hypothetical examples when asked, 'Give me a sentence' or 'What would be a sensible course of action in this situation?' It is the architectonic agency being the structure of spontaneous action or 'real examples' as they feature in the discovery procedure. And it is the source of descriptions and analyses, again on a rather fragmentary level, such as the ability to attach labels like *question, threat* and *promise* to specific locutions.

The discovery procedure, then, should begin with the collection of

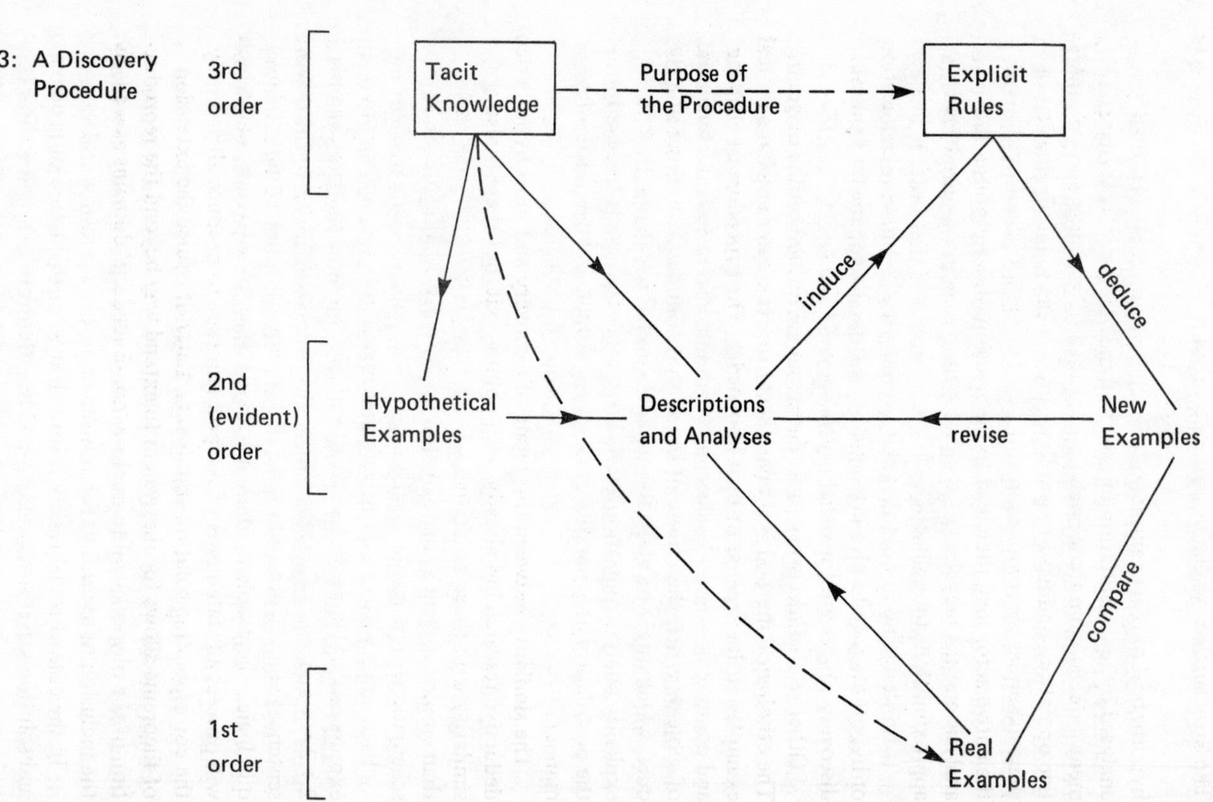

Figure 8.3: A Discovery Procedure

hypothetical or real examples of behavioural structure, which are then analysed by re-consultation of the tacit knowledge. A summary statement induced from these analyses may then be stated as a set of generative operations and used to produce further examples. Evaluation of these examples by comparison with real examples or the intuitions of the native actor may then lead to the revision of descriptions and analysis and the recycling of the discovery procedure to give better approximations to reality.

It is interesting to note that this is a very straightforward application of hypothetico-deductive principles, but at the same time an unusual discovery procedure for social psychology.

Other related discovery procedures may be located on the diagram. The ethological method is similar except for its greater emphasis on real examples at the expense of tacit knowledge. The procedure of eliciting and combining subjects' judgements uses the descriptions and analyses of subjects rather than those of the analyst. Another promising procedure, which might be given the generic name of *simulation,* has no explicitly analytic initiation at all. It proceeds from tacit knowledge to the postulation of generative rules which are then tested in the above manner.

The similarity between this mode of discovery and most hypothetico-deductive research has already been pointed out, but there is also a similarity with those disciplines which might be called rational rather than empirical, such as mathematics, philosophy and linguistics. A schematic representation of these may be found in Figure 8.4.

Each starts with the intuitively inescapable relation between two expressions which might be called *problem* and *solution*. For example $2 + 2 = x$ and $x = 4$ in mathematics; # S # (standing for an exemplary sentence) and 'The cat sat on the mat' in linguistics; and $p \supset q$, p and q in logic. The problem, then, is to find the set of inference rules which will process all statements of the problem type to produce all and only the corresponding solution statements. Later of course the extension of theorems allows for the system to extend way beyond the reproduction of the obvious, and to explore 'non-Euclidean' domains as well, by the inclusion of axioms which mis-represent our familiar world.

In the case of social reality it is unclear what the nature of problem and solution statements might be. Column four in Figure 8.4 shows a naive counterpart to the linguistic formulation in which # I # represents an interaction as problem statement, and the solution statement would be something akin to a script. This conception has been popular among those authors who have attempted to write formal generators for

	Mathematics	Logic	Linguistics	Social Behaviour (Incorrect Model)	Social Behaviour (Correct Model)
Problem	2 + 2 = x	$p \supset q$ p	# S #	# I #	time
Rules of Inference	Number theory Rules of algebra operations ...	Truth tables Rules of tautology ...	S → NP + VP ...	?	?
Solution	x = 4	q	eg. 'The cat sat on the mat.'	Script	

Figure 8.4: Rational Disciplines

interaction (e.g. Păun, 1976) but it seems to be psychologically implausible. No one person (in most interactions) is omniscient and omnipotent, so as to be able to develop the entire structure of the interaction by the hierarchical elaboration of his conception of # I # Rather it is up to each actor to take circumstances at any moment as he finds them, since he is unlikely to have predicted them, and then decide upon a suitable course of action. The appropriate psychological formulation of the problem would be to treat circumstances or 'the story-so-far' as the problem statement and to output a sensible next move by way of the solution statement. From the point of view of the other actors this would add another item to their conception of the problem, so, by passing control from one actor to another, such a group of generators could reproduce whole interactions. Furthermore, it could embody additional constraints to allow for individual differences (of a situation-sensitive type) and the selection of particularly desirable response options from amongst the set of sensible alternatives.

One apparent limitation of this approach might seem to be its reliance on tacit knowledge which appears to make it unsuitable for the study of alien cultures or subcultures (that is, cultural systems of which the analyst is not a member). In practice, however, this is a commonplace problem since nearly all discovery procedures for alien cultures rest upon the putative membership of the analyst (or his informants).

Figure 8.5 shows how such a discovery procedure lends itself to use in the base and alien cultures and how it gives rise to other research of a more empirical nature.

Rational work in the base culture depends on the extensibility of axiomatic systems (such as the proof of ever more complex theorems from a set of geometrical axioms) and the investigation of non-Euclidean systems derived from counter-intuitive axioms. The system of rules and descriptions so produced would then be a vehicle for empirical work in the base culture, testing and falsifying predictive hypotheses. It is important to note that the empirical falsification only applies to certain predicted relations and outcomes and not to the rational system or the empirical meta-language which it furnishes. Physics cannot be used to invalidate algebra, except in the trivial sense that physical experiments may show some algebraical systems to be more or less convenient notations for that purpose.

Turning to the study of alien cultures, rational analysis has really to start again using the tacit knowledge of informants, or an analyst who is becoming gradually equipped for competent membership. Empirical work in the alien culture can then be framed in terms of its own

Figure 8.5: Products of the Rhetorico-Deductive Method

	Base Culture	Alien Culture
Rational	Extensibility of theorems 'Non-Euclidean' Cases	Devise new rules from tacit knowledge of informants
Empirical	Empirical hypotheses falsifiable, but the meta-language is not	Test empirical hypotheses framed in rhetoric of base (dangerous) or alien culture

rationale, or more commonly and more dangerously, in the terms of a base-cultural analysis, at least for the sake of communicability. The pitfalls of this policy are well known to all who have even a passing knowledge of anthropology.

To summarise, then, we need a discovery procedure for the genesis of social order (in its widest and least authoritarian sense) which can make full use of the rich but fragmentary knowledge we all possess of our own social milieu. A synthesis of these fragments into something like a generative grammar would provide a powerful explanatory model for human action and experience, and a resource for practical action in service of the general good.

References

Altman, S.A. (1965). Sociobiology of Rhesus monkeys. II: Stochastics of social communication. *Journal of Theoretical Biology, 8,* 490-522.

Chomsky, N. (1965). *Aspects of the theory of syntax.* The Hague: Mouton.

Clarke, D.D. (1975a). The structural analysis of verbal interaction. Unpublished doctoral thesis, Oxford University.

Clarke, D.D. (1975b). The use and recognition of sequential structure in dialogue. *British Journal of Social and Clinical Psychology, 14,* 333-9.

Clarke, D.D. (1976). Rules and sequences in conversation. In P.Collett (ed.), *Social Rules and Social Behaviour.* Oxford: Basil Blackwell.

Clarke, D.D. (in press a). Discourse analysis as third order psychology. Proceedings of the IKP Conference on Gesprächsanalyse, Institut für Kommunikationsforschung und Phonetik der Universität Bonn, October 1976. Hamburg: Helmut Buske Verlag.

Clarke, D.D. (in press, b). The linguistic analogy, or 'When is a speech act like a morpheme?' In G. Ginsburg (ed.), *Emerging Strategies in Social Psychology.* London: Wiley.

Dawkins, R. (1976). Hierarchical organisation: a candidate principle for ethology. In P.P.G. Bateson and R.A. Hinde (eds.), *Growing Points in Ethology.* London: Cambridge University Press.

Harré, R. and Secord, P.F. (1972). *The explanation of social behaviour.* Oxford Basil Blackwell

Harré, R. (1976). The constructive role of models. In L. Collins (ed.), *Models in the social sciences.* London: Tavistock.

Hutt, S.J. and Hutt, C. (1970). *Direct observation and measurement of behaviour.* Springfield, Illinois: Thomas.

Păun, G. '(1976)A generative model of conversation. *Semiotica, 17,* 31-3.

Slater, P.J.B. (1973). Describing sequences of behaviour. In P.P.G. Bateson and P.H. Klopfer (eds.), *Perspectives in Ethology.* New York: Plenum.

Van der Kloot, W. and Morse, M.J. (1975). A stochastic analysis of the display behaviour of the red-breasted Merganser (Mergus serrator). *Behaviour, L VI,* 181-216.

9 QUALITATIVE KNOWING IN ACTION RESEARCH

Donald T. Campbell

In programme evaluation methodology today, there is a vigorous search for alternatives to the quantitative-experimental approach. In academic social science there is renewed emphasis on the methods of the humanities and increased doubts as to the appropriateness of applying the natural science model to social science problems. From these sources I draw the qualitative versus quantitative polarity implicit in the title. These terms are shorthand for a common denominator among a wide range of partially overlapping concepts: For *quantitative* read also scientific, scientistic, and *naturwissenschaftlich*. For *qualitative* read also humanistic, humanitistic, *geisteswissenschaftlich,* experiential, phenomenological, clinical, case study, field-work, participant observation, process evaluation and common-sense knowing.

While initially my discussion of these issues will involve epistemology and the social sciences in general, the target focus is on the evaluation of the outcomes of deliberately introduced novel social innovations. I have used the term '*knowing*' rather than 'evaluation' to indicate an effort to provide an epistemological grounding for the issues. The phrase *action research* is particularly appropriate to research centred around deliberate efforts at social action. As developed by Lewin and his associates in the heroic Committee on Community Interrelations it involved a wise integration of qualitative and quantitative approaches (Lewin, 1946; 1947; Lippitt and Radke, 1946; Chein, Cook and Harding, 1948a; 1948b; Selltiz and Cook, 1948; Cook, 1962; Harding, 1948; Chein, 1949; 1956; Marrow, 1969, pp. 191-218; Selltiz, 1956). It also had an important feature for this chapter which is not highlighted in my title: the development of procedures whereby action groups can assess their own progress – programme self-evaluation. All of these reasons make *action research* a better label than programme evaluation, in addition to symbolising continuity with the work of Kurt Lewin.

The analysis that follows starts out with epistemological considerations, aspiring to a unified perspective for both quantitative and qualitative knowing, consistent with the modern uprootings in the philosophy of science. It reaches the conclusion that quantitative knowing depends upon qualitative knowing in going beyond it. This dependence is poorly represented in much of quantitative social science. Subsequently, the qualitative grounding of quantitative social sciences is discussed, and the role of qualitative knowing in programme evaluation.

Some Descriptive Epistemology

Non-laboratory social science is precariously scientific at best. But even for the strongest sciences, the theories believed to be true are radically underjustified and have, at most, the status of 'better than' rather than the status of 'proven'. All common-sense and scientific knowledge is presumptive. In any setting in which we seem to gain new knowledge, we do so at the expense of many presumptions, untestable – to say nothing of unconfirmable – in that situation. While the appropriateness of some presumptions can be probed singly or in small sets, this can only be done by assuming the correctness of the great bulk of other presumptions. Single presumptions or small subsets can in turn be probed, but the total set of presumptions is not of demonstrable validity, is radically underjustified. Such are the pessimistic conclusions of the most modern developments in the philosophy of science (Quine, 1953, 1969; Goodman, 1955; Hanson, 1958; Polanyi, 1958; Popper, 1959, 1963, 1972; Toulmin, 1961, 1972; Kuhn, 1962, 1970; Feyerabend, 1970; Lakatos, 1970).

Yet science is much better than ignorance and, on many topics, better than traditional wisdom. Our problem as methodologists is to define our course between the extremes of inert scepticism and naive credulity. An evolutionary epistemology may help because it portrays common-sense knowing as based upon presumptions built into the sensory/nervous system and into ordinary language, presumptions which have been well-winnowed, highly edited, and thus indirectly confirmed through the natural selection of biological and social evolution. For scientific theories, still more presumptive, the natural selection process is continued through the competitive selection from among existing theories (Popper, 1958, 1963, 1972; Campbell, 1959, 1960, 1966, 1970; Toulmin, 1961, 1972; Quine, 1969; Caws, 1969; Shimony, 1970).

The concrete activities of 'methodology' can be subsumed under such a perspective, and in a way somewhat comforting for those in the social sciences, where so much must be presumed in order to come to any conclusions at all. *When a scientist argues that a given body of data corroborate a theory, invalidation of that claim comes in fact only from equally plausible or better explanations of those data.* The mere existence of an infinite number of logically possible alternatives is not in practice invalidating. As we have known since Hume, scientific inductions are unproven, deductively or inductively. We must now allow our critics to point out specific examples of this general scandal of induction as though it were peculiar to our study or to our field.

The Dependence of Science upon Common-Sense Knowing

We must not suppose that scientific knowing replaces common-sense knowing. Rather, science depends upon common sense even though at best it goes beyond it. Science in the end contradicts some items of common sense, but it only does so by trusting the great bulk of the rest of common-sense knowledge. Such revision of common sense by science is akin to the revision of common sense by common sense, which, paradoxically, can only be done by trusting more common sense. Let us consider as an example the Muller-Lyer illustration: Figure 9.1 below.

Figure 9.1

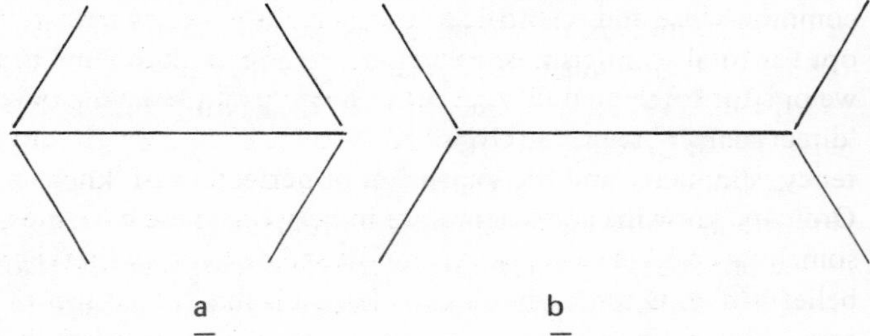

If you ask the normal resident of a 'carpentered' culture (Segall *et al.*, 1966) which horizontal line is longer, *a* or *b*, he will reply *b*. If you supply him with a ruler, or allow him to use the edge of another piece of paper as a makeshift ruler, he will eventually convince himself that he is wrong, and that line *a* is longer. In so deciding he will have rejected as inaccurate one product of visual perception by trusting a larger set of other visual perceptions. He will also have made many presumptions, inexplicit for the most part, including the assumption that the lengths of the lines have remained relatively constant during the measurement process, that the ruler was rigid rather than elastic, that the heat and moisture of his hand have not changed the ruler's length in such a coincidental way as to produce the different measurements, expending it when approaching line *a*, contracting it when approaching line *b*, etc.

Let us take as another example a scientific paper, containing theory and experimental results, demonstrating the quantum nature of light, in dramatic contrast to common-sense understanding. Were such a paper to limit its symbols to scientific terms, it would fail to communicate to another scientist in such a way as to enable him to replicate the experiment and verify the observations. Instead, the few scientific terms have been embedded in a discourse of pre-scientific ordinary language which the reader is presumed to (and presumes to) understand. This language is demonstrably incomplete, elliptical, metaphorical and equivocal. In addition, in the laboratory work of the original and replicating laboratory, a common-sense, pre-scientific perception of objects, solids and light was employed and trusted in coming to the conclusions that revise the ordinary understanding. To challenge and correct the common-sense understanding in one detail, common-sense understanding in general had to be trusted.

The Doubt-Trust Ratio

These two illustrations introduce the theme of continuity between common-sense and scientific knowing and the doubt-trust ratio. If we opt for total scepticism or solipsism, we give up 'knowing' or science. If we opt for total credulity, as some versions of phenomenology and 'direct realism' seem to (Campbell, 1969b, 1974), we give up consistency, simplicity and the expansion or perfection of 'knowledge'. Ordinary knowing and science are in between these extremes, and somehow combine a capacity for focused distrust and revision with a belief in a common body of knowledge claims. One aspect of the process which makes the cumulative revision of science possible is the practice of trusting (tentatively at least) the great bulk of current scientific and common-sense belief ('knowledge') and using it to discredit and revise one aspect of scientific belief. The ratio of the doubted to the trusted is always a very small fraction. This is expressed in the metaphor Quine (1953) borrows from von Neurath: we are like sailors who must repair a rotting ship at sea. We trust the great bulk of the timbers while we replace a particularly weak plank. Each of the timbers we now trust we may in its turn replace. The proportion of the planks we are replacing to those we treat as sound must always be small. Or in Quine's own words:

> The totality of our so-called knowledge or beliefs, from the most causal matters of geography and history to the profoundest laws of atomic physics or even of pure mathematics and logic, is a man-made fabric which impinges on experience only along the edges . . . A conflict with experience at the periphery occasions readjustments in

> the interior of the field . . . But the total field is so undetermined by its boundary conditions, experience, that there is much latitude of choice as to what statements to re-evaluate in the light of any single contrary experience . . . A recalcitrant experience can . . . be accommodated by any of various alternative re-evaluations in various alternative quarters of the total system, . . . but . . . our natural tendency is to disturb the total system as little as possible (Quine, 1953, pp. 42-4).

The presumptive character of even the most ordinary and basic instances of perception and common-sense knowing is currently being referred to through the truism that there are no hard facts that speak for themselves and against which theory may be checked. Instead, the so-called facts are themselves 'theory-laden' (Hanson, 1958; Kuhn, 1962, 1970; Feyerabend, 1970). This is a point worth emphasising. The Muller-Lyer illusion used above may very well be due to an implicit 'theory' of environmental relations built into the nervous system by learning or genetic heredity, to the effect that obtuse and acute angles in the plane of vision are most likely generated by rectangular solids (Segall *et al.*, 1966; Stewart, 1973). The Duncker (1929) dot-and-frame illusion may be more convincing. In an otherwise totally dark room is a large luminous frame with a luminous dot within. The frame is moved several inches to the right. The observer instead perceives the dot move several inches to the left. The perceptual system has built-in pre-conscious decision-trees that convert the evidence of relative motion into an inference of absolute motion. The 'presumption' or 'theory' used is this: in case of doubt, it is the small fragment of the visual field that has moved, the large bulk that has remained still. This is an excellent general rule, but wrong in the ecologically atypical setting of Duncker's laboratory. This is theory-ladenness at the natural knowing level. When we come to reading a galvanometer or a scintillation counter, the theory-ladenness of the resultant facts is still more obviously 'theoretical' because explicit scientific theories must be trusted in order to interpret the meter readings.

This emphasis can acquire a misleading connotation. In Kuhn's (1962) usage, when speaking of scientific revolutions, he seems to assume that all of physical knowing is tied up in one single integrated theory, one single equation, and that the 'facts' against which this theory is checked are all laden with, and only with, this one encompassing theory. When this master-theory is changed, then it is supposed that *all* of the 'facts' change simultaneously. Hanson (1958) and

Feyerabend (1970) are similar on this point.

This assumption of a single overreaching theory is wrong. The actual situation of science is much less 'integrated' or 'unified' than this. The theory-ladenness of 'facts' involves many deep-seated presumptions not overthrown by a specific scientific revolution. Instead, there is an elaborate hierarchy of trusts-presumptions-theories in which the simpler common-sense levels are for the most part depended upon in an unchanged fashion both before and after the revolution. The same trust is also true for 90 per cent of the laboratory-level, instrument-dependent 'facts' in the course of a scientific revolution. Indeed, some of these pre-revolutionary facts provide the anomalies which are the principal leverage for overthrowing the old paradigms.

This is not to deny the relevance of the duck-rabbit ambiguous figure made famous by Jastrow (1900), Wittgenstein (1953), Hanson (1958) and Kuhn (1962). Facts *are* seen in (or from) a different perspective after the shift in the 'theory' of *duck* to the 'theory' of *rabbit*. But there is a continuity of the paper pigment pattern for which the duck or the rabbit is the changed solution or interpretation. The pigment pattern represents a continuing shared restraint on possible interpretations. Duck or rabbit are the 'incommensurable' *interpretations* of a shared puzzle. There are very few such acceptable interpretations practically available, perhaps only these two. Moreover, the pigment pattern which seems a common base of 'fact' underlying these two 'theories' is itself a theory-laden perception. When examined in microscopic detail, its solid linearity disappears into discrete specks of pigment and these in turn into organisations to which attributes of colour or pigment are inappropriate. But this lower-level theory-laden presumptiveness which produces the line pattern is not changed in shifting from duck to rabbit, although the perception of some specific angles or other linear relationships may be.

Figure 9.2: Do you see a Duck or a Rabbit?

Source: Outlined from Jastrow's (1900, p. 295) textured drawing. Jastrow credits *Harper's Weekly* who credit *Fliegende Blätter.* Wittgenstein (1953, p. 194), credits Jastrow, but uses his own smaller casual free-hand drawing, making one wonder why he provides a citation, the only one in his book. Hanson (1958) and Kuhn (1962) credit Wittgenstein, but do not show the drawing. Hanson's antelope-storks are a superior illustration.

Figure 9.3: Hanson's Antelope-Stork Figure

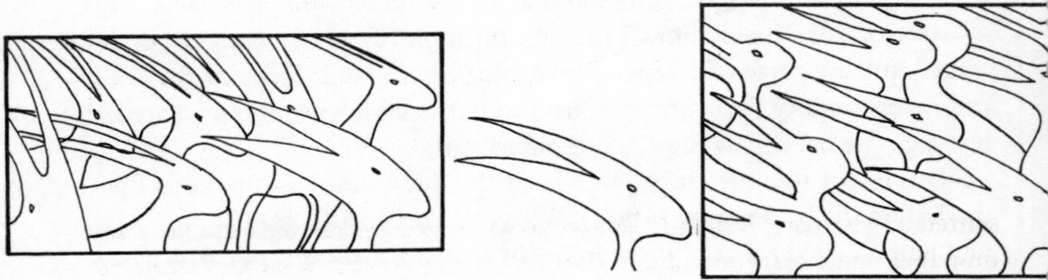

Source: Hanson (1958), pp. 13, 14.

For example, angle *a* in Figure 9.4 is perceived to be much closer to

Figure 9.4

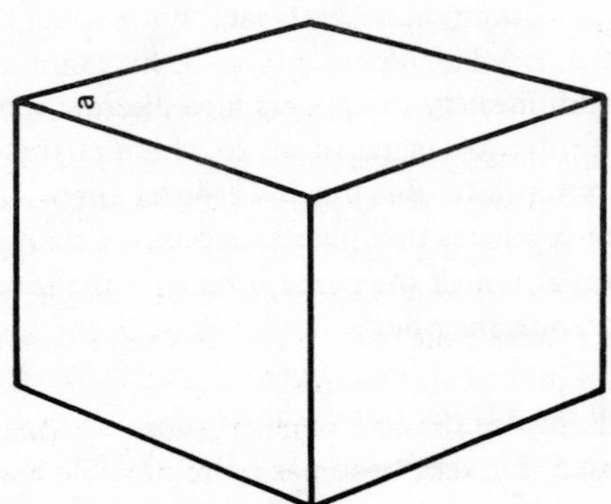

90° when, as there, it is interpreted as a part of a rectangle than it is when this 'theory' is made less compelling by exposing a smaller fragment, as in Figure 9.5. (One might wonder if this is merely a shift in

what one understands to be the question: Is it the on-paper or the repre-

Figure 9.5

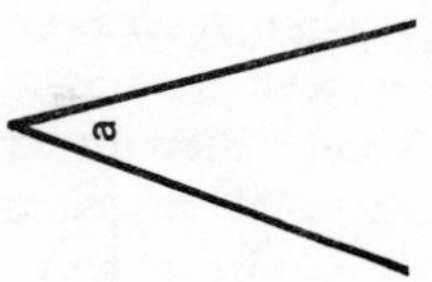

sented angle one is judging? But even when one makes it clear that the on-paper angle is to be judged, the first figure produces larger estimated angles than does the second.) Similar effects might be demonstrable for the duck-rabbit shift. Thus I do not wish to deny Hanson's, Kuhn's and Feyerabend's specific examples of some lower-level 'facts' which change dramatically in the course of a scientific revolution. What I do deny is that all facts, or even most facts, so change. I deny that the pervasive theory-ladenness of all the relevant facts is a matter of a singular integrated encompassing theory either before or after a scientific revolution. This same point is made by Blachowicz (1971) and Kordig (1971).

The Priority of Pattern Identification over Knowledge of Details

Another aspect of this descriptive epistemology is an emphasis on the epistemic priority of patterns rather than particles (Campbell, 1966). Consider the task of identifying 'the same' dot in two prints of the same newspaper photograph. Let each picture be covered with a large sheet of paper with a small hole in it. When this reduction screen exposes only one dot at a time, the task is impossible – the particle in isolation is nearly totally equivocal. When a square centimetre or a square inch is exposed, the task becomes more possible because patterns become identifiable – the larger the pattern, the more certain the identification. In so far as an identification of corresponding dots is achieved, it is because of a prior identification of the patterns. This is an obvious truism, yet epistemological orientations still abound which seek certainty in particles, be it definitions of terms or particulate sense data. All knowing of atoms or minute details is at least as context-dependent and as presumptive as is the knowing of larger or more encompassing patterns. Atomic particles or sense data are the very reverse of dependable building blocks. Qualitative, common-sense knowing of wholes and patterns provides the enveloping context necessary for the interpretation of particulate quantitative data.

Common-Sense Cross-Validation of Science

Not only does science depend upon common-sense knowing as the trusted grounding for its elaborate esoteric instrumentation and quantification, in addition many products and achievements of this esoteric science are cross-validated in ways accessible to common sense. The mysteries of trigonometry are visibly confirmed when the two ends of a tunnel or bridge meet. Faraday's invisible flows of electrical currents produced visible sparks and visible magnetic movement of bars of iron. Thus even non-scientists have the capacity to perceive evidences of the validity of esoteric science in common-sense terms. Engineering achievements visible to the naked eye do thus validly validate science in the public mind.

Among laboratory scientists themselves, this common-sense cross-validating is in continual use, and is a fundamental component in that identification and expectation amalgam which justifies their rejecting much of their meter readings as in error (due to faulty calibration, misconnections, or whatever). This cross-validation of the quantitative by the qualitative is today usually missing in the social sciences, or appears as hostile criticism, discussed below. In well-used scientific laboratories there emerges another fusion of the qualitative with the quantitative, in which mechanical, quantifying instruments become such familiar appendages that they become incorporated into qualitative knowing, like the blind man's cane. Whether we will ever achieve this state in the social sciences is moot, but it will never emerge without an intense prior interaction of common-sense and scientific knowing on the same problems.

Qualitative Knowing in Quantitative Programme Evaluation

The qualitative underpinnings of quantitative data can be discovered by tracing back to its sources any punch on an IBM card or any numerical value on a computer print-out. Behind the test scores in a Head Start Program lie the verbal and demonstrational instructions to the test administrator, the verbal and demonstrational explanations given by the test administrator to the children, the children's qualitative comprehension of the questions, etc. Qualitative knowing on someone's part is also basic to identifying these tested children as the same individuals who participated in the prior Head Start sessions. The Head Start curriculum instructions were conveyed by ordinary language, and if the loyalty of their execution has been checked, it has been by qualitative observations. If interviews with parents have been used, a common-sense trust in shared language and shared motives has undergirded the interview conversation. Recording of responses and the coding of free response answers achieve quantification only as the end product of a qualitative judgemental process. Most of this underpinning of common-sense knowing is so ubiquitous and so dependable that we fail to notice it. But I believe that such a base underlies all quantitative knowing in the social sciences just as in the physical.

It is usually so dependable we fail to notice it, yet the dependence on the qualitative is there even when unwarranted. Critique of the qualitative base is needed and this turns out to depend upon a qualitative knowledge of the more complete context. At the present time we have an unhealthy division of labour in this regard: on the one hand, we have quantitative social scientists who use census data, monetary records and crime rates, forgetting their qualitative judgemental base. On the other hand, we have qualitative sociologists who do critiques on how the numbers get recorded, for example, analysing the social dynamics of a census interview, the incommensurable understandings of the participants, the fears and pressures lying behind the answers and because of the scepticism thus generated, refuse to participate in quantitative analyses.

Particularly in the area of quantified administrative records, a vigorous critical literature has emerged, the flavour of which can be caught from titles such as 'Good Organizational Reasons for Bad Clinic Records' (Garfinkel, 1967), 'The Uses of Official Statistics' (Kitsuse and Cicourel, 1963), 'Police Misreporting of Crime and Political Pressures' (Seidman and Couzens, 1972), 'Nixon Anti-crime Plan Undermines Crime Statistics' (Morrissey, 1972), 'Downgrading of Crimes Verified in Baltimore' (Twigg, 1972). (See also Becker, 1968, 1970; Douglas, 1967; Beck, 1970; Blau, 1963; Etzioni and Lehman, 1967; Ridgeway, 1956.)

Similar studies are needed for the achievement test situation. If multiple independent anecdotes are to be trusted, the computers too often have been processing in stolid seriousness worthless data produced by children who were staging mass boycotts, or deliberately sabotaging the process or making jokes out of their answers. Anecdotes of similar scandals are available for questionnaires, attitude scales and interviews (Vidich and Bensman, 1954). We need such critique to be integrated with quantitative study. At the present time there is a little relating of these two approaches, although not enough. Some of this integration is at least called for in the methodology of field experimentation, under the headings of 'threats to validity' or 'plausible rival hypotheses' (e.g. Campbell and Stanley, 1963 and 1966; Cook and Campbell, forthcoming). A qualitative consideration of the differing contexts of measurement often generates hypotheses as to how differences between pre-test and post-test, or between experimental group and control group, are due to differences in the respondent's or researcher's understanding of the measurement process, rather than to changes in the attribute which the measure is intended to reflect. Some of these rival hypotheses can be ruled out by formal aspects of design, but many of them must remain qualitative even in the most thorough report: in the mode of generating the rival hypotheses, in seeking out other evidence of that hypothesis' validity, and in the overall judgement as to its plausibility. Where the social interactions producing measurement are concerned, this is at least as great a problem for randomised 'true' experiments as for quasi-experimental ones.

For many experimental programme evaluations, especially quasi-experimental ones, a major category of threats to validity are the many other events, other than the experimental programme, which might have produced the measured changes. Generating these specific alternative explanations and estimating their plausibility are matters of common-sense knowing and require a thorough familiarity with the specific local setting.

While these rules regarding the use of qualitative knowing are clearly present in the quantitative methods books, they are rarely exercised. The researcher is apt to feel that presenting such content undermines the appearances of scientific certainty, or that weaknesses on these points are evidence of his own incompetence. The field experimenter's defensiveness *vis-à-vis* his laboratory colleagues leads to further minimising of this content and still more so when he is earning his living as a contractor in programme evaluation.

In current quantitative programme evaluations, qualitative knowing is also regularly present in the narrative history of the programme, as well as in the description of the programme content, the measures and means of data collection, and in the verbal summary of programme outcomes. The numerical evidence would not be interpretable otherwise. Yet such qualitative content is often an unplanned afterthought.

This sketch of the present role of qualitative knowing in the quantitative evaluation of action programmes has already implied the need for increasing explicit cognisance of that role at several points. In what follows, this theme will be expanded. There will also be some grudging consideration of qualitative programme evaluation in the absence of quantitative measures. Before getting to that, it seems well to look at the types of qualitative knowing that might be or have been proposed.

Types of Qualitative Evaluation

Tribes, governments and voluntary groups have for centuries instituted new programmes, which have then been stopped, retained or disseminated. From a social-evolutionary perspective (Campbell, 1965), such programme fates are evaluations, and the decision processes involved constitute evaluation mechanisms. Some of these mechanisms are matters of organisational survival, a social-evolutionary natural selection. But more often, the decisions, and certainly the borrowing decisions, have involved human judgements serving as vicarious representatives of potential survival value. These vicarious judgemental processes presumably have approximate adaptive value as they are themselves products of biological and social natural selection.

The raw material for such evaluations is the *remembered experiences of participants* transformed into an institutional decision by some formal or informal political process. Remembered experiences of participants will be treated as the most primitive and pervasive of qualitative knowing relevant to programme evaluation. Since memory of the past is continually readjusted by current context and recent experience, an important variant becomes *recorded participant experience*, as through writings and recorded votes. For action research, there are other relevant groups of lay observers, persons well placed to observe, incidental to other social roles. These include the programme staff and those groups of citizens who come into regular contact with the recipients.

Qualitative evaluation by evaluation experts (by social scientists) can take many forms. It can involve the social scientist's own qualitative experiences, as in a single time sample in the *site visit*, or over an entire social action experience, including a pre-programme period, as in *participant observation* and *non-participant observation*. But still more common in qualitative social science is the expert's role in recording and collating the participant's experiences, as through *informant interviews, opinion surveys,* or the *experience interview* of the Committee on Community Interrelations.

In the political processes in which groups transform the remembered experiences of participants into evaluative decisions, voting may be used, a kind of quantification of the qualitative for the purposes of pooling subjective judgements. Similarly, the social scientist's role in collating participant experience may involve quantification, as in coding free-response interviews, or in counting the number of participants who had generally negative evaluations of the programme, or in providing rating scales and structured questions on which participants can quantify their own subjective experience. Indeed, much of what we think of as experimental measures, recorded on the occasion of pre-test and post-test for both experimental and control groups, are in fact quantifications of subjective judgements. The qualitative social scientist may also use quantitative translations in recording or summarising his own direct experiences. In what follows I shall try to distinguish qualitative from quantitative collations of qualitative experience, but shall treat both under the overall category of qualitative.

Process evaluation has been offered as a supplement (Freeman and Sherwood, 1970) or alternative to quantitative experimental programme evaluation (e.g. Weiss and Rein, 1970; Guttentag, 1971, 1973). One founding statement presents this challenge in exaggerated form:

> The reason we require 'control groups' in experimental science is that the processes presumably go on in the famous 'black box.' So we cannot observe the significant middle state of 'throughput.' We can only ascertain the input and measure the output. But where it is possible to observe the throughput – the process – then the need for the crude experimental model is by-passed (Bennis, 1968, p. 231).

In practice, process evaluation has meant qualitative consideration of the specific events in programme implementation, including the typical experiences of participants. Process evaluation may be done by the programme implementation staff themselves, or by process evaluation specialists whose full-time job it is, or conceivably by getting participants to keep diaries. Narrative histories of programme experience may be a typical product (such are referred to as the extensive data base for Kaplan's (1973) summary Model Cities evaluation. See also Gilbert and Specht, 1973.) While we as yet lack classic examples and critical reactions, we may be sure that the clairvoyant visibility of causal relations anticipated by Bennis is lacking. None the less, a well-planned and conscientiously executed process description seems a desirable feature in any programme evaluation as a cross-validation and as a critique of the measurement process and the experimental arrangements. (The usual assignment to the process evaluator should be explicitly extended to cover these latter activities.)

If we were to see develop a widespread practice of process evaluation and if process evaluators were to criticise each other and argue about assessments of programme effects, their mutual criticisms would almost certainly lead them to re-invent aspects of experimental design. That is, a need would be felt for similar process records prior to the innovation, and for a record of the process stream for comparable social units experiencing the same historical events except for the programme. Experimental design can be separated from quantification. The equivocalities of inference which experimental design seeks to reduce are present for qualitative evaluation fully as much as for quantitative.

Formative evaluation has been distinguished from the *summative evaluation,* the measurement of programme impact that is the goal of the typical quantitative experimental programme evaluation. Formative evaluation refers to a continuous monitoring of a new programme designed to support immediate revisions in aspects of the programme that prove to be unworkable or obviously ineffective. While conceivably some of this could be done by quantitative experiments on these features, the cumbersomeness resulting, the need for immediate reaction, and the fact that many of the errors in planning are visible to the naked eye, make formative evaluation primarily a matter of commonsense knowing. It is an obviously desirable precursor to quantitative experimentation or full-scale process evaluation, since these expensive procedures should not be wasted on programmes which the programme implementors would not want to see repeated and disseminated in that form. Where feasible, such a debugging formative run of a programme should precede programme evaluation. The need for formative evaluation needs emphasising and scheduling. Otherwise, the project may defensively implement a programme designed only on paper, and in so doing, may blind itself to available qualitative evidence of implementation failure.

Systems analysis is a frequently recommended alternative/supplement to the quantitative experimental approach (Baker, 1968; 1970; Schulberg and Baker, 1968; Schulberg, Sheldon and Baker, 1969; Weiss and Rein, 1970). While in biology and engineering (e.g. Jones, 1973), this is a highly quantified utilisation of experimental findings, it has come to represent in social programme evaluation a generally qualitative approach typified by an attention to organisational functioning, relationships to other systems, and close attention to the actual processes involved in the treatment. In this, it certainly avoids the narrow blindness of many quantitative evaluations. Awaiting the day when we have some full-scale systems analyses of new programmes and their impact, I will not try to distinguish this approach from process evaluation or the field-work methods to be described below, and will repeat the recommendation that it would seem a valuable adjunct to quantitative evaluations.

The use of *anthropologists* as programme evaluators has been undertaken in the Experimental Schools Program of the National Institutes of Education in the United States. While this is not to the total exclusion of quantitative measurement, the anthropological field-work represents the one dominant research expense in several expensive programme evaluations. Reputedly resident anthropologists have also been employed in some Model Cities evaluations.

Prior to Malinowski, most anthropological research represented the compilation of the experience of informants, often with the aim of reconstructing a picture of the local culture prior to contact with Europeans. Since Malinowski, the typical goal has been to describe the current lived culture of a specific village, without regard to its historical sources or cultural typicality. With this has come an emphasis on the anthropologist as a direct observer, as fully a participant in the collective life of the community as possible, learning the local language thoroughly, and living the local life 24 hours a day for some two years or more. It is this latter anthropological model that has been dominant so far in programme evaluation. Particularly influential has been one non-participant-observer study of a school superintendent's office (Wolcott, 1973), although this study was not itself focused on a programme evaluation. The field-work methods of the qualitative sociologists have also been used as models (Nelson and Giannotta, 1974a, 1974b).

A few preliminary samples of this approach in the US Experimental School Program are now available (Nelson, Reynolds, French and Giannotta, 1974). There is also available a methodological essay stemming from a similar experience (Everhart, in press). In a few years, we will have digested this experience and be in a better position to judge it. Already I am willing to affirm that they provide a background that will help the interpretation of quantitative evaluations, if and when the latter are forthcoming. There is a richness of detail on how things happened and what went wrong that would occasionally lead one to throw aside a quantitative evaluation as not worth reading since in the end no real changes were made, or because so many stronger extraneous forces impinged on the scene that the experimental programme's impact had no chance of showing. But it does not seem to me yet that these ethnographies can stand alone as evidence of programme effectiveness, replacing a good quantitative experimental evaluation.

The anthropologists have never studied a school system before. They have been hired after (or just as) the experimental programme has got under way, and are inevitably studying a mixture of the old and the new under conditions in which it is easy to make the mistake of attributing to the programme results which would have been there anyway. It would help in this if the anthropologists were to spend half of their time studying another school that was similar, except for the new experimental programme. This has apparently not been considered. It would also help if the anthropologists were to study the school for a year or two prior to the programme evaluation. (This would be hard to schedule, but we might regard the current school ethnographies as pre-studies for new innovations still to come.)

All knowing is comparative, however phenomenally absolute it appears, and an anthropologist is usually in a very poor position for valid comparison, as their own student experience and their second-hand knowledge of schools involve such different perspectives as to be of little comparative use. The perceptual position of the lay programme participants is in fact superior to that of the anthropologists, as we shall discuss below. (In the Southeast Minneapolis studies (Nelson *et al.*, 1974), the several anthropologists working with the different schools did have the advantage of comparing notes with each other.)

In its prior uses, anthropological and sociological field observation methods have not usually been focused on the causal impact of a single factor or new institution. Instead, the goal has been that of describing things as they are without causal imputation. Indeed, the methodological orientation often includes a denial of the relevance or possibility of attempting to infer causal relationships. In accepting the assignment of evaluating the effects and effectiveness of a programme, the anthropologist or sociologist has lost a significant freedom, and has re-entered the more traditional scientific arena of causal inference. Once at it, he comes to recognise the ambiguities of this task, and indeed may often in the end justify his efforts in terms of the value to anthropology and to education of having some thorough ethnographies of schools, abandoning the focus on programme impact. However well-tested observational field-work methods are for their usual purposes, they are untried for programme evaluation.

There are no reliability or validity studies of observational field-work that I am aware of. I believe that if two ethnographers were sent to study the same culture, or two participant-observer sociologists to study the same factory, considerable agreement would be found. But when you propose such studies, it turns out that the qualitative social scientist would be more interested in differences than in congruences, and would not necessarily expect agreements since each observer is recognised to have a unique perspective, or since there is believed to exist no social reality except as constructed by the observer. Such a perspective on diversity of product can hardly be tolerable to a government agency or a volunteer group trying to decide on expanding or terminating a new programme. The degree to which two anthropologists working independently agree on institutional programme description will certainly soon be tested. I myself believe that there is some firm social reality there to be described and that considerable agreement will be found. But an anthropologist's idiosyncracies will also be present (Campbell, 1964), and I am not sure the agreement will extend to the usually low-contrast details of programme effectiveness.

But it is not only for qualitative evaluations that such replicability needs demonstrating. Quantitative experimental studies involve so many judgemental decisions as to mode of implementation, choice and wording of measures, assembly of data in analysis, etc., that they too should be done in replicate. Our big evaluations should be split up into two or more parts and independently implemented. When the results agree, the decision implications are clear. When they disagree, we are properly warned about the limited generality of the findings. If qualitative and quantitative evaluations were to be organised on the same programmes, I would expect them to agree. If they did not, I feel we should regard it possible that the quantitative was the one in error (I feel this was the case in the first major Head Start evaluation, even though the qualitative evaluation was to my knowledge never systematically collected and assembled. See Campbell and Erlebacher, 1970.)

For qualitative programme evaluation, historians should also be considered. Political scientists are already involved (e.g. Greenstone and Peterson, 1973, although they eschew estimates of impact). If qualitative programme evaluation is to become a frequent procedure, the methodologies of humanistic studies should be re-assembled and re-assessed for this purpose. The most frequent methodological package is the 'case study', combining all available evidence from informants, news reports, documents, archives and first-hand observations. Standards of evidence exist which not all process evaluations and programme ethnographies as yet live up to. There is the anthropological and sociological field-work requirement of field notes, written up each day, and subsequently used to check attempts at generalisation. In the Anthropology Department at Berkeley, Lowie and Kroeber used to require all myths and histories to be obtained independently from at least two informants. Greenstone and Peterson, in a report that boldly names names and events in recounting off-the-record programme history, are able to assert: 'In all cases, reports of the participant's behavior is based . . . on evidence obtained from several actors speaking from various perspectives' (1973, p. 7). Such a requirement is certainly apt to increase the replicability of a study.

In past writings (1961, 1963, 1970) I have spoken harshly of the single-occasion, single-setting (one-shot) case-study, not on the grounds of its qualitative nature, but because it combined such a fewness of points of observation, and such a plethora of available causal concepts, that a spuriously perfect fit was almost certain. Recently, in a quixotic and ambivalent article, 'Degrees of Freedom' (1975), I have recanted, reminding myself that such studies regularly contradict the prior expectations of the authors, and are convincing and informative to sceptics like me to a degree which my simple-minded rejection does not allow for. My tentative solution is that there must exist many 'degrees of freedom' in the multiple-implications attribute space, giving such a study a probing and testing power which I had not allowed for. It is possible that specific examples of case-studies focused-programme effects might eventually convince me that they had the power to evaluate programmes. Particularly, they might validly pick up unanticipated effects missed by more structured approaches. But I await the specific examples. (For other observations on anthropological method, sometimes pushing quantification but usually respecting the qualitative, see Campbell 1955, 1961, 1964, 1972; Campbell and LeVine, 1970; Werner and Campbell, 1970.)

Acquaintance with events and persons extended across time and settings provides even the quantitative scientist with qualitative knowledge that enables him to catch misunderstanding, error and fraud in his data. Where the same person runs the treatment programme, collects the data, and analyses the results, the qualitative support for the quantitative results is apt to be strong. Much or all of this acquaintanceship base can be lost in large-scale modern quantitative programme evaluation. At its worst, four different teams under four separate contracts collect pre-treatment data, administer the programme, collect post-treatment data, and analyse the results. Even on single-contract studies the division of labour within the project produces a similar split. The belief that external evaluators are more objective further prevents the sharing of qualitative experience. Undoubtedly the computer print-outs often provide a pseudoscientific façade which gullibly uses data for which the qualitative basis of the quantitative is in fact invalid.

A project anthropologist, sociologist or historian, assigned to the task of common-sense acquaintance with the overall context including the social interactions producing the measures, could often fill in this gap.

Participant Evaluation

Participants, as we have noted, will usually have a better observational position than will anthropologists or other outside observers of a new programme. They usually have experienced the pre-programme conditions from the same viewing point as they have the special programme. Their experience of the programme will have been more relevant, direct and valid, less vicarious. Collectively, their greater numbers will average out observer idiosyncrasies that might dominate the report of any one ethnographer.

While participants are asked to generate a lot of data in programme evaluations, rarely are they directly asked to evaluate the programme, to judge its adequacy, to advise on its continuance, discontinuance, dissemination or modification. Rather than evaluating programmes, participants are usually asked about themselves and their own adequacy. We are thus wasting a lot of well-founded opinions. Course evaluations are one exception to this, and at their best confirm the competence of participants as observers (Frey, 1973).

In a Head Start programme, many of the mothers have the experience of older children to compare to their Headstarters. In the New Jersey Negative Income Tax Experiment, the participants have gone through three years of a very special income subsidy system. They have both their own prior experience and the concurrent experiences of their equally poor non-experimental neighbours as comparison bases. They know they've been in an experiment, and must have a variety of impressions about its effects on their lives.

We should start trying to assemble these participant judgements. In the spirit of qualitative compilations of qualitative judgements, we should probably let the participants pool their judgements in face-to-face meetings, perhaps first in small groups with recording secretaries and then in delegate groups, buzz-session style. The group's meetings could generate conclusion statements and vote on them, but usually verbal statements of unquantified consensus would result.

Should the control group participants meet with the experimentals to add that comparison base? If one wanted to use such evaluation methods, would it not be desirable to have alternative programmes tried out adjacent to each other, so that the participants could by conversational sharing compare notes on the alternatives all during the course of the study? In any event, it would seem a fruitful way of generating informed qualitative comparisons to have the participants of differing alternative programmes brought together in conferences.

In Head Start programmes, there are other competent observers whose evaluations go unrecorded: the Head Start teachers, the first-grade teachers, the Headstarters themselves. In the Negative Income Tax Experiments, the regular community social workers, the interviewers, and next-door neighbours all suggest themselves as competent qualitative observers, well worth listening to.

Robert L. Wolf (1974), in an impressive, detailed, speculative dissertation has proposed that judicial procedures, adversary hearings, with witnesses such as Head Start parents, teachers and pupils, with attorney cross-examination and an expert jury, be used to generate the integrated decision. He presents a very persuasive case for the extra validity provided by judicial procedures, especially cross-examination, citing Levine (1974) among others. Let us hope he is funded soon for a full-scale try-out.

But qualitative compilation procedures do not seem to me to be essential. Group opinion, if a mature consensus exists, has a stubborn reality that will show through a variety of methods. Thus I think much of the value of participant evaluation could be obtained by direct interview questions on the effects of the programme, etc., which could then be statistically summarised. Occasionally subtleties would be missed that the participants would discover and agree upon in a group discussion. Equally often, however, the minutes of the group discussion would be dominated by a single participant and lack the averaging-out of errors achieved by a statistical summary.

For institutions and groups that will be continuing sites of programme changes, such as the welfare system and schools, Gordon and I (1971) have proposed that all participant groups (social workers and clients, pupils, parents and teachers) fill out an 'Annual Report for Program Evaluation' that would provide the pre-tests and time-series for the quasi-experimental evaluations of changes.

We need to try out a variety of such procedures. As described so far, these would represent methodologically independent cross-validations of the quantitative results. They would have the chance of discovering programme effects on topics not anticipated in the formal measurement devices. They would be likely to confirm the major findings on shared dimensions. If they did not, as I've said, we should consider the possibility that the quantitative procedures are in error. – If I will concede all this, why would I be reluctant to see the qualitative procedures used without the quantitative? It is because I believe that the quantitative, when based on firm and examined qualitative knowing, can validly go beyond the qualitative, and can produce subtleties that the qualitative would have missed.

The issue may be made clearer by considering a second valuable role for participants, or for qualitative social science observers, i.e. as critics of the quantitative results. If our programme ethnographers or historians and the participant discussion groups were to be presented with the major results and allowed to criticise them, an important kind of validation would be achieved. Some of the findings they would concur with. Other results they would disagree with and explain away as artefacts due to aspects of the situation which the quantitative measurers had missed. Still other results would surprise them, but stand up under their cross-examination, and eventually appear valid to the qualitative observers. It is these latter instances in which the quantitative would have gone beyond the qualitative in a valid manner.

Before this analysis is completed, it should go on to make use of our century of research on human judgement and its biases. It should go over the lists of threats to validity of experiments and measures, comparing the susceptibility of qualitative and quantitative on each. It should look to the special threats coming from the politics of evaluation, the internal project politics and the intrusion of the politics of the external setting: in what ways do these political pressures impinge differently on the quantitative and the qualitative? It should discuss in detail the CCI methodology and the current revivals of it.

In summary: the polarity of quantitative versus qualitative approaches to research on social action remains unresolved, if resolution were to mean a predominant justification of one over the other. Social knowing, even more than physical knowing, is a precarious and presumptive process. However approached, there is much room for valid criticism. Each pole is at its best in its criticisms of the other, not in the invulnerability of its own claims to descriptive knowledge.

Accepting my own continued identification with the quantitative experimental approach to action research, I cannot recommend qualitative social science, nor group process lay participant consensus, as substitutes for the quantitative. But I have strongly recommended them both as needed cross-validating additions.

More than that, I have sought to remind my quantitative colleagues that in the successful laboratory sciences, quantification both builds upon and is cross-validated by the scientist's pervasive qualitative knowledge. The conditions of mass-produced quantitative social science in programme evaluation are such that much of this qualitative base is apt to be lost. If we are to be truly scientific, we must re-establish this qualitative grounding of the quantitative in action research.

References

Baker, F. (1968). The changing hospital organizational system: A model for evaluation. Read in General Systems Session of AAAS Annual Meeting, Dallas, Texas, 1968. To be published in *Man in Systems: Proceedings of the 14th Annual Meeting of the Society for General Systems Research.*

Baker, F. (1970). General systems theory, research and medical care. In A. Sheldon, F. Baker and C.P. McLaughlin, *Systems and Medical Care,* pp. 1-26. Cambridge, Mass.: The MIT Press.

Beck, B. (1970). Cooking the welfare stew. In R.W. Habenstein (ed.), *Pathways to data: Field methods for studying ongoing social organizations.* Chicago: Aldine.

Becker, H.M. Geer, B. and Hughes, E.C. (1968). *Making the grade.* New York: Wiley.

Becker, H.W. (1970). *Sociological work: Method and substance.* Chicago: Aldine.

Bennis, W.G. (1968). The case study. *Journal of Applied Behavioral Science, 4,* 2, 227-31.

Blachowicz, J.A. (1971). Systems theory and evolutionary models of the development of science. *Philosophy of Science, 38,* pp. 178-99.

Blau, P. M. (1963). *The dynamics of bureaucracy* (rev. ed.) Chicago: University of Chicago Press.

Campbell, D.T. (1955). The informant in quantitative research. *American Journal of Sociology, 60,* pp. 339-42 (No. 4, January).

Campbell, D.T. (1960). Blind variation and selective retention in creative thought as in other knowledge processes. *Psychological Review, 67,* pp. 380-400 (No. 6).

Campbell, D.T. (1961). The mutual methodological relevance of anthropology and psychology. In F.L.K. Hsu (ed.), *Psychological anthropology: Approaches to culture and personality,* pp. 333-52. Homewood, Ill.: Dorsey.

Campbell, D.T. (1963). Social attitudes and other acquired behavioral dispositions. In S. Koch (ed.), *Psychology: A study of a science.* Vol. VI. *Investigations of man as socius,* pp. 94-172. New York: McGraw-Hill.

Campbell, D.T. (1964). Distinguishing differences of perception from failures of communication in cross-cultural studies. In F.S.C. Northrop and H.H. Livingston (eds.), *Cross-cultural understanding: Epistemology in anthropology,* pp. 308-36. New York: Harper and Row.

Campbell, D.T. (1965). Variation and selective retention in socio-cultural evolution. In H.R. Barringer, G.I. Blanksten and R.W. Mack (eds.), *Social change in developing areas.* Cambridge, Mass.: Schenkman.

Campbell, D.T. (1966). Pattern matching as an essential in distal knowing. In K.R. Hammond (ed.), *The psychology of Egon Brunswik,* pp. 81-106. New York: Holt, Rinehart and Winston.

Campbell, D.T. (1969a). Reforms as experiments. *American Psychologist, 24,* pp. 409-29 (No. 4, April).

Campbell, D.T. (1969b). A phenomenology of the other one: Corrigible, hypothetical and critical. In T. Mischel (ed.), *Human action: Conceptual and empirical issues,* pp. 41-69. New York: Academic Press.

Campbell, D.T. (1970). Natural selection as an epistemological model. In R. Naroll and R. Cohen (eds.), *A handbook of method in cultural anthropology,* pp. 51-85. Garden City, New York: Natural History Press.

Campbell, D.T. (1971). Methods for the experimenting society. Paper presented to the meeting of the American Psychological Association, Washington, D.C., September 1971. To appear, after revision, in the *American Psychologist.*

Campbell, D.T. (1972). Herskovits, cultural relativism, and metascience. In M.J. Herskovits, *Cultural relativism,* v-xxiii (Introduction). New York: Random House.

Campbell, D.T. (1974). Evolutionary epistemology. In P.A. Schilpp (ed.), *The philosophy of Karl Popper.* Vol. 14, I and II. *The library of living philosophers,* pp. 413-63, Vol. 14-I. La Salle, Ill.: Open Court Publishing.

Campbell, D.T. (1975). 'Degrees of Freedom' and the case study. *Comparative Political Studies,* September, 178-93.

Campbell, D.T. and Erlebacher, A.E. (1970). How regression artifacts in quasi-experimental evaluations can mistakenly make compensatory education look harmful. In J. Hellmuth (ed.), *Compensatory education: A national debate.* Vol. III. *Disadvantaged child,* pp. 185-210. New York: Brunner/Mazel.

Campbell, D.T. and LeVine, R.A. (1970). Field-manual anthropology. In R. Naroll and R. Cohen (eds.), *A handbook of method in cultural anthropology,* pp. 366-87. Garden City, New York: Natural History Press.

Campbell, D.T. and Stanley, J.C. (1963). Experimental and quasi-experimental designs for research on teaching. In N.L. Gate (ed.), *Handbook of research on teaching.* Chicago: Rand McNally. (Also published (1966) as *Experimental and quasi-experimental designs for research.* Chicago: Rand McNally.)

Campbell, R. (1974). *The chasm: The life and death of a great experiment in ghetto education.* Boston: Houghton Mifflin.

Caws, P. (1969). The structure of discovery. *Science, 166,* 1375-80.

Chein, I. (1949). On evaluating self-surveys. *Journal of Social Issues, 5,* 56-63.

Chein, I. (1956). Community self-surveys. Lecture given at University of Rochester, 5 November. Mimeo., 23 pp.

Chein, I., Cook, S.W. and Harding, J. (1948a). The field of action research. *The American Psychologist, 3,* 43-50.

Chein, I., Cook, S.W. and Harding, J. (1948b). The use of research in social therapy. *Human Relations, I,* 497-510.

Cook, S.W. (1962). The systematic analysis of socially significant events: A strategy for social research. *The Journal of Social Issues, 18,* 66-84.

Cook, T.D. and Campbell, D.T. (forthcoming). The design and conduct of quasi-experiments and true experiments in field settings. In M.D. Dunnette and J.P. Campbell (eds.), *Handbook of industrial and organizational research.* Chicago: Rand McNally.

Douglas, J.D. (1967). *The social meanings of suicide.* Princeton, New Jersey: Princeton University Press.

Duncker, K. (1929). Uber induzierte Bewegung. Ein Beitrag zur Theorie optisch-wahrgenommener Bewegung. *Psychologische Forschung, 12,* 6, 180-259.

Etzioni, A. and Lehman, E.W. (1967). Some dangers in 'valid' social measurement. *Annals of the American Academy of Political and Social Science, 373,* 1-15.

Everhart, R.B. (In press.) Problems of doing fieldwork in educational evaluation. *Human Organization,* (*ms* May 1974.)

Feyerabend, P.K. (1970). Against method: Outline of an anarchistic theory of knowledge. In M. Radner and S. Winokur, *Analyses of theories and methods of physics and psychology*. Vol. IV, Minnesota Studies in the Philosophy of Science, pp. 17-130. Minneapolis: University of Minnesota Press.

Freeman, H.E. and Sherwood, C.C. (1970). *Social policy and social research.* Englewood Cliffs, New Jersey: Prentice-Hall.

Frey, P.W. (1973). Student ratings of teaching: validity of several rating factors. *Science, 182,* 83-5.

Garfinkel, H. (1967). 'Good' organizational reasons for 'bad' clinic records. In H. Garfinkel, *Studies in ethnomethodology*, pp. 186-207. Englewood Cliffs, New Jersey: Prentice-Hall.

Gilbert, N. and Specht, H. (1973). The model cities program: A comparative analysis of participating cities process, product, performance, and prediction. Marshall Kaplan, Gans and Kahn, Inc. of San Francisco. Washington, D.C.: Department of Housing and Urban Development, Office of Community Development, Evaluation Division. U.S. Government Printing Office, Washington, D.C. 20402, GPO Bookstore Stock Number 2300-00242.

Glaser, B.G. and Strauss, A.L. (1967). *The discovery of grounded theory: Strategies for qualitative research.* Chicago: Aldine.

Goodman, N. (1955). *Fact, fiction, and forecast.* Cambridge, Mass.: Harvard University Press.

Gordon, A.C., Campbell, D.T. *et al.* (1971). Recommended accounting procedures for the evaluation of improvements in the delivery of state social services. Mimeo. Center for Urban Affairs, Northwestern University.

Greenstone, J.D. and Peterson, P.E. (1973). *Race and authority in urban politics: Community participation and the war on poverty.* New York: Russell Sage Foundation.

Guttentag, M. (1971). Models and methods in evaluation research. *Journal for the Theory of Social Behavior, 1,* 75-95. (No. 1, April.)

Guttentag, M. (1973). Evaluation of social intervention programs. *Annals of the New York Academy of Sciences, 218,* 3-13.

Hanson, N.R. (1958). *Patterns of discovery.* Cambridge: The University Press.

Harding, J. (1948). Community self-surveys: A form of combating discrimination. *Congress Weekly: A Review of Jewish Interests.* 5 March.

Jastrow, J. (1900). *Fact and fable in psychology.* Boston: Houghton Mifflin.

Jones, R.W. (1973). *Principles of biological regulation: An introduction to feedback systems.* New York: Academic Press.

Kaplan, M. *et al.* (1973). The model cities program: A comparative analysis of city response patterns and their relation to future urban policy. Washington, D.C.: Office of Community Development Evaluation Division, Department of Housing and Urban Development. U.S. Government Printing Office, Washington, D.C. 20402, GPO Bookstore, Stock No. 2300-00241.

Kitsuse, J.K. and Cicourel, A.V. (1963). A note on the uses of official statistics. *Social Problems, 11,* 131-9. (Fall.)

Kordig, C.R. (1971). *The justification of scientific change.* New York: Humanities Press.

Kuhn, T.S. (1962). *The structure of scientific revolutions.* Chicago: University of Chicago Press.

Kuhn, T.S. (1970). Logic of discovery or psychology of research? and Reflections on my critics. In I. Lakatos and A. Musgrave (eds.), *Criticism and the growth of knowledge,* pp. 1-23 and 231-78. Cambridge: Cambridge University Press.

Lakatos, I. (1970). Falsification and the methodology of scientific research programmes. In I. Lakatos and A. Musgrave (eds.), *Criticism and the growth of knowledge.* Cambridge: Cambridge University Press.

Levine, M. (1974). Scientific method and the adversary model: Some preliminary thoughts. Washington, D.C.: *American Psychologist, 29* (9), 661-77.

Lewin, K. (1946). Action research and minority problems. *Journal of Social Issues, 2,* 34-46. Reprinted in K. Lewin, *Resolving social conflict.* New York: Harper, 1948.

Lewin, K. (1947). Frontiers in group dynamics, Part II-B. *Human Relations, 1,* 147-53. Reprinted as Feedback problems in social diagnosis and action in W. Buckley (ed.), *Modern Systems Research for the Behavioral Scientist,* pp. 441-4. Chicago: Aldine, 1968.

Lippitt, R. and Radke, M. (1946). New trends in the investigation of prejudice. *The Annals of the American Academy of Political and Social Science, 244,* March.

Marrow, A.J. (1969). *The practical theorist: The life and work of Kurt Lewin.* New York: Basic Books.

Morrissey, W.R. (1972). Nixon anti-crime plan undermines crime statistics. *Justice Magazine, 1,* 8-11, 14. (No. 5/6, June/July) (*Justice Magazine,* 922 National Press Building, Washington, D.C. 20004.)

Murchison, C. (ed.) (1931). *Handbook of Child Psychology.* Worchester, Mass.: Clark University Press.

Nelson, H. and Giannotta, F.J. (1974a). Research methodology in alternative education settings: The met plan. Minneapolis, Minnesota: Aries Corporation. (Submitted to the National Institute of Education pursuant to Contract No. OEC-0-71-4752.)

Nelson, H. and Giannotta, F.J. (1974b) (Draft). MET interim report on southeast alternatives ESP project. Volume 1: Project context and rationale of research. Minneapolis: Aries Corp.

Nelson, H. Reynolds, J., French, L.R. and Giannotta, F.J. (1974) (Draft). MET Interim report on southeast alternatives ESP project, Volume IIA: School ethnographic studies: Tuttle, Pratt-Motley, Marcy. Volume IIB: Southeast and Free School and Marshall University High School. Minneapolis: Aries Corp.

Poincaré, H. (1913). Mathematical creation. In H. Poincaré, *The foundations of science.* New York: Science Press.

Polanyi, M. (1958). *Personal knowledge.* London: Routledge and Kegan Paul.

Popper, K.R. (1959). *The logic of scientific discovery.* New York: Basic Books.

Popper, K.R. (1963). *Conjectures and refutations.* New York: Basic Books.

Popper, K.R. (1972). *Objective knowledge: An evolutionary approach.* Oxford: Clarendon Press.

Quine, W.V. (1953). *From a logical point of view.* Cambridge, Mass.: Harvard University Press.

Quine, W.V. (1969). *Ontological relativity.* New York: Columbia University Press.

Raser, J.R., Campbell, D.T. and Chadwick, R.W. (1970). Gaming and simulation for developing theory relevant to international relations. In A. Rapoport (ed.), *General Systems: Yearbook of the Society for General Systems Research, 15,* 183-204. Ann Arbor, Michigan: Society for General Systems Research.

Ridgeway, V. (1956). Dysfunctional consequences of performance measures. *Administrative Science Quarterly, 1,* 240-7. (No. 2, September.)

Salasin, S. (1973). Experimentation revisited: A conversation with Donald T. Campbell. *Evaluation, 1,* 7-13. (No. 3.)

Schulberg, H.C. and Baker, F. (1968). Program evaluation models and the implementation of research findings. *American Journal of Public Health, 58,* 1248-55. Reprinted in Schulberg, Sheldon and Baker, 1969, pp. 562-72.

Schulberg, E.H., Sheldon, A. and Baker, F. (1969). Introduction. In *Program Evaluation in the health fields,* pp. 3-28. New York: Behavioral Publications.

Segall, M.H., Campbell, D.T. and Herskovits, M.J. (1966). *The influence of culture on visual perception.* Indianapolis, Indiana: Bobbs-Merrill.

Seidman, D. and Couzens, M. (1972). Crime statistics and the great American anti-crime crusade: Police misreporting of crime and political pressures. Paper presented at the meeting of the American Political Science Association, Washington, D.C., September. (To appear in *Law and Society Review.*)

Selltiz, C. (1956). The use of survey methods in a citizens campaign against discrimination. *Human Organization, 14,* 19-25.

Selltiz C. and Cook, S.W. (1948). Can research in social science be both socially useful and scientifically meaningful? *American Sociological Review, 13,* 454-9.

Sheldon, A., Baker, F. and McLaughlin, C.P. (eds.) (1970). *Systems and Medical Care,* pp. 1-26. Cambridge, Massachusetts: The MIT Press.

Shimony, A. (1970). Scientific inference. In R. Colodny (ed.), *Pittsburgh studies in the philosophy of science,* Vol. IV, pp. 79-172. Pittsburgh: University of Pittsburgh Press.

Stewart, V.M. (1973). Tests of the 'carpentered world' hypothesis by race and environment in America and Zambia. *International Journal of Psychology, 8,* 83-94.

Tolman, E.C. (1932). *Purposive behavior in animals and men.* New York: The Century Co.

Toulmin, S.E. (1961). *Foresight and understanding: An inquiry into the aims of science.* Bloomington, Indiana: Indiana University Press.

Toulmin, S.E. (1972). *Human understanding.* Vol. I. *The evolution of collective understanding.* Princeton, New Jersey: Princeton University Press.

Twigg, R. (1972). Downgrading of crimes verified in Baltimore. *Justice Magazine, 1,* 15, 18. (No. 5/6, June/July.) (*Justice Magazine,* 922 National Press Building, Washington, D.C. 20004.)

Vidich, A. and Bensman, J. (1954). The validity of field data. *Human Organization, 13,* 1, 20-7.

Weiss, R.S. and Rein, M. (1970). The evaluation of broad-aim programs: Experimental design, its difficulties, and an alternative. *Administrative Science Quarterly, 15,* 97-109.

Werner, O. and Campbell, D.T. (1970). Translating, working through interpreters, and the problem of decentering. In R. Naroll and R. Cohen (eds.), *A handbook of method in cultural anthropology,* pp. 398-420. Garden City, New York: Natural History Press.

Wittgenstein, L. (1953). *Philosophical investigations.* New York: Macmillan.

Wolcott, Harry F. (1973). *The man in the principal's office: An ethnography.* New York: Holt, Rinehart and Winston.

Wolf, R.L. (1974). The application of select legal concepts to educational evaluation. Ph.D. dissertation, University of Illinois at Urbana-Champaign, School of Education. (Mimeo., 204 pp.)

10 HIERARCHIES OF INTERACTION IN SOCIOLOGICAL RESEARCH

Derek L. Phillips

In recent years there has been increased criticism of the dominant assumptions and techniques of sociological research; the direction and tone of these criticisms is well reflected in the present volume. Because the contributors to this volume give so much attention to problems and controversies central to sociological methodology, I intend to utilise this occasion to consider the major methodological controversies from a somewhat different vantage-point than that taken by most persons concerned with the sociology of methodology. I will focus mainly on one particular area of methodological importance that has yet to receive the full attention which it deserves.

To many of us it is no secret that sociology (and social science more generally) is not, and never has been, value-free, that the social sciences are lacking in laws and general propositions which can call upon empirical support, that the cumulation of sociological knowledge is almost non-existent, that our data frequently lack accuracy and validity, that – despite its professed concern with social interaction – most empirical research fails to get at these social processes and interactions which many sociologists believe should be their particular focus. Of course, none of this is a secret, yet unfortunately, at least from my point of view, the bad news has yet to reach the vast majority of social scientists. Or, if it has reached them, it has failed to have much of an impact. Perhaps I exaggerate. If so, let me rephrase my lament in the following way: those of us who have given attention to documenting, and/or trying to remedy, the pretensions and shortcomings of the social sciences have failed to persuade most social scientists that our views are correct. Worse yet, we have often failed to get them to even take our criticisms seriously. Later on, I will try to show that many criticisms are indeed ignored or played down. Further, I will suggest why this is the case, and will consider how it might be partially remedied.

Social Interaction: Three Sets of Relations

Many sociologists profess to be concerned with social interaction, in those social processes where two or more persons respond to one another's actions. Weber notes that 'in general, for sociology, such concepts as "state", "association", "feudalism", and the like, designate categories of human interaction' (H. Gerth and C. Wright Mills, 1960, p. 55). Wilson summarises this viewpoint nicely: 'the process of interaction . . . is at the logical core of sociological interest, even though for some purposes, particularly of a macrosociological sort, this is often left implicit.' Although most sociological research fails to get at (deal with, consider) the social interaction which is often its particular concern, sociological investigators are themselves necessarily involved in two sets of social interactions: with those whom they study, and with their fellow social scientists. It is, of course, true of all scientific investigators that the individual researcher must take account of two sets of relationships: to the phenomena which he investigates, and to his fellow scientists. But the sociologist's relation to the phenomena which he studies is one often characterised by *social* interaction between himself and the subjects of his investigation. Further, as I have noted above, the primary focus of the sociologist's interest – social interaction – is itself a human activity. In other words, the sociological researcher must be concerned with social interaction at *three* levels: (1) that among those whom he studies, (2) between himself and the subjects of study; and (3) between himself and his fellow sociologists. The natural scientist, on the other hand, is concerned with only one set of 'social' interactions: between himself and other scientists.

Much of the current concern with the inadequacies of sociological methodology can be viewed as dealing with one or more of these sets of social relationships. In the remainder of this chapter, I will briefly consider the first two sets of interactions (subject-subject, and subject-sociologist) and will then discuss at greater length those interactions between the individual scientist and the scientific community in which he shares membership. This last set of social relations, I will argue, is crucial to the eventual alteration (and replacement) of those methodological assumptions and techniques which are now dominant in sociology. It is at *this* level of social interaction that disagreement about the other two levels of interaction are, in one sense, settled. Thus, the chapter title.

Interaction as a Focus of Sociological Research

Max Weber (1947) defined sociology as a science which 'attempts the interpretive understanding of social action in order thereby to arrive at a causal explanation of its course and events'. Here, in one sentence, Weber joins the two terms which have come to divide sociologists (and, often times, philosophers who are concerned with these matters) into two opposing camps: 'social action' and 'causal explanations'.

It is not my intention to discuss here the various fine points of Weber's approach, as that is done quite adequately elsewhere. Rather, I want to point out that with the exception of those few sociologists who advocate an exclusive emphasis on observable behaviour, all sociologists in varying degrees are concerned with social action in the Weberian sense:

> In 'action' is included all human behavior when and in so far as the acting individual attaches a subjective meaning to it. Action in this sense may be either overt or purely inward or subjective: it may consist of positive intervention or acquiescing in the situation. Action is social in so far as, by virtue of the subjective meaning attached to it by the acting individual (or individuals), it takes account of the behavior of others and is thereby oriented in its course (Weber, 1947).

As I said, there are few sociologists who would totally reject the importance of social action for sociological enquiry. Even those positivists such as Brodbeck (1963, p. 309) who hold that individual behaviour must be accounted for by deducing it from some general laws governing such behaviour, acknowledge that a mere bodily movement is distinguished from an action by 'the *meaning* of that movement'.

What distinguishes those holding the view that social action can be accounted for by the usual processes of causal explanation from their opponents is the differing conclusions which are drawn regarding the *emphasis* which should be given to the 'meaning' of social actions. On the one side we have those sociologists in the tradition of logical positivism, behaviourism and structural-functionalism who argue that sociology should follow the methods of the natural sciences. They advocate (as did Durkheim) the focusing on social facts as external forces exercising constraints on the individual actor, the 'discovery' of these social facts, the distinction between independent and dependent variables, a generally deterministic view of nature, and the establishment of causal laws (see Phillips, 1963). They also attack what they see as their opponent's narrow preoccupation with capturing the meaning of an individual's action, since this does not in itself constitute a causal explanation of the action. At the same time, however, they hold that a concern with the meaning of a social action does not preclude causal explanations (see, for example, Ayer, 1967; Davidson, 1963; MacIntyre,

1971).

On the other side are those who argue that the social sciences differ from the natural sciences, both in regard to their subject matter and to their methods. Here we find social scientists and philosophers from several different traditions: people in the *verstehen* tradition of Dilthey and Weber, phenomenologists, symbolic-interactionists, ethnomethodologists, and some followers of Wittgenstein (see, for example, Hodges, 1944; Schutz, 1970; Filmer *et al.*, 1972; Harré, in this volume). There are, of course, differences among those advocating these various approaches, but all share the view that a heavy emphasis must be given to the *meaning* of social actions. Dilthey and others in the *verstehen* tradition see the social sciences as concerned 'with a world which has meaning for the actors involved' (Riekman, 1967). Phenomenologists like Schutz, Husserl and Berger, and symbolic-interactionists such as Mead and Blumer, similarly emphasise the importance of viewing social interaction as an interpretive process in which meanings evolve and change during the course of interaction (see Berger and Luckmann, 1967; Blumer, 1966). Ethnomethodology, a more recent development among the viewpoints advocating interpretive understanding, also focuses on the subjective meanings of social actors and the ways in which people plan and explain their own behaviour and that of others (see Garfinkel, 1974; Turner, 1973). And Peter Winch (1958), partially following Wittgenstein, holds that the focus of social science should be on those activities 'of which we can sensibly say that they have a meaning', and argues that enquiries concerning social life are exempt from causal explanations.

In one way or another, all of those stressing meaning emphasise the importance of placing the individual's action within a context of social rules. For them, all social activities are rule-ridden. Since the task of sociology is to grasp the meaning of an individual's action within one or another context of rules, so as to understand the meaning of his actions for him and for others, this is viewed as incompatible with a causal explanation of the same actions. Speaking of the difference between causal explanations and statistical regularities, on the one hand, and interpretive understanding, on the other, Winch (1958, p. 45) writes:

> The difference is precisely analogous to that between being able to formulate statistical laws about the likely occurrences of words in a language and being able to understand what was being *said* by someone who spoke the language . . . 'Understanding', in situations like this, is grasping the *point* or *meaning of what is being done or said.*

One methodological consequence of this interpretive conception of social action is that the techniques now most frequently employed in the study of social phenomena – interviews and questionnaires – will not suffice. This brings us to the second set of social interactions which concern the sociological investigator: those between himself and the subjects of study.

Interaction Between the Investigator and Those Studied

Within the past few years there has been a growing literature concerned with showing not only the *inappropriateness* of the dominant research techniques in the social sciences but also their *inadequacies*. With regard to their inappropriateness, there is an increasing realisation that social interaction must be studied from within actual social settings. In Blumer's words (1966, p. 542):

> On the methodological or research side the study of action would have to be made from the position of the actor. Since action is forged by the actor out of what he perceives, interprets, and judges, one would have to see the operating situation as the actor sees it, perceive objects as the actor perceives them, ascertain their meaning in terms of the meaning they have for the actor, and follow the actor's line of conduct as the actor organizes it – in short, one would have to take the role of the actor and see his world from his standpoint.

If sociologists are really concerned with social process and interaction, and wish to understand the construction of meanings and of social relations, then it would seem that they can best do so on the basis of more direct involvement and participation than is presently the case. As Whyte (1969, p. 47) notes: 'We need data on social processes, and questionnaires do not provide such data. Who is to provide such data? Somebody who is out in the field observing what is going on, perhaps even a participant observer.'

The reason why questionnaires (and interviews) do not get at social processes and interaction is self-evident. These techniques typically obtain verbal reports of interaction from one individual, then from another, and another, and so on, until everyone in the sample has completed the research instrument. Following this 'scientific' data-gathering process, individuals are then grouped together on the basis of one or more variables of interest to the investigator, and are then discussed *as if* interaction had actually been studied. Among other shortcomings of the use of such techniques is the researcher's assumption that he knows the meaning of his measures (questions, indices, whatever) for those whom he is investigating; i.e. that he understands the meanings which they attach to his enquiries (see Phillips, 1971).

Not only are questionnaires and interviews inappropriate for those concerned with social interaction, but they are inadequate as well in that they fall short of those standards which their own supporters advocate. By now it is obvious that, in these studies utilising causal explanations, the independent variables of major interest to investigators explain only a small portion of the variance in their dependent variables. One reason for this is that the interview process itself constitutes a source of influence on the respondents' replies and reports. This is not to say, of course, that various observational techniques are not also subject to the influence of interaction between the investigator and the subjects of his or her enquiry. Cicourel (1964) captures the problem in a nutshell: 'researchers in the social sciences are faced with a unique methodological problem: the very conditions of their research constitute an important complex variable for what passes as the findings of the investigation.' Paradoxically, attempts to control for biasing effects, over-rapport, 'going native' and the like presume knowledge and understanding of the very social processes which much sociological research has as its central concern.

As with my very limited consideration of the various positions regarding social interaction as the focus of sociological enquiry, my brief discussion of interaction in the data-collection process, i.e. between the researcher and his subjects, is only intended to set the stage for the major concern of this essay: the interaction between the sociological investigator and his fellow sociologists.

Interaction Between the Sociologist and His Fellows

Discussions about the proper focus of sociological enquiry and about the appropriate methods for studying social phenomena are, I intend to argue, attempts to persuade others of what sociology (and sociologists) 'should' be doing. Arguments about causal explanations, a *verstehen* approach, ethnomethodology, surveys or observational techniques can all be viewed as attempts to *legislate* the types of sociological explanations which should ideally be given and the types of methodological approaches which should ideally be followed. What we have, then, are a set of arguments (statements, claims, propositions) which represent different standpoints about what sociology is and ought to be, and a group of persons (Dilthey, Weber, Schutz, Garfinkel, Winch and so on) who have enunciated these various positions. That is, we have these things which men and women have written (or said) and we have the men and women who have written them.

My concern in the remainder of this essay is with the question of how scientists get other scientists to pay attention to, take seriously, accept, act upon, and sometimes warrant as true or correct, what they have written. This means that we can ignore the contents of this or that position and, instead, concern ourselves with that interaction which constitutes (part of) the relationship between the individual sociologist and the scientific community (or elements thereof) to which he directs his claims. In short, I am concerned here with the issue of how the sociologist goes about eliciting agreement with his particular position.

Since my interest is in the interaction between the individual sociologist and those to whom he is speaking or for whom he is writing, it is necessary to begin by considering those to whom his utterances are directed. Most especially as regards writers, authors, and men and women of science, sociologists have given attention to the place of the audience in intellectual life. Coser (1965, p. 3), for example, regards an audience as one of the conditions essential for the intellectual vocation, saying that 'intellectuals need an audience, a circle of people to whom they can address themselves and who can bestow recognition'. Duncan (1953) points to the importance of an author's knowing his audience: 'When an author desires to arouse or to dissipate a certain emotion in his audience, he must know the public he is addressing. He must know what kind of stimulus will produce what kind of response.' Speaking specifically of men of knowledge, Merton (1970, p. 362) places considerable emphasis on the importance of audiences:

> Men of knowledge do not orient themselves exclusively toward their data nor toward the total society, but to special segments of that society with their special demands, criteria of validity, of significant knowledge, of pertinent problems, etc. It is through anticipation of these demands and expectations of particular audiences, which can be effectively located in the social structure, that men of knowledge organize their own work, define their data, seize upon problems.

The physicist, Ziman (1968, p. 9) also points to the role of the scientific audience: 'The audience to which scientific publications are addressed is not passive; by its cheering or booing, its bouquets or brickbats, it actively controls the substance of the communications that it receives.'

All of these writers recognise the importance of the audience in intellectual and scientific life. In the case of men of knowledge, it is emphasised that they orient themselves to particular audiences, receiving their problems, theories, methods, rewards and recognition from these audiences. This is a recurrent theme in the work of Kuhn, Feyerabend, Polanyi and Toulmin, all of whom are concerned with understanding the practice of science. To varying extents, these latter writers emphasise that it is the scientific community itself which creates scientific knowledge. Consider Kuhn's (1963, p. 395) assertion that:

> It is not, after all, the individual who decides whether his discoveries or theoretical inventions shall become part of the body of established science. Rather it is his professional community, a community which has and sometimes exercises the privilege of declaring him a deviant.

Polanyi (1958) writes, 'Scientific truth is defined . . . as that which scientists affirm and believe to be true.'

Quarrels about the focus and study of sociology, then, are ultimately (though never, of course, forever) decided by the sociological community. It is they who decide what is to be accepted as sociological knowledge or, in Kuhn's words, becomes part of the body of established science. The defenders of the various viewpoints concerning social interaction are involved in trying to evoke the assent of other scientists. This requires communication and a common language. In the natural sciences, this common language is to a large extent (though not exclusively) the 'technical' language shared by the members of a particular scientific discipline or sub-speciality. But in the social sciences, it is not only the technical language that is important for communication, but also the everyday language shared by many outside the boundaries of the discipline. In all scientific fields, however, scientific truth and knowledge are created or constructed by the members of various professional communities. As far as the individual scientist is concerned, it is the scientific community which makes the final judgement as to the truth or falsity (correctness or incorrectness) of his knowledge-claims. The decisions and consensus of the community warrant scientific truth and knowledge.

It is important to stress the term 'scientific' in the above, for we can imagine ourselves – even without the existence of a scientific community (though not without human communities) – possessing practical knowledge. We can conceive of ourselves understanding and knowing about things, although it would not be considered as bona fide 'scientific' knowledge unless it were warranted as such by one or another scientific community. (Hanson (1971) makes a similar point.)

In asserting here that it is the professional community in which the individual scientist shares membership that determines the scientific nature of his (her) work, I am assuming that practising scientists can and do share criteria which allow them to distinguish between 'good' and 'bad' science. At issue here, of course, is the whole demarcation controversy, a controversy involving Kuhn, Feyerabend, Toulmin, Lakatos and Popper as major figures. Lakatos speaks of three major philosophical traditions with regard to this problem, and they require brief mention: scepticism, elitism, and demarcationism.

Scepticism, as represented by Feyerabend, holds that scientific theories occupy no privileged epistemological status as compared with other families of beliefs; no one belief system is any more 'correct' or 'truer' than another. Since for the sceptic there are no universal criteria (of anything), there is no possibility of producing an acceptable solution to the problem of appraising scientific products. Thus, one theory cannot be adjudged – on purely scientific grounds – as better or superior to another. The sceptic's major point is that all beliefs, including his own, are arbitrary in that they lack rational warrant.

Elitists share with the sceptics the view that formal, universal, explicit criteria are not sufficient to account for the evolution of theories or judgements about conflicting claims for scientific status. On the other hand, they hold that good science *can* be distinguished from bad science, that theories *can* be compared and evaluated. According to Kuhn, Polanyi and Toulmin, scientists do share standards but these cannot be fully articulated. Thus they accept the impossibility of articulating universal scientific criteria while, at the same time, making a distinction between good and bad scientific practice. With a change of paradigms, Kuhn claims, we have a change of standards and criteria. His own explanation of scientific practice, Kuhn (1970, pp. 237-8) emphasises, is 'irreducibly sociological':

> Take a *group* of the ablest available people with the most appropriate motivation; train them in some science and in the specialties relevant to the choices at hand; imbue them with the value system, the ideology, current in the discipline (and to a great extent in other scientific fields as well); and, finally, *let them make the choice*. If that technique does not account for scientific development as we know it, then no other will.

Lakatos (1970 and 1973) and Popper (1970) are horrified by the views of the elitists. They accuse them of being authoritarian, of advocating psychologism, sociologism, historicism and pragmatism, they speak of 'mob psychology', 'fashions' and 'uncontrolled dogmas'. For demarcationists like Lakatos and Popper, there exist *universal criteria* by which knowledge claims can be compared and appraised. Further, they insist upon *full articulation* of the criteria by which scientific achievements are judged and evaluated, while the so-called elitists accept that not everything can be articulated – since tacit knowledge and conventional wisdom are inevitably involved in scientific practice. In the absence of universal, explicit criteria by which scientific judgements are made, Kuhn and Toulmin hold that only *practising scientists* themselves are competent to make judgements about questions of scientific practice. Lakatos and Popper, on the other hand, believe that the demarcationist *philosophers of science* should lay down the criteria for appraising scientific practice – although they note that these are the results of reconstructions of the standards followed by great scientists in the past. Since I discuss this controversy at length elsewhere (Phillips, 1977), I will say no more about it here except to declare that my own sympathies are with Kuhn and the elitists – although, as will be seen later, I also share with Feyerabend the view that scientific judgements are often made (partially) on the basis of beauty, taste, attention-getting arguments and the like.

Competition and Persuasion

What is generally missing from the whole demarcationist debate is a full recognition of the *competitive* nature of science; it is not only ideas that are in competitition, but human beings as well. Instead of viewing scientists as being engaged in a struggle with Nature to learn her secrets (an image frequently set forth by scientists and philosophers of science), we can also view scientists as being engaged in a struggle with one another for the ascendancy of the ideas of particular individuals and groups. A recognition of this competitive element in science is voiced by Planck (1949), who remarks: 'A new scientific truth does not triumph by convincing its opponents and making them see the light, but rather because its opponents eventually die, and a new generation grows up that is familiar with it.' Darwin expresses a similar view at the end of the *Origin of Species*:

> Although I am fully convinced of the truth of the views given in this volume . . . I by no means expect to convince experienced naturalists

> whose minds are stacked with a multitude of facts all viewed, during a long course of years, from a point of view directly opposite to mine.

It is interesting that both Planck and Darwin speak about 'convincing' one's opponents or colleagues of the truth of one's view. The same attitude is expressed by one of the subjects in Mitroff's (1974) study of Apollo Moon scientists, forty-two eminent scientists who studied the moon rocks. He says that scientists 'are extremely subjective and intuitive. They invent elaborate analytic justifications to *convince* their colleagues.' Other scientists in the same study speak of *selling* their point of view, and of trying 'to *sell* the possibility you think most likely'. All of these statements represent the conviction that scientists are in competition with one another. What is involved in science are numerous attempts to understand reality, various ways of explaining the scheme of things, different accounts of the way things really are. But we should not forget that all of these standpoints and positions are set forth (and defended) by human beings.

If we regard the scientific viewpoints held by various scientists as possible ways of viewing things, we must ask why some of these 'possibilities' have greater survival power than others. Obviously, there is a hierarchy *within* every scientific discipline which follows their own processes of submission and domination among various individuals and groups. For example, there are the 'gatekeepers' of science, as well as certain individuals with so much credibility and/or so many disciples that their positions gain widespread attention and (possibly) acceptance. There are also hierarchies *among* the different scientific disciplines; physics and mathematics, for example, are generally considered more prestigious, more important, and more 'scientific' than sociology and psychology. Thus the 'tools' characteristic of the more dominant disciplines may come to be utilised in the lower-status disciplines. The emphasis on hypothetico-deductive theory, and the use of mathematics and statistics in sociology, represent clear instances of this phenomenon. At the same time, however, even the lowest disciplines in the pecking order of science are in a dominant position *vis-à-vis* non-scientists. Thus the 'same' viewpoint (idea, claim) advanced by a layman and a sociologist is generally given more credibility by the public if it is put forth by the latter than by the former. Obviously, there are a great variety of constraints – political, cultural, socio-economic, individual, as well as mere 'purely' scientific – that play a part in the survival power of possibilities.[1] Later in this chapter I will discuss a few of the factors within science that may be important to the competition between individual scientists (and schools or traditions) and their ideas.

First, however, I want to consider one aspect of the individual scientist's interaction with his or her professional community. Specifically, I will focus my discussion here on the major vehicle through which the scientist makes his or her ideas (truth- and knowledge-claims) available for professional scrutiny and judgement: scholarly *writing*. A scientist's reputation, as C. Wright Mills (1959) has pointed out, is expected to be based 'upon the production of books, studies, monographs – in sum, upon the production of ideas and scholarly works, and upon the judgments of those works by academic colleagues and intelligent laymen'. The reason for this is obvious; a scientist's competence or incompetence is then available for inspection. This inspection takes place not only in the particular university where a scientist works but, more importantly, in wider scientific circles. That is to say, judgements concerning an individual's knowledge or understanding are made less by his immediate colleagues than by other scientists in his field: other physicists, mathematicians, historians or sociologists. The individual scientist's work is directed towards a scientific audience *outside* his own department or institute, towards a scientific audience that is often international in scope. In order to communicate with them, in order to try to persuade them of the correctness of his looking at things his (her) way, then, he must write.

Engaging in research may be a necessary condition for the creation of scientific knowledge and for evaluation, but it is not a sufficient one. Every university contains numerous individuals who engage in research but do not communicate the results to their colleagues in other universities and elsewhere. Some men and women cannot bring themselves, or are unable, to write; some know of no journal or publisher that is interested in the kinds of problems that concern them; and still others are simply afraid or unwilling to expose themselves and their ideas to the criticism and scrutiny of their professional peers. Whatever their reasons and however convinced they, their immediate colleagues, or their students may be of their competence, unless scientists put their ideas in writing they are unable to meet the expectation of evaluation by their scientific peers. In short, research that is unreported is unavailable for judgements concerning the scientist's understanding or competence, and, equally important, does not enter into the arena of scientific competition.

In order to see more clearly exactly how the process of writing about and publishing the result of one's work operates, let me review the steps involved in that process. To begin with, of course, it is necessary that the individual has engaged in research (in the broadest sense of the word) and obtained some results, ideas, or conclusions. He then faces the often burdensome task of 'writing up' these results, either in the form of articles intended for publication in scientific journals or in the form of monographs or books. Frequently he sends early drafts of his work to colleagues both inside and outside his university, so as to receive their comments and criticisms. This means that other scientists in his field have access to his written, but so far unpublished, work. Also, sometimes before submitting his work for publication, the individual presents his results and ideas verbally at scientific meetings. Again, this is an opportunity to communicate with other scientists, to profit from their reactions, and to make claims for the correctness of one's particular viewpoint or findings.

In most cases, the scientist then submits his or her paper to one or another scientific journal, where it is evaluated by specialists in the field of his work. The probability of his paper being accepted by the journal's referees varies greatly with different countries, disciplines and journals. If someone's paper is not accepted by one journal, he is free to send it to another, with different editors, and continue doing so until it is eventually accepted for publication or until he gives up in his attempt to publish that particular paper. Once again, his work is available for the enlightenment of and evaluation by other scientists — in this instance, journal editors. Assuming that his paper is accepted for publication and appears in print, it enters the next step of testing and evaluation: it is read by others in the field, expert and novice alike. An individual's paper may be greeted with enormous (sometimes, deafening) silence and indifference, or it may receive considerable comments and perhaps acclaim. In this final stage, the scientist may find that other scientists cite his or her paper or that it may even play an important role in the future work of others. Of primary importance here is the fact that in the steps intervening between the scientist's early draft of his paper and its eventual publication in a scientific journal, there are several steps where the individual is engaged in *interaction* (though often not face-to-face) with other scientists working in his or her speciality area.

The above is obviously a rather sketchy (and somewhat idealised) picture of what is involved in the process intervening between the initial writing and the final publication of a scientific article. I include it mainly as a necessary reminder that it is through *these* processes that one or another possible way of viewing things comes to find its way into print and becomes – sometimes, at least – a source of debate and controversy.

Having provided this picture, I now want to return to Peter Winch's book *The Idea of a Social Science*. Although this book has been sadly neglected by most sociologists (especially in the United States), it has also – I believe – been responsible for encouraging some persons to defend a view of social science that I consider totally unsociological.

For the most part, Winch's book is an attempt to distinguish the problems and focus of the social sciences from those of the natural sciences. Among other things, Winch emphasises that whereas the natural scientist has to deal with only one set of rules – those governing the investigation itself – for the social scientist, *what* he is studying, as well as his study of it, is a rule-ridden activity. Thus, for the social scientist, Winch says, there are two sets of rules: the procedural rules of his discipline and the rules involved among those whom he is studying. (There is also, I claim, a third set of rules: involving the researcher and those studies.) Winch's book is mainly concerned with the study of social phenomena in terms of grasping the rules of human activity, and he has little to say about the other set of rules involving the investigator and other scientists. He makes some passing comments, but then generally ignores the issue of rules as they pertain to the practice of science. Winch does, however, note the following about the individual scientific investigator's relations to his fellow-scientists:

> The phenomena being investigated present themselves to the scientist as an object of study; he observes them and notices certain facts about them. But to say of a man that he does this presupposes that he already has a mode of communication in the use of which rules are already being observed.

The investigator 'notices certain facts' about phenomena, then, only in terms of rules shared with other scientists. As Winch notes: 'What is important is that they have all *learned* in similar ways; that they are, therefore, *capable* of communicating with each other about what they are doing; that what any one of them is doing is in principle intelligible to the others.'

What Winch apparently fails to see in his consideration of the scientific rules directing the interaction between scientists is that it is *these* rules – and these rules alone – which are involved in the settling of truth- and knowledge-claims in science. In fact, he generally fails to recognise that scientific truth and knowledge are fully the products of scientific communities. While scientists do speak of discovering laws that explain this or that, it is not 'laws' or 'theories' that explain the phenomena of concern to scientists. Instead, it is *scientists* themselves who explain; it is physicists who 'explain' physical phenomena, biologists who explain biological phenomena, and sociologists who explain social phenomena. The explanatory activities of a scientific discipline – including their theories, procedures and techniques – are collective activities which make *communal* sense.

Not only does Winch fail to consider this, but, in the case of sociology, he advances a thesis directly opposed to this viewpoint. He notes that Max Weber, whose genius it was to emphasise the importance of interpretive understanding – i.e. grasping the point or meaning for the actors themselves of what is being done or said – believed that the ultimate test of the correctness of an explanation was the establishment of statistical regularities. Winch criticises this view, saying:

> Against this, I want to insist that if a proffered interpretation is wrong, statistics, though they may suggest that this is so, are not the decisive and ultimate court of appeal, for the validity of sociological interpretations in the way Weber suggests. What is needed is a better interpretation, not something different in kind. The compatibility of an interpretation with the statistics does not prove its validity.

In stressing the importance of rules and interpretive understanding, Winch is, of course, criticising the heavy emphasis on quantification (and measurement by fiat) in the social sciences. He is trying to show that the terms of an explanation must be familiar to the subjects of enquiry themselves as well as to the investigator. Instead of adopting the external point of the observer, the investigator must, says Winch, take full account of the subjectively intended sense of the behaviour. In other words, Winch is arguing that the 'correctness' of an explanation is determined by the subjects of enquiry themselves rather than by the sociological investigator. If, for instance, a sociologist reports that people were engaged in 'Warfare' and the people themselves report that they were 'playing a game', then, Winch holds, the latter is what they were *really* doing. For Winch, the final court of authority as to the meaning of this or that, and the scientific correctness of this or that interpretation, lies with the subjects of enquiry and not with the sociological investigator who frequently imposes the meanings and interpretations from outside (see Benton, 1976 and Ingleby, 1973).

The problem with Winch's line of reasoning is that it fails to recognise that it is one or another *scientific community* – and *not the individual investigator or the subjects of enquiry* – which is the final arbiter as regards the correctness of scientific explanations. So that when Winch says that if a proffered interpretation is 'wrong' and what is needed is a 'better' interpretation, he fails to see that what counts as a 'right' or 'wrong' explanation is decided by the scientific community. The individual sociologist, then, 'explains' social phenomena by following procedures (rules) whose *correctness* is a communal matter. In other words, his explanatory achievements are dependent upon the judgements of the scientific community or the speciality area in which he works.

At issue with regard to Winch's formulation of the focus of sociology is his failure to recognise the full extent to which *all* science is a social enterprise. Moreover, to some extent he mistakenly exempts the natural sciences from his discussion of the problems characteristic of social scientific enquiry. He argues that we must distinguish between 'physical' and 'conceptual' changes in the phenomena of interest, and provides the following example:

> By how many degrees does one need to reduce the temperature of a bucket of water for it to freeze? – the answer has to be settled experimentally. How many grains of wheat does one have to add together before one has a heap? – This cannot be settled by experiment because the criteria by which we distinguish a heap from a non-heap are vague in comparison with those by which we distinguish water from ice: there is no sharp dividing line.

Winch's point here is that the change from water to ice is a physical change, whereas that from a non-heap to a heap is a conceptual one. But, in a sense, *they are both conceptual*. Shared standards among scientists allow for full agreement as to what *counts* as 'freezing' or 'ice'. Granted that there will be far less agreement within any group as to what is necessary for grains of wheat to *count* as a heap, and that, further, what counts as a heap in one group or culture may not count as such in another; nevertheless, there are rules (sometimes explicit, often not) which determine what counts as this or that in the natural and social sciences alike.

With both the natural and social sciences, it is human agreement that underlies scientific practice. In judging the correctness of a proffered interpretation, therefore, the relevant scientific community does not consult the interpretation itself (for example, that 'there is an inverse relation between the number of suicides and worker-satisfaction because . . . '), but rather the procedural rules used to decide if what the interpretation proposes is correct.

If, in the case of Winch's example, these procedural rules in sociology were to include (as they presently do not) the requirement of the investigator's (a) having familiarised himself with the concepts and way of life in terms of which the people studied view their situation and conduct their daily lives; and (b) having 'checked' his explanation with these studies and found it consistent with their subjectively intended sense, then – and only then – would these considerations (procedural rules) play a part in the warranting of an interpretation based on 'interpretive understanding'. And even in that case, it is the sociological community which decides what *counts* as adequate familiarisation with a people and having checked with them. But as it now stands, this close familiarity with the way of life of those studied is not a heavily emphasised requirement in sociology.

Since the scientific correctness of a scientist's claims are warranted only by one or another scientific community, so that it is *they* who establish scientific knowledge, this means that there will frequently be clashes between the claims of various scientists and different schools of thought. This is, of course, the competitive element in scientific life. Let me now consider some of the elements in this competition more closely.

During the last several pages I have emphasised – in a somewhat one-sided manner, I now acknowledge – the importance of procedural rules in science. These rules (which are never completely explicit) help determine what constitutes theorising, observing, testing, experimenting, etc., as well as what counts as 'proper' or 'correct' theorising, observing and the like. But I have also pointed out that science involves competition between and among individual scientists, schools and traditions. If we accept the conclusion of Kuhn, Toulmin and others who advocate a new image of science, that there are no permanent, unchanging standards of rationality and scientific practice (and I accept the conclusion with qualifications), and we recognise the competitive element in science, then we will not be surprised to see that scientific practice is characterised by powerful groups (and individuals) competing to perpetuate *their* views of rationality, proper scientific standards and the like. From this point of view, science is a political struggle with competing ideologies trying to gain dominance.

With regard to these debates surrounding the focus and study of social interaction (discussed earlier in this essay), the views now dominant in sociology may come to be altered or revised. They may prove sufficient for a particular intellectual epoch. By recognising that scientific standards (including, of course, those pertaining to the focus and methods of sociology) are human constructions which can be changed, we are perhaps better able to work towards bringing about such changes. An awareness of the social nature of scientific practice may help strengthen our resolve to cling to our own views while, at the same time, attempting to persuade the wider community of sociologists to alter their standards and revise their criteria.

This raises two questions of critical importance to the general issue of social interaction, for neither of which I have space to more than touch upon here. Why have large segments of the sociological community failed to accept the view that social interaction must be studied from the perspective of the actor(s) and that, therefore, sociologists must obtain 'data' about social processes? And what might be done to help convince them of the correctness of conceiving of sociology in this way?

As to the first question, I will begin by repeating the familiar charge that sociology has long been busy imitating what is (often mistakenly) seen as the practices of the natural sciences. This has meant a stress on hypothetico-deductive theory and a heavy emphasis on the collection of 'hard' data, quantification, the use of statistics, and so forth. Most especially in the United States, the desire to assure that sociology would be regarded as respectable in academic circles was probably partially responsible for the unwillingness of sociological practitioners to give much attention to those criticisms which, if taken seriously, might undermine the achievement of 'real' scientific status toward which so many were working (see Eisenstadt and Curelara, 1976). Certainly during the war years, the use of sociology by the government (for example, *The American Soldier*) totally ignored the more problematic elements of sociological practice. Whether or not this resulted in the suppression of some 'deviant' viewpoints is difficult to say. The appearance of a series of articles by Herbert Blumer which were highly critical of the focus and methods of sociology suggests that dissenting views were often able to find their way into print. And, of course, the existence of the 'Chicago School' shows that there have long existed dissenting views as regards the dominant, positivist, direction of American sociology.

Nevertheless, these dissenting views seemed to have little influence on the assumptions and research techniques that were dominant in American sociology up through the 1950s and the early 1960s. If one looks at the textbooks on 'research methods' during that period (and even now), it is clear that the advocates of one or another version of 'interpretive' sociology received little attention. It is necessary in this connection to stress the enormous importance of these textbooks in propagating a certain version of correct sociological enquiry, since it is mainly through *shared methods of investigation* that sociology (or any discipline) earns the right to be called a 'science'. There are approximately 2,000 colleges (two- and four-year) and universities in the United States, and the vast majority of sociologists teaching in these institutions are themselves not involved in research and publication. Since most of these sociologists define themselves primarily as teachers, it seems likely that dissenting views as to the proper methods of sociological research receive even less attention in the curriculum of sociology students than in the scholarly works of sociology more generally.

In the late 1960s and early 1970s, when sociology had come to occupy the status of respectable science (as evidenced by the participation of large numbers of sociologists in government commissions and in other advisory posts), when there was a relative abundance of university positions, and thus a possibility for individual sociologists to pursue and advocate new (or dissenting) directions without fear that they would be unable to obtain (and keep) a 'good' position, there was a considerable increase in the proportion of books and articles (even in so-called establishment journals) advancing viewpoints in opposition to the dominant images of sociology and sociological enquiry. But even then, the appearance of Cicourel's excellent *Method and Measurement in Sociology* did not occasion the attention from the sociological community that one might have expected or hoped for. It was not even reviewed in the two leading sociology journals in the United States: the *American Sociological Review* and the *American Journal of Sociology*. Since its initial appearance, this book has of course been widely discussed and debated – but mainly by ethnomethodologists and others who are sympathetic to Cicourel's position. It has not, however, had a discernible influence on the assumptions and techniques characteristic of mainstream sociology. This is not to say that Cicourel's work, or my own, or that of Deutscher and others has been totally unrecognised. In fact, there is an interesting phenomenon in this regard.

Objections to the dominant viewpoints and documentation of the shortcomings of much sociological research have not escaped notice, but they are often acknowledged in a particular way. Allow me to give a personal example. Over a period of several years I published a number of articles in which I utilised something called the 22-Item Mental Health Inventory in my research. In those articles I used the inventory without any real questions about its validity. Since that time, however, I have published several additional articles in which I explicitly *call into question* the adequacy and validity of this instrument. These latter articles have not been completely ignored by those sociologists who themselves use the same inventory. Indeed they do cite those articles along with the ones that uncritically assumed the inventory's validity – but they fail to acknowledge that some of these articles of mine call into question the inventory's adequacy and, *if taken seriously,* the very utilisation of such a measuring device. It is not that they attend to, and rebut, my criticisms, but they ignore them altogether. In other words, they pay lip-service to the scientific norm of covering the relevant literature without acknowledging that part of that very literature has the consequence of undermining their own research aims and assumptions. Similarly with Cicourel's work, where textbooks presenting the most widely held conception of sociological research often contain a footnote reading: 'For a somewhat different view, see Cicourel.'

Anyone who accepts the dominant description of scientific practice (for example, Merton's) should be astonished by such occurrences. After all, anomalies and unexpected findings – most especially those which call into question our procedures and techniques – are expected to give reason for pause and reflection. But if one accepts the fully social nature of science, including its competitive element, one finds such occurrences rather understandable. Until various dissenting views are not only *noticed* but also *taken seriously* and *acted upon* by large segments of the sociological community (or perhaps more importantly, the 'gatekeepers' of the discipline), the presently dominant assumptions and techniques of sociology will continue to hold sway.

This brings me to the second question concerning the general issue of social interaction. By what processes can these assumptions and viewpoints characteristic of the dominant modes of sociological thought be discredited and abandoned in favour of an alternative mode? What might be done to help persuade other sociologists to view things the way 'we' do? There are obviously no simple answers to such questions. If there were, we would already possess the very sociological knowledge toward which our enquiries are often directed. Still, I would like to offer some suggestions in this regard.

It is important to keep in mind that the medium of *language* is always involved in the communication between the individual scientist and the audience whom he addresses. He uses both the technical language of his society in attempting to obtain the adherence of others to his position. Most especially in their textbooks, sociologists employ ordinary, everyday language as a means of getting the student or novice to accept the correctness of one or another extraordinary (technical) language. So in addition to the technical language of sociology (or one or another sub-area), there are important elements of everyday language which are used by the individual sociologist in handing along to the reader/audience a vision, a mood, a way of looking. Among these are examples, illustrations, comparisons and contrasts, analogies, metaphors, quotations, humour, irony, epithets, repetition and amplification; as well as, of course, the very richness of the written word itself. That is, not only the *what* but also the *how* of a written (or spoken) argument needs to be recognised as a factor in the settling of truth- and knowledge-claims (see also Phillips, 1977, where the issue is dealt with at length and Gusfield, 1976).

In calling into question the established ways of looking, the individual sociologist has the task of getting the audience's *attention* and engaging them in dialogue. He or she must get them to look at phenomena (including the practice of sociology) from a different perspective. He may begin by communicating his way of seeing to a small circle of friends, students, and colleagues, perhaps an 'invisible college' in which he shares membership. Beyond this immediate circle, he will usually have considerably more trouble in getting wider segments of the scientific community to take notice. Considering this problem of arousing an inclination on the part of others to be interested in our position, Feyerabend (1975, p. 111) speaks of the necessity of propaganda and extreme positions. He writes:

> Extreme positions are of extreme value. They induce the reader to think along different lines. They break his conformist habits. They are strong instruments for the criticism of what is established and well received. On the other hand, the current infatuation with 'syntheses' and 'dialogues' which are defended in the spirit of tolerance and of understanding can only lead to an end of all tolerance and of all understanding.

Thus one might adopt an extreme position in order to break the reader's usual habits of thought. This 'extreme' position may be formulated by the use of extreme (polemical, or highly emotive) language, or by a highly unusual viewpoint. (This is, I believe, *one* of the reasons why the work of Feyerabend himself, Kuhn, Gouldner and Goffman has received considerable attention.) Evidence of this phenomenon comes from Mitroff's Apollo Moon study where one scientist is quoted as saying: 'In order to be heard you have to overcommit yourself,' and another states: 'There's so much stuff in the system that if one wants to be heard over the crowd, one must adopt a position more extreme than one believes in' (Mitroff, 1974, pp. 588-9).

If a scientist's ideas are to be considered and discussed, it is generally necessary that they be published. Whatever the actual contents of sociological articles and books (and however the sociologist employs language and presents his position), the reception of someone's work depends primarily on where it is published and who reads it. An article in the *American Sociological Review,* the *American Journal of Sociology*, the *British Journal of Sociology* or *Sociology* will reach a far larger audience and (potentially, at least) command more attention than the 'same' article in a lesser-known or more specialised journal. The rejection rates of these journals are all extremely high (90 per cent in the case of the *ASR* and *AJS*), and the probability of any given article being accepted for publication in these particular journals is rather small. It is undoubtedly even smaller for those advocating a position (or doing the kind of sociology) that is in opposition to (or out of step with) the dominant viewpoints in the discipline. Nevertheless, there is something to be said for submitting one's work to these journals – even though it is highly unlikely that it will be accepted for publication.

In the first place, it allows one to obtain editorial comments from 'experts' in the field. Whether or not one shares their standpoints, such comments can be extremely useful. This is especially so for those individuals who are not tied into an invisible college and/or do not have colleagues readily available who are knowledgeable enough to comment on their work. Second, editorial comments may serve as an indicator of exactly how receptive 'establishment' journals are to dissenting or new ideas. That is, they may show the degree to which one is (or is not) out of step with current definitions of what constitutes good sociology or, in fact, with what constitutes sociology. Again, I offer a personal example.

Some time ago, I submitted a paper on 'The Demarcation Problem' to the *American Sociological Review*. The paper was not accepted for publication. This is not the first nor last time that I have had an article rejected, but what is interesting about this particular rejection is the comments of the two editors who evaluated it. One editor did have some substantive criticisms of the paper, but also noted: 'It is an unfortunate fact of life that very few sociologists read in the philosophy of science, hence for most sociologists the discussion and analysis in this paper will be almost totally beside the point.' The second editor was very positive about the paper itself, but was even more explicit about most sociologists' unfamiliarity with current issues in the 'philosophy of science'. In his words:

> This article will not be understood by one in one hundred readers of the *ASR*. This is not because the paper is poorly written or poorly argued, but because it deals with a very specialized literature in the philosophy of science, that 99 percent of *ASR* readers are simply unfamiliar with. I would hazard a guess that only 3 or 4 in 100 sociologists have ever heard of Imre Lakatos, much less have dipped into his provocative work. Indeed, there are only a limited number of those who call themselves sociologists of science who are familiar with the work. Of course, they should be, but they simply are not. This paper will not introduce them to that work, since it really assumes at least a working knowledge of the main positions of Kuhn, Popper, Feyerabend and Lakatos.
>
> In sum, the paper should be submitted to a specialty journal in the philosophy, history, or sociology of science.

If these two editors' viewpoints are representative of these held by the editors of the *ASR* and by the 'gatekeepers' of sociology more generally (as I believe they are), then it seems clear that the chances of my bringing certain ideas to the attention of the wider sociological community (the *ASR* has a paid circulation of over 18,000) are somewhat limited. Of course, I can – as the one editor suggests – submit the paper to a speciality journal in the philosophy, history or sociology of science. But I am a sociologist and I believe that the demarcation controversy is to a large extent a sociological issue: it concerns the social nature of science and various arguments, pro and con, about Kuhn's self-professed sociological approach to science. It is not only, as Mills (1959, p. 19) puts it, that 'every cobbler thinks leather is the only thing, and for better or worse, I am a sociologist,' but also that I wish to direct my argument *to* sociologists. Were I to send the article to one of the speciality journals, and were it to be accepted, it would presumably be read by very few sociologists. That is, I suspect, exactly what happens with much that is written concerning the whole issue of meaning and social action; it does get published but not where it catches the eye of many sociologists.

In this regard, I want to speculate on the possibly different roles of articles and books in science. It seems to me that, in American sociology at least, 'careers' are usually made on the basis of publications in journals; while 'reputations' are more dependent upon the publication of books. In the handful of colleges and universities where research and publication are a major requirement, journal articles – which in the case of the major sociology journals are often highly quantitative, and scientific in the positivist sense – frequently serve as the principal basis for decisions about tenure and scientific advancement (decisions which are generally made rather early in the sociologist's career). Articles often rely on what Perelman (1963 and 1971) terms 'demonstration'. Demonstrative proof is impersonal; it is binding on any normal mind, and its correctness is not seen as dependent on any particular persons. In the practice of science (including sociology), demonstration involves the application of rules enumerated beforehand; it is binding on any normal mind, and its correctness is not seen as dependent on any particular persons. In the practice of science (including sociology), demonstration involves the application of rules enumerated beforehand; it is intended to guarantee the truth of a scientist's affirmations.

So far as 'reputations' are concerned, however, I suspect that it is book-length presentations which are most influential. It is not only that books are longer and perhaps represent more work and a larger achievement but, most importantly, they allow the individual to utilise argumentation, to give numerous examples and illustrations, and to employ more fully various elements of everyday language (for example, humour and irony) which are generally absent in shorter, more closely reasoned, articles. 'Argumentation', in contrast to demonstration, grants the status of knowledge to viewpoints which have survived the criticisms and objections of the particular audience to whom they are directed. Both argumentation and demonstration are addressed to an audience, whom the individual tries to persuade. But arguments are non-compelling, while demonstration involves necessary truths, results or outcomes, and, ideally, mathematical certitude. Demonstration rests on the force of logical deduction, experimental evidence, and scientific method. Argumentation, however, is a persuasive device which men and women employ to bring about the free adherence of other minds. Hence, the author of a book is less likely to be narrowly dependent upon the technical language of sociology (demonstration and rule-following) and is able to explore more fully the potentialities of argumentation.

Most especially when the sociologist is presenting a somewhat deviant view or is defending a new way of looking at things, a book is a superior vehicle to the journal article for accomplishing this aim. Since the practice of sociology depends upon a complicated structure of interactions between the individual sociologist and his fellows, there may be instances when the individual must make a strategic decision about how best to communicate with them in order to persuade them of the correctness of viewing things his way. In some instances, the choice of a book-length presentation rather than articles may represent the best strategy for persuading one's fellow sociologists.

Now all this talk about persuasion, convincing, getting people to take notice and pay attention, careers, reputations, strategies and the like may strike the reader as crass and vulgar in the extreme. It sounds as if we were competing businessmen trying to sell our wares in the marketplace. To some extent, I would agree with such a characterisation of what I have written; it does appear to be vulgar and crass, and is in direct opposition to the norm of 'disinterestedness' stressed by many sociologists of science. At the same time, however, I believe that it is a necessary corrective to those versions of scientific practice where the elements of persuasion, competition and power differentials are so sadly neglected.

If we are persuaded that there are indeed hierarchies of interaction in sociological research, then we must give more attention than heretofore to that level of interaction (between the sociologist and his fellows) where conflicts and controversies about the other two levels of social interaction (subject-subject, and subject-sociologist) are settled. That is the message of this essay. As Wittgenstein (1972, p. 27) once said: 'What I'm doing is also persuasion. If someone says: "There is not a difference," and I say: "There is a difference," I am persuading. I am saying: "I don't want you to look at it like that."' I, too, have been engaged in persuasion; I have been trying to get you to look at sociology *my* way. Whether I have been successful or not depends entirely upon (the collective) you.

Note

1. To touch only briefly on one such constraint, the success of any given possibility may depend partially upon its usefulness for one or another powerful interest group in society or on its 'fit' with certain accepted beliefs. Russian biology under Stalin in the 1930s, where political constraints prevented certain possibilities from entering the arena of scientific competition, is one clear instance of this. Unfortunately, I do not have room to consider these 'external' constraints here.

References

Ayer, A.J. (1967). Man as a Subject for Science. In P. Laslett and W.G. Runciman (eds.), *Philosophy, Politics and Society*. Third Series. Oxford: Blackwell.

Benton, T. (1976). Winch, Wittgenstein and Marxism. *Radical Philosophy, 13*.

Berger, P. and Luckmann, T. (1967). *The Social Construction of Reality*. Harmondsworth: Penguin.

Blumer, H. (1966). Sociological implications of the thought of George Herbert Mead. *American Journal of Sociology, 71*, 535-44.

Brodbeck, May (1963). Meaning and Action. *Philosophy of Science, 30*.

Cicourel, A.V. (1964). *Method and Measurement in Sociology*. New York: Free Press.

Coser, L.A. (1965). *Men of Ideas*. New York: Free Press.

Davidson, D. (1963). Actions, Reasons and Causes. *The Journal of Philosophy, 60*, 685-700.

Duncan, H.D. (1953). *Language and Literature in Society*. Chicago: University of Chicago Press.

Eisenstadt, S.N. and Curelara, M. (1976). *The Form of Sociology*. New York: Wiley.

Feyerabend, P.K. (1975). *Against Method*. London: New Left Books.

Filmer, P., Phillipson, M., Silverman, D. and Walsh, D. (1972). *New Directions in Sociological Theory*. London: Collier-Macmillan.

Garfinkel, H. (1974). *Studies in Ethnomethodology*. Harmondsworth: Penguin.

Gerth, H.R. and Mills, C. Wright (1960). *From Max Weber: Essays in Sociology*. New York: Oxford University Press.

Gusfield, J. (1976). The Literary Rhetoric of Science: Comedy and Pathos in Drinking Driver Research. *American Sociological Review, 41* (February).

Harré, R. and Secord, P. (1972). *The Explanation of Human Behaviour*. Oxford: Blackwell.

Harrison, N.R. (1971). *Observation and Explanation*. London: George Allen and Unwin.

Hodges, H.A. (1944). *Willhelm Dilthey: an Introduction*. London: Routledge and Kegan Paul.

Ingleby, D. (1973). Review of Harré and Secord (op. cit.) in *Radical Philosophy, 6*, 42-6.

Kuhn, T.S. (1962). *The Structure of Scientific Revolutions*. Chicago: University of Chicago Press.

Kuhn, T.S. (1963). Response to Critics. In A.C. Crombie (ed.), *Scientific Change*. London: Heinemann.

Kuhn, T.S. (1970). Reflections on my Critics. In I. Lakatos and A. Musgrave (eds.), *Criticism and the Growth of Knowledge*. Cambridge: Cambridge University Press.

Lakatos, I. (1973). Untitled paper read at seminar, Programmes of knowledge and growth in Science. Europaisches Forum, Altbach, Austria.

Lakatos, I. and Musgrave, A. (eds.) (1970). *Criticism and the Growth of Knowledge*. Cambridge: Cambridge University Press.

MacIntyre, A. (1971). *Against the Self Images of the Age*. London, Duckworth.

Merton, R.K. (1970). Paradigms for the Sociology of Knowledge. In J.E. Curtis and J.W. Petras (eds.), *The Sociology of Knowledge*. New York: Praeger.

Mills, C. Wright (1959). *The Sociological Imagination*. New York: Oxford University Press.

Mitroff, I. (1974). *The Subjective Side of Science*. New York: Elsevier.

Perelman, C.H. (1963). *The Idea of Justice and the Problem of Argument*. London: Routledge and Kegan Paul.

Perelman, C.H. and Oltrechts-Tytecha, L. (1971). *The New Rhetoric*. Notre Dame, Indiana: University of Notre Dame Press.
Phillips, D.L. (1971). *Knowledge From What*? Chicago: Rand McNally.
Phillips, D.L. (1973). *Abandoning Method*. San Francisco and London: Jossey-Bass.
Phillips, D.L. (1977). *Wittgenstein and Scientific Knowledge*. London: Macmillan.
Planck, Max (1949). *Scientific Autobiography and Other Papers*. Translated by F. Gaynor. New York: Philosophical Books.
Polanyi, M. (1958). *Personal Knowledge*. New York: Harper and Row.
Popper, K. (1970). Normal Science and its Dangers. In Lakatos and Musgrave (eds.).
Riekman, H.P. (1967). *Understanding and the Human Studies*. London: Heinemann.
Schutz, A. (1970). Concept and Theory Formation in the Social Sciences. In B. Emmet and A. MacIntyre (eds.), *Sociological Theory and Philosophical Analysis.* London: Macmillan.
Toulmin, S.E. (1972). *Human Understanding.* Vol. I. Princeton: Princeton University Press.
Turner, R. (1973). *Ethnomethodology*. Harmondsworth: Penguin.
Weber, Max. (1947). *The Theory of Social and Economic Organization*. Translated by Talcott Parsons. New York: Oxford University Press.
Whyte, W.F. (1969). Reflections on My Work. In I.L. Horowitz (ed.), *Sociological Self-Images.* Beverly Hills, California: Sage Publications.
Wilson, T.P. (19) Conceptions of Interaction and Forms of Sociological Explanations. *American Sociological Review, 35,* 698.
Winch, P. (1958). *The Idea of a Social Science*. New York: Humanities Press.
Wittgenstein, L. (1972). *Lectures and Conversations*. Berkeley, California: University of California Press.
Ziman, J. (1968). *Public Knowledge: The Social Dimension of Science*. Cambridge: Cambridge University Press.

11 DISCUSSION CHAPTER: AN APPRAISAL OF THE NEW APPROACH TO THE STUDY OF SOCIAL BEHAVIOUR

Michael Argyle

I do not regard myself as a paid-up member of the group of psychologists and sociologists whose views are represented in this book. However I have known many of them well, over a number of years, as friends and colleagues, and have learnt a lot from them. While I consider that what they have to say is very important, I believe that they have gone too far in the abandonment of procedures of verification, in giving up hope of discovering useful generalisations, and in rejecting nearly everything that has gone before. I believe that their main doctrines can be incorporated in a broadened but still rigorous kind of social science.

The contributors to this book and other members of this group are sociologists, social psychologists and philosophers, who share certain views. They do not, however, speak with a common voice. Some of them do research involving rigorous experimental designs, statistics and other trappings of the old methodology – but with a difference. Others see themselves as methodologists, and not only do not do any research, but actively persuade others not to do any either. They all reject or are deeply critical of the methods traditionally used in psychology and the social sciences, and most reject causal explanations. They are aware of themselves as a social movement and realise that they are in a minority position, and that a lot of persuasion will be required to convert the others (Phillips, Ch. 10).

The New Approach to Social Behaviour

The contributors to this book hold a variety of points of view, but they hold a number of beliefs in common.

1. Rejection of Traditional Research Methods

Brenner (Ch. 6) has shown how interviewing, on which social surveys depend, is far from an objective procedure, and that the responses obtained are affected by misunderstandings and complex interactions between interviewer and respondent. Similar points could no doubt be made about observational techniques which also depend on a human observer, who may interact with those observed. Harré and Secord

(1972) criticised social psychology experiments on the grounds that subjects are forced into a passive role, and that they may perceive the situation, i.e. the experimental manipulations, differently; they argue that experiments often involve the destruction of complex situations. Ginsburg (Ch. 5) has criticised them as unethical; indeed many experiments are no longer allowed for this reason. Ethnomethodologists have criticised social statistics of suicide rates, etc., on the grounds that a variety of complex social processes and human decisions are involved in the production of these statistics.

Most members of the group think that we should not be trying to find universal laws, and certainly not *causal* laws. The emphasis is more on 'deepening and enlarging our understanding of actual everyday life activities' (Shotter, p. 33). The approach of physics is rejected in favour of activities more akin to literature, biography or journalism. The general research method favoured is the collection of verbal accounts, in order to find the meanings and intentions of individuals. Harré argues that traditional psychology and social science often consisted of blind empiricism, whereas true science requires an underlying theory which directs the collection and interpretation of data.

Many others, outside the group, and including myself (Argyle, 1969) have been critical of the artificiality and sterility of much traditional research. Campbell (Ch. 9) draws attention to the value of qualitative evaluation of programmes, such as remembered experiences of participants, as opposed to quantitative research – although he himself is mainly concerned with the latter.

2. Emphasis on Cognitive Processes

The central doctrine is that behaviour can only be understood in terms of the way the individual perceives, interprets and creates situations. The importance of the individual's 'definition of the situation' has long been recognised in sociology though it is overlooked by behaviourists and most experimentalists. A number of 'emic' concepts are used. (a) Menzel (Ch. 7) discusses the meanings of actions to the actors who perform them, by which he means the purposes of the behaviour in a particular setting, e.g. mowing the lawn to annoy idle ethnic neighbours, throwing stones at a street theatre because it was felt to be invading territory. (b) The categories of behaviour in the minds of actors in a particular setting may be established, as opposed to the investigator imposing his own (etic) units. (c) Rules of behaviour, i.e. which behaviour is felt to be socially unacceptable, acceptable or mandatory, can be found (Collett, 1976). (d) The intentions of actors, i.e. the goals they are consciously seeking, may be found, as opposed to the causes of their behaviour, as ascertained by the investigator (Bruner, 1977). (e) Infants are socialised into an objectively existing shared social world, and learn to produce social acts with shared social meaning in the culture, like (in later life) a kiss, suicide, lighting a cigarette (Harré, Ch. 3). However, Harré believes that accounts need to be supplemented by the observation of behaviour. This dual approach is examplified by Marsh's work on football hooligans (Marsh, Rosser and Harré, 1978).

3. The Importance of Language

It is recognised that social behaviour and communication are only possible if two or more people use signals which have shared meanings, though as Rommetveit (Ch. 1) points out, there are often discrepancies of meaning. There is also a structuralist point here (Harré, p. 50): in any situation a group of signals may be equivalent (a wave and saying 'goodbye'), and signals partly have meaning through their contrasts with other signals in that situation. Social acts have meanings which are thought to be conveyed by largely verbal means, hence language can play an important role in making behaviour intelligible, when accounts of it are given.

Some members of the group think that language is such a pervasive aspect of our social life that it can serve as a model for social behaviour in general. Clarke (Ch. 8) uses a generative grammar model to account for the properties of conversation, where the units are speech acts. Instead of parts of speech, there are categories of speech act, instead of rules of grammar there are rules of sequence of speech act types, and so on.

4. The Explanation of Behaviour

In the new approach, an event is explained in terms of the actor's intentions or goals, his beliefs about what behaviour will bring the goals about, and his awareness of rules governing this behaviour (Cushman and Pearce, 1977). The traditional approach to explanation is quite different. In the first place what is to be explained is an empirical generalisation, rather than a particular event. A generalisation in psychology is explained in terms of real or postulated physiological processes, mechanical analogies or mathematical models.

It must be admitted that this procedure has not been very successful in social psychology, and my approach is rather different. (1) It is necessary to recognise the importance of cultural factors, including definitions of social acts, and rules; these are the product of historical development and it is usually impossible to explain them further. (2) Some aspects of social behaviour can be explained or partly explained in terms of biological evolution, though the processes involved are partly speculative, such as the explanation of altruism in terms of preservation of genes (Dawkins, 1976). (3) Part of the explanatory process consists of a 'mapping out' of the main variables and how they work; for example we now know that gaze acts during interaction to collect feedback, to send signals, and to help synchronise utterances (Argyle and Cook, 1976). (4) Part of the process of explanation consists of an empirical and conceptual analysis of the main components, for example of social situations (Argyle, 1976). (5) Part of the explanation lies in the derivation of generalisations from basic cognitive and social processes, such as reinforcement, response-matching, displacement of drives, and cognitive balance. Parts (1) and (4) of this approach overlap with the new paradigm, but the remaining three components lie outside the reach of verbal accounts.

The Effects of the New Approach on Research

The most important test of the new approach is surely its capacity to generate research which is generally accepted as making a useful contribution to knowledge. However, there are such wide differences between the contributors to this book that it is difficult to generalise. One effect which has usually been overlooked is that a number of people have abandoned research altogether. They were trained in conventional methods, then heard the new doctrines and were persuaded that the old methods were wrong, but did not see what methods could be used instead.

The most common kind of data collection comes from studying the behaviour of a number of individuals in a particular situation by collecting of their accounts. A small-scale local phenomenon may be understood similarly – like Menzel's stone-throwing at a street theatre (p. 143). This is very similar to the activities of a journalist, who interviews people to find their point of view and the reasons for their actions.

More interesting is the systematic sampling of accounts and analysis of behaviour. One example is Marsh's research on football hooligans, based on extensive informal interviews, participant observation, and study of videotapes. This led to the conclusion that much of the apparent violence is a kind of ritual, governed by rules which usually prevent anyone getting hurt. Another is Elizabeth Rosser's study of the cognitive world of disorderly schoolchildren; she found that children have 'rules' which the teachers are expected to keep, like not having favourites and not demanding too much work. If these rules are broken, the teachers get 'punished' (Marsh, Rosser and Harré, 1977). Another example is the research on industrial sabotage; accounts from those responsible showed that there were three main kinds of individual goals involved: (1) reducing tension and frustration – by smashing things up or having fun; (2) making the work easier – by adjusting the machinery, and (3) trying to assert control – for example by creating breakdowns (Taylor and Walton, 1971). These three examples of new-style research differ from journalism in their more rigorous and extensive collection and analysis of data, the attempt at verification, and the use of social science concepts. This is more akin to normal social science, the difference being that the means of verification are weaker, and more importance is attached to the point of view of participants.

Gauld and Shotter (1977) suggest that there is a particular kind of research which fits the new approach – study of the socialisation of children, with emphasis on 'the transformation of the neonate into a concept-possessing, intention-possessing and socialised little person' (p 211).

Another effect the new paradigm has had is on the conduct of more conventional studies. It is hard to isolate such an effect since there has been an increasing awareness in any case of the importance of cognitive processes, and an increasing availability of relevant measuring instruments, like the semantic differential, the repertory grid, and multi-dimensional scaling. For example, more care may be taken to ensure that independent and dependent variables correspond to meanings in the minds of subjects. It has been widely confirmed that frequency of interaction leads (on average, and by no means always) to liking. Harré (p. 53) suggests that it is better to distinguish between frequency of interaction 'as a result of accidental propinquity, marriage, of common job location, of deliberate contrivance by an interfering relative etc.', and so it would. Similarly it would be useful to distinguish between 'love' and 'liking', and this can be done (Rubin, 1973).

In addition to improving the research methods used for existing problems, a whole range of new problems has been opened up. A good example is the study of social rules. We can now investigate such questions as what are the rules for different situations, why do certain rules appear in these situations, what different kinds of rule are there (e.g. intrinsic, conventional, moral, legal), what are the effects of different kinds of rule-breaking, how is order restored, and so on (Collett, 1976).

Another research problem concerns the semiotic structure of events, in terms of contrasts, as seen by participants.

There is another kind of result of work in the new paradigm tradition – the development of a more adequate model of man. Traditional research excluded certain important features of human nature – our freedom, creativity, and consciousness, for example. Many people have been attracted to the new approach, as they have been to humanistic and existential psychology, because of the broader, more generous, model of man offered, which seems much closer to everyday experience than the conception of man as low-grade computer that may be found in behaviouristic psychology. On the other hand, this broader model of man is not apparently based on any detailed research findings but is based on broad considerations of cultural diversity and complexity, derived from anthropology and history (Harré, personal communication). More important, it does not seem to be open to empirical investigation.

Can this kind of research lead to useful applications in solving social problems? The traditional approach is to find the causes of a phenomenon, and then to manipulate them. The new approach is to gain deeper understanding, which also leads to the possibility of manipulation, as Menzel's solution of the street theatre problem shows. There is a further kind of application – informing people of the findings, in the hope that this will give them insight and increase their power to direct their own behaviour (Rommetveit, 1976). However there is no evidence that providing insight has such effects.

Evaluation of the New Approach

Is it a new paradigm?

Harré and Secord (1972) describe this approach as a 'new paradigm', Shotter (Ch 2.) describes it as a 'Copernican revolution', and others use the Kuhn (1962) terminology here. But is the new approach a new paradigm in Kuhn's sense? The examples of new paradigms he gives are the Copernican view of the solar system, Einstein's relativity, the wave theory of light and so on – new theories which required a totally new way of looking at phenomena, but which none the less incorporated and explained all the facts covered by the previous paradigm. The demise of alchemy was rather different: the new chemistry rejected much of what went before as nonsense, and reinterpreted the empirical findings which had been obtained. The new paradigm under discussion is similar: it does not incorporate most existing work, but rejects experimental findings, for example, as applying only to meaningless behaviour between strangers in a social vacuum.

So we have the curious situation that a minority movement in sociology and social psychology 'rejects' most of the work of the majority, on criteria of their own choosing, which are of course not accepted by the majority. (The new movement is, however rather *closer* to the common sense approach to behaviour, which had been rejected by traditional social science.) The majority could of course defend itself by pointing to the robustness in extensive replication of many of its findings, and to the areas of useful application of its findings and methods. In fact it will do nothing of the sort, since it rejects most of the work of the new movement as being inadequate in empirical rigour. If the carefully controlled interviews used in social surveys are inaccurate, how about the uncontrolled interviews favoured by the new movement? If sophisticated ethological studies of behaviour are not good enough, are participant observation studies any better?

To some extent the testing of causal hypotheses and the analysis of subjective meanings and intentions are simply different approaches to the same problem. They can lead to very similar results. Take Menzel's street theatre example again: the causal analysis approach here could be rather cumbersome, and might consist of an analysis of variations in aggression against street entertainments under different circumstances. This would no doubt lead to the conclusion that removal of group play territory was one factor – as was discovered by interviewing. Even what looks at first sight like purely behavioural studies can find the meaning of events to subjects. Kendon (1975) in an analysis of a courtship sequence found that the girl used two kinds of smile, which produced different results – kiss or withdrawal. The fascinating and influential work of Goffman has been based mainly on informal participant observation, with no interviews, though he consistently accounts for behaviour in terms of the inferred point of view of interactors.

Harré (p. 58) suggests that events need to be explained both in terms of external causes and also of their meaning to the agent in relation to 'templates' available in the society. The synthesis I would like to propose is somewhat different. I believe that the emphasis should be on the establishment of causal laws of the traditional kind, together with explanatory theories which can be tested by experiments and other well-controlled studies. However, the behaviour to be explained and the causal variables need first to be categorised in a way that is meaningful to those involved. Sometimes it is desirable to impose problems and variables as seen by the investigator. Informal interviewing and observation should be used for preliminary pilot studies only. For the serious work they need to be replaced by cognitive testing methods and systematic observation.

Clarke (Ch. 8) argues that traditional psychological research, in emphasising causality, is at a lower level of scientific sophistication than, say, physics, which is concerned with structures and processes, with deduction rather than induction. This leads to a kind of research different both from traditional work in psychology, and from that by other followers of the new paradigm, and more akin to linguistics and systems analysis.

The limits of meaning and perception

As we have shown, the central tenet of the new movement is the importance attached to the subjective, emic point of view, to the meanings of events, categorisations, rules and intentions, which can be discovered by collecting verbal accounts. Often it is impossible to understand what is happening without this information. On the other hand, subjective reports are sometimes incomplete, and they are sometimes misleading. (I am indebted to the discussion by Nisbett and Wilson (1977).)

(a) Awareness of own behaviour. People have a very low level of awareness of (a) their own non-verbal behaviour (gaze, facial expression, posture, etc.), and are often surprised when they see a video-recording of themselves; (b) their own physiological state, as measured by GSR and heart-rate, which often has little or no relation to verbal reports, in experiments; (c) changes in their own behaviour or attitudes as a result of experimental manipulations.

(b) Awareness of stimuli affecting behaviour. People are quite unaware of (a) small non-verbal cues like pupil-dilation, and have a very low level of awareness of more molar cues like another's percentage of gaze, and bodily orientation; (b) there is an extensive literature on subliminal perception – influence by stimuli which are too weak to produce conscious awareness; (c) problem-solving has been shown to be assisted by visible hints of which subjects have no memory immediately afterwards; (d) perceptual judgements are influenced by halo effects, anchoring effects, prestige suggestion and a host of similar factors, of which people appear to be unaware.

(c) Awareness of causal factors in behaviour. Psychoanalysts have extensive case-materials on people who are not aware of the sexual and other drives affecting their behaviour. Experiments on post-hypnotic suggestion can show the working of 'unconscious motives': a person is hypnotised, instructed to (say) stand on the table at a certain hour, but to forget that the suggestion was made, and is then woken up. At the appointed hour he stands on the table, and makes up a quite different explanation for doing so. Experiments on helping behaviour show that subjects claim not to have been influenced by the presence of others, yet the likelihood of helping decreases rapidly with the number of other people present. In cases like this verbal accounts are highly misleading. One reply to this is to accept that verbal accounts are misleading, but that nevertheless we need to know how people are making sense of events themselves. In such cases it is clearly essential to analyse behaviour as well.

In his discussion of Vietnam atrocities, Menzel argues that concentrating on the meanings of these events to the actors 'deflects us from even considering' explanations in terms of social structure, social pressures, frustration, and allied sociological and psychological concepts (p. 150). Indeed the meanings could be regarded as a consequence of these factors, and accompaniments or *post hoc* justifications rather than a cause of atrocities. This takes us to the heart of the argument – it is an instance where meanings do not reveal the true generative processes, and where a causal analysis could do so.

(d) Awareness of cognitive and generative processes. People seem to be aware of the results of cognitive processes, but not of the processes themselves. In cognitive dissonance experiments, for example, subjects have sometimes been asked to account for their behaviour, but have never given replies bearing any relation to the processes now generally believed to be responsible. For example, in an experiment in which subjects were induced to eat grasshoppers, a subject said, 'Well, it was just no big deal whether I ate a grasshopper or not' (Zimbardo, cited by Nisbett and Wilson, op. cit.). In experiments in the attribution theory tradition, there are numerous instances in which subjects have wrongly attributed the causes of their behaviour. In earlier experiments in which subjects learned concepts (e.g. 'shapes with an odd number of corners') a stage was often reached were subjects could judge correctly which shapes fitted the concept, but could not name the concept. Similarly, most people who can speak correctly have little idea of the rules of syntax and phonology, unless they happen to be linguists.

Clarke (Ch. 8) maintains that social behaviour also has an underlying grammar, or set of generative rules, of which people are unaware.

(e) Distorted accounts in cases of mental disorder. Large sections of the 'normal' population suffer at times from mental abnormalities, so this is a common problem. Mental defectives are not able to give adequate accounts of their behaviour. Nor are schizophrenics. Paranoids can give accounts, but these bear little relation to the real origins of their behaviour, and do not suggest what might be done to help them – it would not help much to try to reduce the level of death rays for example. Epileptics have fits without being aware of any cause, and endogenous depression is set off without any depressing events. Brain damage produces a variety of distortions of consciousness, such as knowing where a light is, but not being able to see it (Weiskrantz *et al.*, 1974).

Shotter (Ch. 2) does not share the view that all social behaviour is consciously planned. Some of it is, but some of it is more like a motor skill which people perform fast without time to think. Harré (1977) now thinks that account collection is suitable for the study of meaningfull social acts, but unsuitable for the smaller, automatic features of non-verbal behaviour. This fits my own ideas, of behaviour as a social skill: in a skill the larger moves are consciously planned, the smaller ones are automatic and habitual. Shotter also maintains that social behaviour is a joint accomplishment by different interactors, and that reasons for actions and social grammars do not 'exist in-the-heads of individuals, but are . . . spread out in the social practices by which individuals relate themselves to one another' (1977). In so far as I understand this notion, it takes us straight back to experimental social psychology.

The Philosophical Basis of the New Movement

The new movement takes a very definite position on two of the most controversial topics in philosophy – the mind-body problem and free will. There are many philosophical views about the mind-body problem, several of them still widely held today. The new movement assumes a version of one of them – what used to be called one-sided interactionism, i.e., the view that mind and body are separate, but that mind can influence body. Gauld and Shotter (1977) present arguments in favour of this theory. This philosophical debate has gone on for so long that I see little hope of it being resolved by philosophical argument, and believe that empirical research may in the end be more relevant. Some of the research we have just been looking at goes against this theory – by showing, for example, that behaviour may be influenced by physiological states and external stimuli of which the actor has no knowledge, and that the account he gives of his behaviour may be simply wrong.

Free will *v*. determinism is the other famous insoluble philosophical problem. Where traditional social science has assumed a deterministic model, the new approach assumes free will. However, as Shotter (1975) points out, some acceptance of causality of human behaviour must be retained – 'the very possibility of acting deliberately and effectively requires that we should be able to rely upon the causal efficacy of our actions' (p. 87). Again I doubt whether philosophers will ever be able to solve the problem, but research workers may be able to find out all we need to know. There are indeed several lines of research, *all using traditional methods*, though with a broadened conceptual base, which have told us a lot already. I mention them here because they show that the much despised traditional, rigorous, 'old paradigm', is capable of almost indefinite extension, including the study of free will.

(a) Reactance. If individuals expect that they will be able to make a free choice and then find that they can't, they often become very upset and make strenuous efforts to gain control of the situation. If lack of control continues for a longer period, however, 'learned helplessness' may set in (Wortman and Brehm, 1975).

(b) Internal-external control. There are consistent individual differences in the extent to which individuals believe that what will happen depends on them or on other people and chance. The internal controllers are less affected by social pressures and make more effort to find out all they can about a situation (Phares, 1976).

(c) Behavioural self-control is a new form of do-it-yourself behaviour therapy, in which, for example, the patient makes a decision to give himself certain rewards, when he has done four hours' work, or to entertain certain images, or say certain verbal instructions to himself – to make himself work harder, eat less, and so on (Thoreson and Mahoney, 1974).

(d) Cognitive dissonance. There are maximum effects of dissonance (i.e. on attitude change following counter-attitudinal behaviour) if subjects are given a free choice and exposed to minimal influence.

(e) Reciprocity. Helping behaviour is more likely to be reciprocated if the other's help was seen to be freely given, and not a result of the experimenter's instruction.

From these and other studies we learn that the important sense of 'freedom' is absence of situational pressures and constraints. Austin (1961) argues that individuals want this kind of freedom, that they differ in the extent to which they have it, that it is possible to increase the inner direction of one's behaviour, and that freely chosen behaviour in this sense has consequences for the actor and the way others respond to him.

But is there behaviour which is free in the sense of not being determined by past events, so that it is in principle unpredictable? This creates problems for research on creativity. The position here is most interesting: there is plenty of causal research on such topics as the conditions for maximum creativity, and the childhood experiences and personalities of creative individuals. There is no research, however, on what creative people create, which is assumed to lie outside the scope of psychological research. It is not known whether creative products are produced in some complex but law-governed and predictable way, or whether in some more fundamental sense there are new and unpredictable creations. Even this, in principle, could probably be found out.

A second area where non-determination has been postulated is the development of the personality. In fact socialisation research has been very unsuccessful in predicting the shape of the mature personality from earlier experiences. Erikson (1956) postulated that there can be a kind of creation of the self-image, and supports this with case-materials, such as the emergence of the new G.B. Shaw after a period of withdrawal in late adolescence. Sartre maintains that there is continuous self-creation of the personality. Secord and Backman (1974) suggest a way in which such changes can come about: a small change in behaviour is tried out first on the immediate circle of friends, and if it is accepted, becomes stabilised and used in wider circles. Behavioural self-control (see p. 247) is another way, rather in line with the new approach, for producing development of the personality.

The possibility of non-determinism has also affected linguistics. Here no attempt is made to predict what anyone will actually say; indeed it is recognised that most utterances have never been uttered before, which increases the difficulty of prediction. What linguists do instead is to find the generative rules, which afford a weak degree of prediction – that all acceptable utterances will conform to these rules. The study of conversation, and other sequences of social behaviour inspired by the linguistic model, takes a similar form. In both cases there is creativity combined with lawful regularity.

How should research proceed when confronted by such a basic threat to established procedures as the possibility of non-determination? I believe that it is no good simply giving up and falling back on weak methods not providing for falsification. On the other hand, it is obvious that methods have to be extended and modified to find out all we can about the phenomena in question. If there is real free will, then experiments may be impossible, at least for the aspects of behaviour which are unpredictable. However we should still study these kinds of behaviour by the most rigorous methods possible.

A Re-appraisal of Social Science Research Methods

I now want to take a brief look at the main social science research methods, in the light of new movement criticisms and practice.

Interviewing

Brenner (Ch. 6) criticised social survey interviews on the grounds that uncontrolled interaction between interviewer and respondent, and failure to communicate with shared concepts, introduce error. Analyses of such interviews show that they can be very chaotic, and that respondents often do not keep to the rules of this situation. There are a number of more familiar sources of error in survey interviews, and techniques for minimising them have been developed. For example, the tendency to say 'yes' is avoided by using multiple-choice rather than yes-no items, and the tendency to giving socially desirable answers is avoided by offering equally respectable alternatives. The danger of fabrication is avoided by the use of filter questions to find out whether a respondent has the necessary experience, or knowledge, to answer a group of questions usefully (Kahn and Connell, 1957). The problem of misunderstanding and lack of shared concepts is already tackled by the use of pilot studies, in which the concepts and verbal labels commonly used by respondents are discovered. In market research surveys the concepts used by the population to be surveyed are found, for example by use of semantic differential or rep grid, and these terms are then used in the final survey (Lunn, 1968). This is very much in tune with new paradigm thinking, though it was not inspired by it. Failure to keep the rules on the part of respondents is usually dealt with by patiently explaining again the purpose of the interview or the meaning of the question – though some additional social skills training for interviews would probably be useful here. I conclude that the survey interview is a valuable research tool, and that any further sources of error in it can probably be minimised just as more familiar ones have been. This is as well, since the interview is the main method used in new paradigm research.

Individual Cognitive Testing
This is a more sophisticated alternative to ordinary interviewing. New methods emerged rather earlier than the new movement and provide a rigorous way of assessing subjective concepts. The semantic differential (Osgood *et al.*, 1960) imposes the investigator's scales, but the factor analysis can reveal the dimensions used by subjects. The repertory grid (Fransella and Bannister, 1977) elicits their own concepts from subjects, and can be used to explore an individual's classification scheme. Multi-dimensional scaling (Shepard *et al.*, 1973) is based on similarity judgements of pairs of stimuli, and produces the dimensions a judge is implicitly using. All three methods have been in general use by social and clinical psychologists for some time, and are also used as a preliminary to social survey work as indicated above.

To study rules, similar methods can be used. For example, instances of rule-breaking can be presented or described, and subjects asked to rate them on a number of scales. The ratings can be analysed statistically to show how many types of rules there are, and how they vary between situations.

The discussion above suggests that cognitive testing may be of limited validity, if individuals do not have perfect conscious insight. I believe however, that the contributors to this book are right in stressing the importance of categories, rules and other cognitive structures. Some can be elicited directly, some can be elicited indirectly, e.g. by repertory grid and multi-dimensional scaling, and obtaining reactions to rule-breaking. This is very similar to the rules of grammar – few can state them, but most people can tell when they have been broken.

Observation
This has not been discussed in this book, but it is easy to see what the criticisms would be. Systematic observation, e.g. of the Bales type or in the ethological tradition (Kendon *et al.*, 1976) uses the observer's categories rather than the actor's, and may not discover the true meaning or purpose of the behaviour observed. Duncan and Fiske (1977), on the other hand, maintain that the introduction of meaning, intention, etc., only adds error to behaviour analysis. It must be admit-

ted that research in this behaviouristic tradition has produced valuable findings, for example about greetings (Kendon and Ferber, 1973), and the synchronising of utterances (Duncan and Fiske, op. cit.).

In our work at Oxford, some of which is reported by Clarke (Ch. 8), we have been doing observational research modified by new movement considerations. We have found the repertoire of social acts distinguished by actors in different situations. We have asked observers to parse (or chunk) video-tapes of the behaviour stream, we have played back video-tapes to actors asking them for their plans at different points. and we have elicited the rules of sequence for different situations (Argyle, Clarke and Collett, 1977).

Menzel (p. 140) argues that it may sometimes be useful for the investigator to decide on the meanings of acts. In the use of category systems it is found that interactors will readily accept a variety of quite different systems. In the analysis of social behaviour in the classroom, for example, over 100 systems have been used – mainly by teacher trainers to get teachers to recognise and use different social acts – like 'asks higher order question', 'structures', and so on (Simon and Boyer, 1974).

Laboratory Experiments

These have been criticised as being unethically deceptive, forcing subjects into a passive role, producing different interpretations of the experimental conditions on the part of subjects, and lacking external validity. Ginsburg (Ch. 5) suggests that active role-playing is the best alternative, and cites a small number of celebrated examples of this. Mixon (1972) maintains that role-played behaviour may be more valid than that of experimental subjects. His role-played version of the Milgram experiments showed that shocks were not given if subjects believed that they would really hurt the recipient; there is considerable doubt over what Milgram's subjects thought was happening. In a different experimental situation,

> The demand on the role player is to throw or not throw the acid as if the consequences were real; the demand on the conventional experimental subject is to throw it because they are *not*. The same point can be put another way: the deceived subject acts within the rules and conventions of the laboratory; the actor acts within the rules and conventions of the pretended episode (Mixon, op. cit., pp. 169-70).

However it is possible to design experiments which evade the above criticisms. They need not be deceptive – the subjects are told as much as possible, only the main hypothesis is withheld from them. They are certainly not passive – they deal actively with the situation with which they are confronted. The possibility of erratic interpretation of conditions is commonly checked by a post-experimental interview or completion of rating scales showing perception of the conditions. Low validity can be minimised by increasing the resemblance of the experimental setting to a real-life situation, which involves an element of role-playing. And in so far as subject measures are used as the dependent variable, the central tenet of the new paradigm is adhered to.

Field studies

Some new movement researchers carry out very informal pieces of participant observations and experimentation in field settings, like dinner parties, and the like. This may be regarded as a kind of pilot study, but is open to numerous objections as a serious research procedure. Marsh's study of football hooligans (op. cit.) is based on more systematic (participant) observation and (informal) interviewing, with some attempt at quantification. It is a familiar criticism of participant observation that the investigator becomes part of, sometimes a leader of, the group he is observing, and thus affects the behaviour taking place. This can only be avoided by (unethical) disguise, which is any case reduces the ability to ask questions. This kind of study lacks a design, so that it is impossible to arrive at causal explanations.

There are other kinds of field study which are designed to test causal hypotheses. There is a well-established tradition of field experiments on the conditions under which helping behaviour will occur. Another kind of field study uses changes inside an organisation, produced with the co-operation of administrators – changing leadership, group size, incentive schemes, and so on (Argyle, 1972).

Quasi-experimental Research Designs

It has long been recognised within the orthodox tradition that most field studies do not enable causal inferences to be drawn, that laboratory experiments tend to lack external validity, and field experiments are very difficult to carry out. An important way out of this trilemma is the use of field studies designed to make causal inference possible. One of the most widely used is path analysis (Jencks, 1972), in which the causal contributions of, for example, father's occupation, and own education, to later income, are inferred from regression equations. Another is the use of cross-lagged correlations by means of which it has been found for example that ignoring infant crying in the first 3 months of life is correlated with frequency of crying between months 6 and 9 (Ainsworth *et al.*, 1974).

Another method is the study of impact of historical events by appropriate kinds of before and after comparison. Ross, Campbell and Glass (1970) found that the introduction of the breathalyser had a definite but relatively short-lived effect on the rate of drunken driving in Britain.

Conclusions

Positive Contributions of the New Movement

1. The criticisms of traditional research methods are partly justified and have helped to improve them. In particular much research in the past was too artificial, and subject to errors in the collection of data.

2. The emphasis on the cognitions of the actor is valuable, in leading to a better analysis of both independent variables and of the actor's own behaviour. This analysis can best be done by one of the new methods of cognitive testing.

3. The new approach has stimulated some new kinds of research, including apparently disorderly behaviour, various aspects of rules and rule-breaking, and analysis of interaction sequences using analogies from language.

4. A model of man has been presented more in keeping with common experience.

Criticisms of the New Movement

1. It is not a new paradigm, since it does not explain the previous body of findings by social scientists. It is difficult to see what point there is in 'rejecting' this body of material.

2. The criticism of previous research methods went too far; the informal methods of interviewing and observation put in their place are in turn rejected as invalid from the traditional point of view. Furthermore this criticism has had the effect of preventing many people from doing any research at all.

   It has been argued here that the combination of emic cognitive analysis with rigorous, etic, causal designs is best, and that traditional procedures are capable of expansion to deal with a very wide range of problems.

3. The exclusive emphasis on accounts went too far; there are many cases where accounts have been shown to be incomplete accounts of the genesis of behaviour, or to be completely mistaken.

4. A firm position is taken on certain philosophical problems hitherto found to be insoluble. It is argued here that more can be found out about these problems by various kinds of psychological research, than by philosophical debate.

References

Ainsworth, M.D.S., Bell, S.M. and Stayton, D.J. (1974). Infant-mother attachment and social development: 'socialisation' as a product of reciprocal responsiveness to signals. In M.P.M. Richards (ed.), *The Integration of a Child into a Social World.* Cambridge: Cambridge University Press.

Argyle, M. (1969). *Social Interaction.* London: Methuen.

Argyle, M. (1972). *The Social Psychology of Work.* Harmondsworth: Penguin.

Argyle, M. (1976). Personality and social behaviour. In R. Harré (ed.), *Personality.* Oxford: Blackwells, pp. 143-88.

Argyle, M. and Cook, M. (1976). *Gaze and Mutual Gaze.* Cambridge: Cambridge University Press.

Argyle, M., Clarke, D. and Collett, P. (1977). The sequential structure of social behaviour. Report to the Social Science Research Council.

Austin, J.L. (1961). *Philosophical Papers.* Oxford: Clarendon Press, pp. 128-9.

Bannister, R. and Fransella, F. (1971). *A Manual for Repertory Grid Technique.* London: Academic Press.

Bruner, J.S. (1976). Psychology and the image of man. *Times Literary Supplement,* 17 December.

Campbell, D.T. and Stanley, J.C. (1966). *Experimental and Quasi-experimental Designs for Research.* Chicago: Rand McNally.

Collett, P. (ed.), (1976). *Social Rules and Social Behaviour.* Oxford: Blackwells.

Cushman, D.P. and Pearce, W.B. (1977). Generality and necessity in three types of human communication theory – special attention to rules theory. *Hum. Communication Res.*

Dawkins, R. (1976). *The Selfish Gene.* Oxford: Oxford University Press.

Duncan, S. and Fiske, D.W. (1977). *Face-to-Face Interaction.* Hillsdale, N.J.: Erlbaum.

Erikson, E.H. (1956). The problem of ego-identity', *Amer. J. Psycho-anal., 4,* 56-121.

Gauld, A. and Shotter, J. (1977). *Human Action and its Psychological Investigation.* London: Routledge and Kegan Paul.

Harré, R. (1977). The ethnogenic approach: theory and practice. *Advances in Experimental Social Psychology, 10,* 283-314.

Jencks, C. (1972). *Inequality.* Harmondsworth: Penguin.

Kahn, R.L. and Connell, C.F. (1957). *The Dynamics of Interviewing.* New York: Wiley

Kendon, A. (1975). Some functions of the face in a kissing round, *Semiotica, 15,* 299-334.
Kendon, A. and Ferber, A. (1973). A description of some human greetings. In R.P. Michael and J.H. Crook (eds.), *Comparative Ecology and Behaviour of Primates.* London: Academic Press.
Kendon, A., Harris, R.M. and Key, M.R. (1975). *Organization of Behavior in Face-to-Face Interaction.* The Hague: Mouton.
Kuhn, T.S. (1962). *The Structure of Scientific Revolutions.* University Chicago Press.
Lunn, J.A. (1968). Empirical techniques in consumer research. In D. Pym (ed.), *Industrial Society.* Harmondsworth: Penguin.
Marsh, P., Rosser, E. and Harré, R. (1978). *The Rules of Disorder.* London: Routledge and Kegan Paul.
Mixon, D. (1972). Instead of deception. *J. Theory Soc. Beh., 2,* 145-77.
Nisbett, R.E. and Wilson, T.D. (1977). Telling more than we know: verbal reports on mental processes. *Psychol. Rev., 84,* 231-59.
Osgood, C.E., Suci, G.J. and Tannenbaum, P.H. (1957). *The Measurement of Meaning.* Urbana: University of Illinois Press.
Phares, R. (1976). *Locus of Control in Personality.* Morristown, N.J.: General Learning Press.
Rommetveit, R. (1976). On 'emancipatory' social psychology. Lecture at Oxford Summer School of European Association for Experimental Social Psychology.
Ross, H.L., Campbell, D.T. and Glass, G.V. (1970). Determining the social effects of a legal reform: the British 'breathalyser' crackdown of 1967. *Amer. Beh. Sci., 13,* 493-509.
Rubin, A. (1973). *Liking and Loving.* New York: Holt, Rinehart and Winston.
Shepard, R.M., Romney, A.K. and Nerlove, S.B. (1973). *Multidimensional Scaling.* New York: Seminar Press.
Shotter, J. (1975). *Images of Man in Psychological Research.* London: Methuen.
Shotter, J. (1977). Agency and 'accounting': in criticism of Harré and Secord's 'open souls' doctrine. Paper to Social Psychology Section, B.P.S. Durham.
Simon A. and Boyer, E.G. (1974). *Mirrors for Behavior III.* Wyncote, Penn.: Communication Materials Center.
Taylor, L. and Walton, P. (1971). Industrial sabotage: motives and meanings. In S. Cohen (ed.), *Images of Deviance.* Harmondsworth: Penguin.
Thoreson, C. and Mahoney, M. (1974). *Behavioral Self Control.* New York: Holt.
Weiskrantz, L., Warrington, E.K., Sanders, M.D. and Marshall, J. (1974). Visual capacity in the hemianopic field following a restricted occipital ablation, *Brain, 97,* 709-28.
Wortman, C.B. and Brehm, J. W. (1975). Responses to uncontrollable outcome: an integration of reactance theory, and the learned helplessness model *Advances in experimental Social Psychology, 8,* 278-336.

INDEX